COUNTRY CABINETWORK AND SIMPLE CITY FURNITURE

WINTERTHUR CONFERENCE REPORT 1969:

Country Cabinetwork and Simple City Furniture

Edited by John D. Morse

WINTERTHUR

Published for
The Henry Francis du Pont Winterthur Museum
Winterthur, Delaware

The University Press of Virginia
Charlottesville

Copyright 1970 by The Henry Francis du Pont
Winterthur Museum, Inc.
First published 1970
Second printing 1970
The University Press of Virginia
Standard Book Number: 8139-0298-3
Library of Congress Catalog Card Number: 77-114194
Printed in the United States of America

CONTENTS

PARTICIPANTS

Conclusions

Bruce R. Buckley, Assistant Director, Cooperstown Graduate
    Program
Nancy Goyne Evans, Assistant Registrar, Winterthur Museum
E. McClung Fleming, Head, Education Division, Winterthur
    Museum
Benno M. Forman, Research Fellow, Winterthur Museum
Wendell D. Garrett, Managing Editor, *Antiques* Magazine
Craig Gilborn, Associate, Education Division, Winterthur
    Museum
Charles F. Hummel, Curator, Winterthur Museum
Edward F. LaFond, Jr., Keeper, Pennsylvania Register of
    Historic Sites & Landmarks
Charles F. Montgomery, Senior Research Fellow, Winterthur
    Museum
R. Peter Mooz, Teaching Associate, Education Division,
    Winterthur Museum
Charles S. Parsons, Author and Research Specialist
Raymond V. Shepherd, Jr., Assistant Curator of Decorative
    Arts after 1700, Philadelphia Museum of Art

Conservation of Furniture

James K. Barr, Research Supervisor, Fabrics and Finishes
    Department, E. I. du Pont de Nemours & Company
Richard M. Candee, Research Specialist, Old Sturbridge
    Village, Sturbridge, Massachusetts
Jonathan L. Fairbanks, Associate Curator in charge of
    Conservation, Winterthur Museum
Benno M. Forman, Research Fellow, Winterthur Museum
Timothy Jayne, Paintings Conservator, Winterthur Museum
John W. Melody, Furniture Conservator, Winterthur Museum
Charles F. Montgomery, Senior Research Fellow, Winterthur
    Museum
Theodore Penn, Researcher in Technology, Old Sturbridge
    Village, Sturbridge, Massachusetts

ILLUSTRATIONS

Unsophisticated Furniture Made and Used in
Philadelphia and Environs, 1750-1800

An Art Historian's View: A Commentary on Style
in Country Art

From the Check List of Furniture Exhibited During
the Conference

FOREWORD

THE theme of Country Cabinetwork and Simple City Furniture adopted for the Fifteenth Annual Winterthur Conference on Museum Operation and Connoisseurship points up what has been recognized as a thorny subject at Winterthur for many years. Numerous lectures and tours relating to country furniture, given both to our graduate students and to the public, have made us aware of the many unanswered questions involved.

Does "country furniture" constitute a single category of furniture forms with distinguishing characteristics, and if so, what are those characteristics? If there is such a body of furniture, was it made and used chiefly in villages and small towns? If so, can its construction and design be ascribed to the limited skills of rural craftsmen and the limited wealth and taste of their rural clients?

Or was furniture characterized by the term "country" also made and used in the cities? And in this case, was it made by craftsmen who also made high-style furniture, and was it used by clients who could afford more expensive furniture? Do the differences between the work of city and country cabinetmakers in one region and period hold true for other regions and periods? Do we have valid criteria for an esthetic evaluation of this furniture? Is "country" the proper term for this furniture, or should it be replaced by "folk," "vernacular," "traditional," or something else? The conference could not, of course, provide definitive answers to all these questions, but it did successfully point the way toward solution of many of the problems raised.

The conference program committee consisted of Charles F. Montgomery (chairman), E. McClung Fleming, Benno M. Forman, Charles F. Hummel, and R. Peter Mooz. In the early stages of planning, Mr. Montgomery drew up the following suggested objectives for the papers to be solicited; these indicate, as well as anything can, the direction of the committee's initial thinking:

1. To study a corpus of "non-high-style" American furniture, documented as to maker, date, area, and user, covering the widest possible date and geographical range, probably from the late seventeenth century through the early nineteenth century.

2. To explore as far as possible the social-economic group or class to which one maker and one user belonged, thereby hoping to throw light on the other clients served by this furniture maker or the other furniture makers patronized by these clients.

3. To suggest where different income groups bought their furniture and how they used it, that is, where the lowest income groups secured their furniture, where the highest income groups used whatever unsophisticated furniture they purchased, what urban groups preferred unsophisticated furniture, and the like.

4. To describe contacts between rural and urban craftsmen (services and products exchanged, etc.) rural contacts of urban furniture makers, and urban contacts of rural furniture makers.

5. To explore parallels that may exist between the furniture of London and Philadelphia, on the one hand, and between Philadelphia and Lancaster, Pennsylvania, on the other, that is, the relationship of style and workmanship between central and regional style centers.

To make a frontal assault on this subject the committee selected seven speakers: four to present data papers dealing with bodies of documented furniture and three to present interpretative papers suggesting ways of analyzing and understanding this data. The three interpreters were to be a culture historian, an art historian, and a folk-culture specialist. The inclusion of the latter represented a desire by Winterthur to explore the relevance of a related but unfamiliar discipline. Happily, the seven persons at the head of our list all agreed to serve.

The conference proved to be one of the most successful we have held. An exhibition of thirty-one pieces of

furniture from the Winterthur collections was assembled
in the Rotunda by the program committee to illustrate
various phases of the conference theme.   The pieces were
listed in a catalogue prepared by Mr. Forman, who was
present during visiting hours to interpret the exhibition.
Friday afternoon was reserved for tours of the collections,
the libraries, and the new Research Building. Saturday
afternoon was devoted to a feature which it is hoped to
include in all future Winterthur Conferences--a discussion
of the technical problems associated with the conservation
aspects of the conference theme. This year's technical
session studied the conservation of furniture. It was held
in the Rotunda, and was well attended. To obtain a more
complete and accurate record of discussions during the
conference, we employed for the first time a court recorder
to supplement tapes. One hundred and fifty-nine persons
attended, including seven speakers, forty-four members
of the Winterthur staff and the University of Delaware
faculty, thirty-three Winterthur graduates, fourteen
fellows-in-residence, twenty-one resource specialists,
six special guests, and thirty-four wives.

   This report was prepared for publication by John D.
Morse and his staff in the National Extension Office.
Our thanks are due to them, particularly for their per-
severance in working out a new, topical format for the
presentation of discussion sessions. Our thanks are also
extended to the members of the program committee and to
all the other staff members whose cordial collaboration
contributed so much to the success of this Conference.
We are happy to be able to announce that all photographs
of Dunlap furniture are gifts of Charles S. Parsons to the
Decorative Arts Photographic Collection of Winterthur
Museum.

   The Annual Winterthur Conference on Museum Operation
and Connoisseurship was first held in 1954.   It was originally conceived as a contribution to the course of study
offered to the first- and second-year fellows of the
Winterthur Program in Early American Culture.   Over the
years its purpose has been extended to include an

opportunity for the entire Winterthur community--fellows,
graduates, staff, and university colleagues--together
with a few professional associates, to meet for a three-
day study of some major problems concerning the arts in
early America and their preservation.

E. McClung Fleming

COUNTRY CABINETWORK AND
SIMPLE CITY FURNITURE

URBAN ASPECTS OF MASSACHUSETTS FURNITURE
IN THE LATE SEVENTEENTH CENTURY

Benno M. Forman

WHEN we think of the case furniture made in eastern
Massachusetts in the late seventeenth century, a vision of
oak cupboards and linen chests with applied spindle ornamentation and of chests of drawers with geometrically decorated
panels and elaborate moldings appears to the mind's eye. If
we broaden the view of our imagination to include Connecticut
and the Connecticut River valley, the "Sunflower" chests and
cupboards and "Hadley" chests--with their low-profile
carving--must be added. The image, in short, is of furniture
in the oak styles.

An easily remembered landmark in eastern Massachusetts
oak furniture of this period is Winterthur's famous "Vocabulary Chest" of drawers (fig. 1), which bears the carved date
1678. Insofar as published commentary is concerned, this
chest of drawers would seem to be the epitome of New
England craftsmanship as the last quarter of the seventeenth
century began.

If the work of New England's best-known joiner, Thomas
Dennis of Ipswich--who there is good reason to believe made
the Vocabulary Chest--is compared with the scriptoire that
was added to the furnishings of Ham house in Surrey, England,
prior to 1679, the American example, with its carved drawer
and polychromed facade, seems incredibly behind the times.[1]
Its decoration seems to be a lingering survival from the
Middle Ages, provincial and rural, despite its charm: it
seems to be "country furniture."

John Dunton, an English bookseller who toured eastern
Massachusetts, wrote that "Ipswich is a country town"
shortly after visiting there in 1686.[2] Could we defend an
assertion that anything but "country furniture" could have

Fig. 1. The Staniford-Heard chest of drawers, probably made by Thomas Dennis of Ipswich, Massachusetts,
for John and Margaret Staniford, in 1678--the year
carved on the bottom drawer. H. 42"; W. 44 3/4"; D.
19 7/8". Winterthur Museum (57.541)

been made in this "country town?" Indeed, were not--in
actuality--all the towns of Massachusetts country towns
in the last decades of the seventeenth century insofar as the
decorative arts are concerned?

What about Salem, where Winterthur's Woodbury family
wainscot cupboard was made in 1680? Was it yet a city?
Salem supported five joiners in 1680, in contrast to the one
known to have been working in Ipswich. Unquestionably,
Salem was the economic, social, and cultural focus of Essex
County. Yet, despite the presence there of several ambitious
and aggressive merchants, Salem inventories in the period
1680-1720 reveal the surprisingly conservative character of
the town, which by the standards of the decorative arts historian, precludes its being considered a truly urban center
at that date.[3] Even as late as 1760, it was "little more than
a village," whose main street was not paved until 1773, according to Salem's respected historian James Duncan Phillips.[4]

On the other hand, there is contemporary evidence that
one true city did exist in seventeenth-century Massachusetts
--perhaps more than for any other reason, because its residents thought of it as a city. In the spring of 1677, the
citizens of Boston addressed a petition to the General Court
of the Massachusetts Bay Company for a charter, "that this
town may be a corporation."[5] The court rejected the petition,
for political reasons, however, and not for any lack of evidence that Boston was indeed the only settlement in British
America worthy of being called a city.

As early as 1645 Edward Johnson, a joiner by trade, called
Boston "this city-like town." Perhaps he exaggerated, but
Johnson continued his description enthusiastically: "[the
buildings are] beautiful and large; some fairly set forth with
brick, tile, stone and slate, and orderly placed with comely
streets whose continual enlargement presages some sumptuous
city."[6]

Fifteen years later the traveler John Josslyn noted that
Boston's buildings "are handsome, joyning one to the other,
as in London, with many large streets, and so forth."[7] Indeed, by this time Boston had experienced a number of growing pains, as is amply evidenced by the records of town

ordinances regulating the collection of trash, the removal of
pendills overhanging the highways, the leashing of dogs, and
even the establishment of speed limits for carts using the
town's streets.

There is an early hint that craft life in Boston was different
from that in its neighboring communities. A very unusual
petition was submitted by 129 Boston craftsmen to "The
Honored Governour and Deputy Governour, Assistants
and Deputies" on May 23, 1677. It requested the
enactment of laws forbidding persons who had not served an
appropriate apprenticeship or who had not been admitted
residents of the town from setting up trades there. In the
body of the plea, two phrases suggested the part played by
the crafts in the life of the community. It maintained that
"a very considerable part of the Town of Boston doth Consist
of Handcraftsmen" and later pointed out that "the way of our
subsistence . . . [is] so differing from other towns."[8]

Fifteen joiner's names are among the signatures to this
petition. This large number suggests that Boston was without question the center of New England furniture craftsmanship at that time, if not the leader in quality, then at least
the leader in potential output.

Furniture craftsmen were at work in Boston in 1635. In the
ensuing ninety years, 196 of them worked in the town. This
total is made up of 134 joiners, 11 cabinetmakers, 16 turners
(not including blockmakers who specialized in shipwork), 9
chairmakers, 17 upholsterers, and 9 carvers. These figures
include only the craftsmen whose trade is specified in the
surviving public documents of the Town of Boston. Not included are several dozen names published by previous researchers which I have not been able to connect positively
with the trade they are said to have practiced. When the
survey of Massachusetts furniture makers working before
1726 is completed, Boston's total of 196 will probably exceed
the number of those who worked in the rest of Massachusetts
during the same period.

The story of Boston furniture begins with the joiners of
Boston, those skilled workers of wood who made panels out

of oak and pine, fitted them into grooved frames, and pinned
the frames together to make linen chests and cupboards,
wainscot chairs and cradles, chests of drawers and bedsteads. To appreciate their art, we must think in terms of
the particular skills and the inherent limitations of these
first furniture makers who came to New England early and
worked late, whose craft was old when they came, but whose
methods, techniques, and sensibilities grew and matured
through three generations, into the eighteenth century. The
result was a group of furniture that is unique, made at a
moment in decorative arts history when the finest work the
American joiner had ever done was still not good enough to
keep him from becoming superannuated.

To some extent, research is hampered by the fact that we
do not know how long the joiners of New England continued
to make oak-style furniture in the eighteenth century.
Apparently practices varied from place to place. A joined
oak chest made in Connecticut bearing the painted date 1705
is in the Sage Collection at the Metropolitan Museum of Art.
I am not aware of a dated joiner-made chest from eastern
Massachusetts later than the Salem example with the carved
date 1700 described by Russell Hawes Kettell in the 1943
<u>Walpole Society Notebook</u>. [9] Undoubtedly oak furniture
continued to be made in Massachusetts, just as it was in
rural England. [10] At the very moment, for example, that
London cabinetmakers were busily turning out their late
works in the Queen Anne style, somewhere in England in the
year 1712 a joiner made the dated cupboard illustrated in
figure 2. [11] A great oak chest of English or Welsh origin
bearing the carved date 1727 is displayed in the Ironmaster's
House at Saugus, Massachusetts.

While it may be assumed that joined oak furniture continued to be made as long as furniture craftsmen who had
been trained in the joiner's tradition were working, hard-
woods found their way into the furniture of Boston near the
beginning of the last quarter of the seventeenth century.
Obadiah Walker of that town had "A Square table of black
Walnutt" valued at £1 5s., April 18, 1676. [12] During
the next decade, walnut and olivewood are mentioned with

Fig. 2. An English cupboard, dated 1712. H. 70";
W. 60"; D. 23½". Formerly Philadelphia Museum of Art

Fig. 3. "Chest of drawers with doors," Boston, ca.
1675. The Zeeland /Dutch/ prototypes of this popular
English form have shelves in place of drawers, which
suggests that the doors are vestigial in function,
although excellent surfaces for ornamentation.
H. 49"; W. 45 3/16"; D. 23 3/8". Yale University
Art Gallery, Mable Brady Garvan Collection

increasing frequency. In the 1710 inventory of Thomas
Livermore, a young Boston joiner, no oak at all appears,
perhaps an indication of the diminished popularity of that
wood for furniture making. He did have, however, "two
cases of Draws p[art] made & 100 foot of black Walnut,
worth ₤2 15s.[13]

Any idea of what was happening in the furniture crafts of
Boston toward the end of the seventeenth century is complicated by the fact that there is no oak furniture that can be
traced to Boston with the usual type of documentation. No
cupboards or chests descended in the Cabot, Winthrop, or
Savage families have come out of ancestral homes within
the memory of living man. Progress, fire, the dictates of
fashion, the hobby of "antique" collecting, and the mobility
of the American people have long since dispersed the
furniture of Boston's seventeenth century.

Does this mean that we can never hope to identify that
furniture? Perhaps we can make a beginning。

The chest of drawers in figure 3 has been called "the
most sophisticated piece of American seventeenth-century
furniture。" It is referred to by Wallace Nutting as a "court
cabinet," a phrase that does not appear in New England
documents of the colonial period. [14] The form corresponds
to the 1698 inventory description of " 1 chist drawers with
doors," valued at twenty shillings mentioned in the estate
of Timothy Lindall of Salem. [15] It is doubtful that it could
have been made anywhere else in seventeenth-century New
England but in Boston, and to assign to it a date somewhere
in the third quarter of the seventeenth century is not un-
reasonable. It is the only American example in this form
which has been identified. Was it outmoded by English
standards? I think that similar chests would have been
found in the homes of Englishmen of the same time and same
socio-economic class.

Probably the group of chests of drawers known as Dedham
chests can be most justifiably associated with the Boston
area. Some of the type--generally characterized by plain
top and bottom drawers with broad moldings, flanking two
middle drawers outlined with smaller and more complexly

profiled moldings--were doubtless made in Boston. They are
called Dedham chests because one of the type was found in
Dedham in the late 1920s. An examination of several of them
shows that while they are generically similar, they vary
sufficiently in quality of execution to suggest that several
different shops produced them. One of the finest examples
illustrated is figure 4. It does not have a family history but
is quite similar to the chest of drawers, now in the Shelburne
Museum, that stood in the Fairbanks house at Dedham and,
also, to the chest of drawers that descended in the Pierce
family of Dorchester. It is related to the former in the dis-
placement of the drawers and the method of decoration. With
the latter, it shares these features and the fact that it is in
reality made up of a two-drawer chest placed atop another
two-drawer chest.

These chests of drawers are typical examples of what must
have been a popular variation of the chest of drawers as it
was designed and made in and around Boston near the turn of
the century. They were itended to look like furniture made
in the cabinetmaker's fashion whose broad surfaces and
smooth transition from plane to plane is associated with board,
rather than joined, construction. But they are all made in the
joiner's traditional way: the carcass of each is framed and
pinned, the side panels are set into grooves in the frame,
while the half-round moldings between the drawers are purely
decorative and not the molded edges of dust boards that one
might expect. The drawers themselves slide on side runners
of oak, just as drawers did when Governor John Winthrop first
set foot on American soil. The chest of drawers in figure 5
bears sufficient resemblances in construction and appearance
to the chest of drawers in figure 3 to suggest that both were
made by the same craftsman or group of craftsmen. Apparently
the form in figure 5 quickly superseded the chest of drawers
with doors. It is remarkable for the extensive use in its
construction of the tropical wood Cedrela--sometimes known as
Spanish cedar, although it is a porous wood rather than a
conifer. This may well be the earliest surviving example of
Massachusetts furniture that employs as its primary wood a
hardwood not native to New England.

Fig. 4. Dedham chest. Acquired by Hollis Franch
prior to 1913, probably in the Boston area. See
Richard Randall, <u>American Furniture in the Museum of
Fine Arts</u>, Boston, plate 26. H. 36 1/2"; W. 41 1/4";
D. 22 1/2". Museum of Fine Arts, Boston (40.602)

Fig. 5. Chest of drawers, Boston, ca. 1680. See
Richard Randall, American Furniture, plate 38.
H. 51¼"; W. 47 3/16"; D. 23 1/16". Museum of Fine
Arts, Boston (32.219)

The chest in figure 6, found in Marion, Massachusetts, was
one of the first objects acquired by Nina Fletcher Little for
her famous collection of early New England furniture. It has
never been restored and is the mate to a completely restored
example illustrated in Nutting's Furniture of the Pilgrim
Century as figure 56. Except for its ebonized spindles and
triglyphs, the chest originally was not painted. It is likely
that this chest originated in the Boston area sometime
between 1660 and 1680.

Some of the examples mentioned here may have been made
at a date when this furniture was as much in the high style as
any available in eastern Massachusetts. Many of the later
examples, however, such as the Dedham chests and the
toilet table in figure 7, are in reality what this conference is
about: they are, as I will attempt to show, "simple city
furniture."

If this furniture cannot be tied to Boston craftsmen by the
usual methods of documentation, upon what evidence can an
assertion of its Boston origin be based?

First, I must quickly sketch the results of the research of
Miss Patricia Kane and myself during the past few years. In
our years as fellows in the Winterthur Program, we explored
the best documented examples of seventeenth-century case
furniture of Essex County, Massachusetts, and Hartford
County, Connecticut, to determine, if possible, who could
have made it, what its styles and forms were, and whether
its construction fitted into a recognizable pattern. [16] During
that period we also examined a number of examples that are
traditionally believed to have been made in the Plymouth
Colony. The study of construction methods, especially the
ways in which drawers were made, was particularly revealing.
We found that, without exception, the drawers of the seventeenth-century furniture from these essentially rural areas
were made without dovetails. This fact is in itself significant, but becomes of even greater importance when cor-
related with the information that all the joiners who could
have made this furniture came from rural England. Presumably they brought the techniques of their crafts with them
from their native parishes.

Fig. 6. Joined wainscot chest, Massachusetts, ca.
1675, oak. H. 31½"; W. 46½"; D. 30 3/4". Collection
of Nina Fletcher Little

Fig. 7. Toilet table, Boston, ca. 1700. Originally
painted red, black moldings, crimson accents,
possibly with floral design on panels simulating
inlay. H. 38 1/8"; W. 31 1/8"; D. 17 7/8".
Winterthur Museum (58.686)

On the other hand, the drawers of every example of furniture illustrated (which I have suggested are all of Boston
origin) have well-articulated dovetails. How can they be
accounted for? The obvious suggestion is that the joiners
or the masters who trained the joiners who made these
American cupboards and chests came from a place in England
where the dovetail was used. We now believe that place was
London. The dovetail as a London technique is mentioned in
a famous legal decision of 1632 specifying the rights of the
Joyner's Company of London as opposed to those of the London
Carpenter's Company. Among other things, the decision
stated that London's joiners were entitled to the exclusive
manufacture of "All sorts of chests being framed, duftalled,
pynned or glewed"; also "All sorts of Cabinets or Boxes
duftalled, pynned or glewed." [17]

Among the first ten joiners who came to Boston between
1635 and 1641, three--Ralph Mason, John Davis, and Henry
Messenger--came from London. The two most important,
Mason and Messenger, had several sons each who followed
their fathers' trade in the next generation. [18] It seems likely
that these London-trained craftsmen brought with them the
technique of constructing drawers with a dovetail. This may
be the clue we have sought to help us identify some of the
seventeenth-century Boston furniture that has so long gone
unrecognized.

The idea that the dovetail was present in the early seventeenth century in New England and was passed on as a technique of construction from master to apprentice has the merit
of suggesting a possible explanation to an otherwise knotty
problem. First, it explains the anomalous presence of the
dovetail in a few pieces of oak furniture that stylistically
seem to be fairly early but must be dated quite late if, in
fact as well as legend, the dovetail does not "appear" in
American furniture until "around the beginning of the eighteenth century," as we have long believed. If this idea may
be accepted, then it is no longer necessary to believe that
all oak furniture whose drawers are constructed with a dovetail was made in the eighteenth century. Second, it relieves
the strain of trying to rationalize the sudden appearance of

the dovetail in walnut-style furniture without understanding
how it "evolved." The dovetail could hardly have evolved
simultaneously in Massachusetts, Connecticut, New York,
and Philadelphia: it is more probable that the technique was
introduced into this area. Indeed, it seems likely that it was
introduced into New England twice--first and earliest, into
Boston, from where it was undoubtedly disseminated somewhat by apprentices and the movement of craftsmen. Its
second introduction came about through the arrival of a new
generation of craftsmen in America near the beginning of the
eighteenth century, after which time it became common.
What appears to be virtually inexplicable "evolution" when
one looks only at the furniture involved, instead becomes
the more believable case of introduction by immigration, and
dispersal as the demand for cabinet wares increased with the
increase of New England's population in the eighteenth
century.

If this line of reasoning is correct, then it seems likely
that the dovetail in seventeenth-century furniture may prove
to be as much a regional preference of construction, and
subject to the same exceptions, as the open tenon in the
back stiles of Philadelphia rococo chairs and the triangular
front-corner blocks of Massachusetts Federal chairs.

Through the period of the English civil wars and the
Commonwealth, the flow of immigrants and new craftsmen to
America virtually ceased. During these years, the ranks of
Massachusetts furniture makers were increased solely by the
sons and apprentices of craftsmen who had immigrated before
the middle of the century. It was not until after the restoration of the Stuart monarchy in 1660 that immigration once
more picked up. At the beginning of the fourth quarter of the
century, the population of rural Essex County was growing
very slowly, but the town of Boston was growing at an enormous rate. Into all of Essex County, only one new English-
trained joiner came during the last quarter of the century. He
was George Booth, and he came to Salem, probably from
Horsemonden, County Kent, in 1676--the first English-trained
joiner in Salem furniture making in thirty-four years! If the
£16 that comprised his worldly estate at the time of his

death in 1682 is any indicator, Booth was neither a rousingly successful nor an enthusiastically accepted craftsman. It seems apparent that whatever changes took place in the joining and turning crafts of Essex County were the result of growth from or modification of the traditional base that had existed there since the early years of settlement.

In Boston, the story is quite different. During the third quarter of the seventeenth century, at least seven new joiners began to work in the town, not including the sons of older joiners. From 1685 to 1695 Salem had one and only one up-holsterer working, George Herrick. He seems to have had no predecessor and no immediate successor. During that same decade, the citizens of Boston were able to provide work for six men who practiced this trade. [19]

Because the records of the town of Boston so consistently identify men by their trades, a chronological arrangement of the numerous references to Boston craftsmen has recently yielded a nugget of information that eluded those furniture historians of the past who called all woodworking craftsmen "cabinetmakers." Not one joiner who had worked in seventeenth-century Boston was called a cabinetmaker in the eighteenth century. [20] In like manner, the sons of those joiners remain "joyners" insofar as the legal documents of the town are concerned. Thus it would appear, if the documents are to be believed and can be assumed to be accurate, that the craftsman who was thought of as a cabinetmaker in early Boston did not evolve from Boston's seventeenth-century joiners.

The earliest reference I have found to a cabinetmaker in all of New England occurs on October 31, 1681, when "John Clark, cabinetmaker," was admitted a resident of Boston. I have not found the word used again in seventeenth-century New England records or further mention of this John Clark. From 1700 onward, however, cabinetmakers are frequently mentioned. It is perhaps significant that Boston seems to have been the first place in America to refer to its cabinet-makers consistently by that name.

Thus far, ten men called cabinetmakers are known to have been working in Boston between 1696 and 1726. Of the ten,

the work of only one--Job Coit--has been identified. Coit, a
native of New England, was at work by 1713, but his signed
desk and bookcase bears the date 1738 and is more or less in
the Queen Anne style.

Four more of Boston's ten earliest cabinetmakers were
native New Englanders: George Thomas, working by 1706, and
his cousin John Maverick, working by the next year, were
probably born in Boston or Charlestown; James Mattocks, who
was working in 1726, was a native Bostonian, the son of a
tailor named Samuel Mattock: Fifield Jackson, who was working by 1723, was the youngest of the group and came to Boston
from Cambridge to learn his trade. But none of them has the
distinction of being the first to practice that trade in the town.
That honor belongs to John Brocas (sometimes spelled, as it
was pronounced, Brockhurst), who was in Boston in May 1696,
with his wife, Catherine. [21] He died in 1738. Four other
cabinetmakers immigrated to Boston in the next decade.
William Howell and William Price both were working there in
1714, and William Robinson and a Mr. "Andrews," whose first
name is not recorded, emigrated from London in 1716.[22]

If, as we have long suspected, the verbal distinction between a joiner and a cabinetmaker represents a distinction
in fact, namely, that the cabinetmaker did something which
the joiner did not do, then the difference should somehow be
reflected in the furniture each produced.

Of Boston's ten cabinetmakers who worked during the period in which the William and Mary style was the high style,
only one died before 1725. "William Howell, the cabinetmaker, an honest servant of mine, was buried yesterday,"
Samuel Sewall wrote his brother Stephen, on December 23,
1717.[23] Howell's inventory, taken a few days later, represents the earliest instance in which a Boston cabinetmaker's shop goods and tools are itemized. In addition to
the great variety of tools one might expect to find in any
versatile joiner's inventory, Howell possessed "walnut
Fenere" valued at £8 18s., "1 Finereing Hammer, one
tooth Plain, 2 Glew Potts, 15 lb. of Glew," and "80 lb. of
Lead [weights]" --all items associated with veneering. [24]
If Howell's inventory presents a picture of the normal Boston

cabinetmaker's shop of his time, it would indicate that veneering was the primary technique used by the cabinetmaker of
William and Mary Boston which was not used by the joiner.
The resulting product was doubtless very much like the high
chest of drawers in figure 8.

Merely because cabinetmakers appeared in Boston at the
end of the seventeenth century, the joiners of the town who
were known as furniture makers did not close up shop. Neither
did they cease to take apprentices, nor did their customers
cease to patronize them. William Parkman, for example, who
was working in 1706, was called a joiner in a 1714 lawsuit;
yet his advertisement of 1723 says that his place of business
is at the sign of "the case of drawers," [25] and it seems
obvious that he was making furniture.

In Boston, however, the history of the joiner as furniture
maker in the eighteenth century is a story of slow retreat. As
the biographies of the sons of seventeenth-century joiners
are pursued further into the eighteenth century, they are referred to, with increasing frequency, as "housewrights," a
term very rarely used during their fathers' lifetimes. Most
informative of all is the fact that their tools--some of which
undoubtedly had made fine furniture half a century earlier--
are often listed in their inventories as "carpenter's tools."

In the rural towns of New England, the local joiners and
their sons and apprentices were even further removed from the
influence of the cabinetmaker's techniques. They continued
to make furniture, as well as to perform the hundreds of
miscellaneous tasks a skilled woodworker would be called
upon to do. But the introduction of new forms, as well as
changes in their work both stylistically and technically,
proceeded at a much slower pace than in the competitive
situation of their urban counterparts.

This is not to say that the term "joiner" immediately or
even quickly passed out of usage for a furniture maker in
urban America. For example, the term "cabinetmaker" was
slow to appear in New York, where the work first occurs in
the Freeman's List on June 19, 1739, to describe the trade of
Nicholas Baker. In 1748, when Gilbert Ash, whose lovely
chairs in the Chippendale style have been identified, was

made a freeman of New York, he was listed as a "Joiner and
Carpenter." [26] In Salem, when a list of the town's crafts-
men was compiled around 1760 or 1761, thirteen furniture
makers, among them the elder Thomas Needham and Abraham
Watson, were called "Shop Joyners," [27] and when the Oc-
cupation Tax List of 1783 was drawn up in Philadelphia,
Thomas Affleck, Daniel Trotter, John Gillingham, and William
Savery were all listed as "joiners." [28]

It is not a coincidence that cabinetmakers and American
furniture made in the William and Mary style appeared in
Boston at the same time. While Bostonians took the arrival
of the new type of craftsman in stride, the demand for the
new style of furniture must have been traumatic for the joiners
of New England, who were the third generation working in the
tradition brought by their grandfathers in the 1630s. There is
also, however, evidence that the new style was not acceptable to many of the remaining Puritans of Massachusetts--
regardless of whether they lived in the country or the city.
If ever a style of furniture represented a foreign culture,
it was the William and Mary style. To that majority of late
seventeenth-century New Englanders who were Puritans not
only by belief but by temperament, the style symbolized not
only the worldly decadence of Restoration England, and the
style of the court circle and its hated representatives in the
colony, but the forcible appearance of the previously not
tolerated Anglican communion in Boston.
For these reasons, it seems unlikely that furniture in the
true William and Mary style was frequently imported into New
England or was being made there as early as 1680--twelve
years after the restoration of the Stuart monarchy to the
English throne in the person of Charles II.
When, then, did the new style appear, and on what social
level was it introduced? This information is virtually impossible to determine from inventory references to case
furniture because what was later called a "high chest of
drawers" was merely called a "chest of drawers" in inventories of the period with which we are concerned. Nor
does the value assigned to these chests of drawers aid us in

Fig. 8. Burl maple veneer on white pine gives distinction to this high chest of drawers, one of the
earliest masterpieces of the Boston cabinetmaker's
art. The birch legs--virtually identical to others
known to have been turned in Boston--have been
painted to echo the grain pattern of the veneer.
Although this form appears to have been popular
between 1675 and 1710, it probably was made around
1700. H. 58"; W. 40¼"; D. 23". Winterthur Museum
(58.579)

any way, for apparently high chests cost no more than the
joiner's most elaborate chests of drawers.

One form of furniture associated with the new style, however, cannot elude us, the cane chair. "Six cane chairs . . .
£2: 08:00," are listed in the July 9, 1688, inventory of
the estate of Giles Master of Boston. [29] James Savage, the
genealogist, informs us that Master "probably lived here a
very short day, and with no sympathy towards our people, as
in Sewall's Diary he is described merely as 'the King's
attorney.'"[30] Master's inventory is slightly more informative.
That he possessed a "hatchment" suggests that he at least
had some connection or pretensions to family status, and his
profession--confirmed by the "two and twenty skinnes of
parchment with the Kinges Effigie" in his inventory--places
him in the privileged class, despite the slight amount of
£36 14s. at which his estate in New England was
appraised.[31]

I have not located a documentary reference to cane chairs
earlier than Master's inventory, although Sir Edmund Andros,
the first royal governor of Massachusetts (December 1686 to
February 1689), undoubtedly possessed a few among the "considerable quantity of Goods for the Governour" which Sewall
noted in his diary as arriving on December 14, 1686.

The inventory of John Ragland of Boston (died 1691), whose
total value was £313, mentions "six cane back chairs, 6 bass
bottomed chairs. . .£3: 10:00." Biographical material on
Ragland is entirely lacking, and inasmuch as he owned no
property in Boston, nor was ever admitted a resident, it seems
likely that he was in some way connected with the royal
government. [32]

Fully caned charis do not occur again in the probate records
of Boston until "six cane chairs" valued at £5: 02:00 are
mentioned in the 1693 inventory of Dr. Thomas Pemberton,[33]
a "chirurgeon," and an intimate of Sir William Phips. Pemberton
was a New Englander, as was Sir William, who had been made
the second royal governor. Pemberton also possessed a number of other items that would seem to indicate that--at least
in the governor's circle--the new style was in use. In addition to the cane chairs, there was a "slate table" valued at

Ł1 sterling, and "a chest of drawers and a table" valued at
Ł8 --enough to suggest that perhaps these latter were a high
chest and dressing table en suite.

From 1693, onward, cane chairs and other William and Mary
forms appear in Boston inventories with increasing frequency.
Moreover, they are found in the homes of people of lower
rungs of the social and economic ladder. In September 1694
William Gross of Boston, whose total estate amounted to only
Ł50, had "a dozen of Cain chaires," appraised at Ł3: 10:00.[34]
During the five years between the death of Giles Master
in 1688 and that of Dr. Pemberton in 1693, times had changed
a great deal, politically, economically, and spiritually.

In February 1695 Captain John Ware possessed "A marka
tree looking Glass Split . . . Ł1: 10:00" and "1 doz. of
caine chaires" valued at 20 shillings each. [35] The next
year Hezekiah Usher, a wealthy merchant, died possessed of
" 1 broken Olive Wood Table . . . 10s., 1 Olive wood Scrip-
tore", and "1 olive Chest of Drawers." [36] By 1696 the appraisers who took Boston's inventories were clearly familiar
with the distinction in styles. When Edward Cowell's estate
was appraised on May 11, 1696, it included: "1 old-fashioned
broken cupboard . . .8s.; 5 old Turkey workt chairs; 3 very
old Leather chairs much broken . . . 3s.; sundry very old
worne out Towells & napkins not worth the naming to the
number of 17 . . . 1s.; one Shovelboard table . . . 12s.; an
old Clock which is decayed and quite out of order," appraised at Ł2: 5:00. [37] Altogether, the word "old" occurs
fifty-seven times in Cowell's inventory, and since there was
only one new fashion--the William and Mary style--the date
and place are of extraordinary importance.

In Essex County, the William and Mary style first appeared in the new merchant class. Oddly, it is not found earliest in Salem, the county's most cosmopolitan community,
but rather in Marblehead, an ironic happenstance in view
of the way John Barnard, the town's faithful minister, described the possibilities of Marblehead upon his arrival in 1707:

There was not so much as one proper carpenter, nor

mason, nor tailor, nor butcher in the town, nor any
thing of a market worth naming; but they had their
houses built by country workmen, and their clothes
made out of town, and supplied themselves with
beef and pork from Boston, which drained the town
of its money. [38]

The Reverend Mr. Barnard had come a little late to Marblehead
and had missed the greatest show ever to take place in the
town--before or since: the building and furnishing of the mansion house of "Captain Andrew Cratey of London, Eng., mariner," as he is described in the understated language of the
Essex County deeds.[39]

On Friday, May 18, 1688, Samuel Sewall noted the captain's
first appearance in New England: "This day Cratey comes to
Marblehead." [40] The thirty-seven-year-old captain apparently
liked what he saw; indeed, there is probably no more agreeable place on earth than Marblehead on a spring day. Slightly
more than a year later, Captain Cratey bought an orchard lot
on "The Broad Street" for Ŀ60, and two months later the little
lot next to it for Ŀ30. He then proceeded to erect his three-
story mansion, which undoubtedly presented an astounding
contrast to its nearest rival in splendor, if it had a rival.

On the street floor were an entry, a great hall, a parlor and
a little parlor, a kitchen, a shop, and a little room behind the
shop. [41] On the second floor were chambers over each of
these rooms, and on the third floor were garrets over them all.
The land, as we have seen, was worth Ŀ90, when he purchased it in 1689, but at the time of his death on May 10,
1695, the house and land were appraised at Ŀ700. The interior was appointed most lavishly, and judging from the
elaborate descriptions in Cratey's inventory, there would seem
to be little question that most of the furnishings had been
brought over from London in one of his ships:

In the great hall [were]: one doz. of caine chears
. . . 7:4:0; 6 Turkey Work chears . . . 3:12:0;
1 Looking Glass, 1 Inlaid table & pr. stands . . .
14:0:0; 1 clock 10:0:0; 4 pictures . . . 4:0:0; and

one ovil table 1:0:0. In the chamber over ditto
hall [were]: 1 doz. of Lackered Cane chears . . .
12:00:00; 1 ditto couch 3:00:00; 1 Japan case of
draws . . . 10:00:0; 1 ditto case for plate . . .
10:00:0; 1 gilded leather screen . . . 3:00:0; 1
Jappan table, a looking glass. . . .

There were also 350 ounces of silver to go in the japanned
plate case--the largest collection of plate in New England at
that date--and in other rooms, an "olive wood Case of Draws
and table" valued at Ł8, a "looking glass and inlaid table,"
at Ł10, an "inlaid case of draws & looking glass" at Ł10,
and so on and on, to a total of Ł600 worth of "movables."[42]
Captain Cratey had equipped himself handsomely to endure
the hardships of New England living.

One searches in vain among the inventories of Captain
Cratey's social and economic peers, who had long been
settled in Essex County, for such a worldly collection of
furnishings. Bartholomew Gedney of Salem was a wealthy
merchant and public servant, probably the most solid of
Salem's solid citizens. At the time of his death in the early
summer of 1699, his inventory amounted to just a few hundred
pounds less than Captain Cratey's, but Puritan sensibility
and habit are reflected by every item in it: "In the parlor: 1
square table . . . 30 shillings; 1 round table . . . 45s.; 6
worne turkey work Chairs . . . 9s. [a] piece; 6 ditto . . .
12s. [s] piece; 1 large Iron Candlestick . . . 18s. "however,
along with the "grate chaire," appraised at 4s., and the
"Joynt stool" valued at 18d., we find 6 caine chairs" at 8s.
apiece, only slightly more expensive than the "map of Canan"
than hung on the wall in merchant Gedney's hall.[43] These
chairs are the only hint of the new style in his extensive
inventory.

The inventory of Captain John Price of Salem, who died
just a few years before Captain Cratey--late in the winter of
1691--amounted to Ł70 more than Cratey's. It contained:
"1 old Jack and 1 old cupboard . . . 20s.; 5 old chaires . . .
5s.; 6 old Turkey Wrought Chaires, 1 1/2 dozen Leather
chaires [probably "Cromwellian" chairs], 6 Searge chaires."
As sometimes happens, by a bit of luck, we find that Captain

Price--one of the half-dozen wealthiest men of Salem in his
day--had recently acquired a dozen expensive chairs. They
were not, however, cane chairs but were described as "New
Turkey Wrought Chaires . . . 4:16:0,"[44] of a type that had
been popular during his father's lifetime.

The presence of simple furniture in Salem at this time was
not totally a matter of economics. While the Gedneys and the
Prices may have been rather slow to acquire new furniture because of Puritan habits, the barely tolerated Salem Quakers
apparently felt the same way. To Joshua Buffum, the man who
had gone to England in 1659 to persuade the authorities to stop
the Massachusetts Theocrats from persecuting the Quakers,[45]
the William and Mary style was virtually of no interest. His
inventory of 1705 reveals only one suggestion of the new style
intermixed with the "joynt stools," "fformes," and the "Cub-
bord with Drawers," and that was a "couch," appraised with a
square table, a chair, and pillows at £2:17:00.[46]

When John Maule, a merchant of some standing in Salem's
Quaker community, died in 1730, his inventory betrayed no
hint of faddish furniture, although his estate amounted to £723
and he could easily have afforded it. As a matter of fact, he
was still using "6 Turkey wrot chairs," valued at 5s. each,
in his "best" chamber over his shop. The inventory also item-
izes a "voyder" in the same room--a very late mention of a
type of tray or basket popular in the time of Henry VIII.[47]

Yet a famous but atypical chest-on-frame with its five legs
in the form of S-scrolls, illustrated by Walter A. Dyer on page
15 of the Antiquarian Magazine for June 1931, is signed by
Edmund Titcomb of Newbury, and must have been made prior
to his death in 1723.[48] The present location of this chest is
not known to the author, but if it came from the same hand as
the almost identical chest in the Wadsworth Atheneum
(Nutting, Pilgrim Century, Fig. 103), rather coarse construction would seem to contradict its stylistically advanced
appearance. The fact that the unique group of chests, of
which these are examples, were made in Newbury, a very
rural village in the first quarter of the eighteenth century,
qualified our present knowledge and concepts of style diffusion: it appears to represent a direct European influence

not filtered through Boston or Salem.[49]

While the William and Mary style was well on its way to popularity in Boston in 1695, the inventories of Salem reveal a much slower adoption of its baroque grandeurs there. Except for the mentions in the Cratey and Gedney inventories, only John Tawley, a newly successful but unpopular merchant, had any items that suggest an interest in the fashionable.[50] The style seems not to have come into general use on the North Shore until the second decade of the eighteenth century.

It has long been the custom of American furniture historians to think of the changes that came about in New England furniture as a sequence of changes in style. It may rather be that the first change of style in American furniture--the progression from the oak (jacobean) style of joined furniture to the hardwood (William and Mary) style of board construction-- represented a fundamental change in method of construction rather than the application of new ornament to existing forms, as was common throughout the remaining decades of the colonial period. As such, it is probably the first instance in American furniture making of the common phenomenon of today: technological unemployment. The change in construction brought an end to the careers of many Boston joiners as furniture makers.

The suggestion is very strong that the more fashionable clientele of the town availed themselves of the services of the cabinetmaker, while the "common sort" continued to trade with the furniture-making joiner. It seems likely that furniture in the new high style was the product of the cabinetmaker, while "simple city furniture" continued to be made by Boston's joiners. It appears probable that little, if any, William and Mary high-style furniture was made in Boston prior to the appearance there of John Brocas in 1696. Additional research may provide specific instances that can demonstrate that what happened in Boston also occurred in the smaller towns of America. How many questions would be answered if we knew that the rural maker of case furniture was not only the spiritual descendant of the seventeenth-century joiner but his lineal descendant, too--working in the old way, producing furniture in new styles as he conceived the new styles to be--without ever having had the opportunity of knowing the significance of those styles from the firsthand experience of regular apprenticeship under an urban or English-trained cabinetmaker.

Although we still cannot separate the work of the urban joiner who trained himself to make cabinetmaker-style furniture in the first quarter of the eighteenth century from that of his rural counterpart, we can at least proceed to explore the later styles of American furniture with confidence in the knowledge that we have some idea that at a specific time in history the two traditions diverged, although the joiner never really disappeared from the craft life of colonial America.

Notes

1. See Ralph Edwards, The Shorter Dictionary of English
Furniture (London, 1964), p. 73, fig. 1. The comparison suggested here seems particularly ludicrous when we read in John
Evelyn's Diary his August 27, 1678, description of Ham house:
"After dinner, I walked to Ham, to see the house and garden
of the Duke of Lauderdale, which is indeed inferior to few of
the best villas in Italy itself; the house furnished like a great
Prince's" ([London, 1906], III, 18).
2. George Francis Dow, Two Centuries of Travel in Essex
County (Topsfield, Mass., 1921), p. 41.
3. See Donald W. Koch, "Income Distribution and Political Structure in Seventeenth-Century Salem" Essex Institute
Historical Collections, CV (Jan. 1969), 50-71, for a different
point of view. Mr. Koch's essentially statistical analysis
never suggests that a comparison with Boston in the same
period might make a relative judgment of urbanity more three-
dimensional. The attributes of urbanity, at any rate, would
appear to be multifarious.
4. Salem in the Eighteenth Century (Boston, 1937), p. 174.
5. Report of the Record Commissioners of the City of
Boston, VII, Boston Town Records, 1660-1700, ed. William H.
Whitemore (Boston, 1881), 111 (hereafter Boston Record Commissioners).
6. Edward Johnson, The Wonder Working Providence of
Sion's Saviour in New England, ed. William Poole (Boston,
1867), p. 43. Johnson's accuracy and veracity have often been
questioned by historians and literary critics alike. In this one
instance, it is likely that Johnson reported the appearance of
Boston accurately. A map of the town as it existed in 1643-44
has been painstakingly reconstructed by Samuel C. Clough,
based upon the surviving comtemporary MS Possessions of the
Inhabitants of Boston, printed in Boston Record Commissioners,
II (Boston, 1877), Pt. 2. Clough's map (Publications of the
Colonial Society of Massachusetts, XXVII [Boston, 1927],
12-13) shows that in Johnson's time Boston was settled from
present Boylston Street eastward to the harbor at the point
where the Charles River flows into the Bay. The 208 heads of

household listed in the "Book of Possessions" implies a population of approximately 1,000.

The Royal Commissioners who viewed the king's colonies
in 1662 described the Bostonians thus: "Their houses are
generally wooden, their streets crooked, with little decency
and no uniformity." Far from contradicting Johnson, their
comment merely shows how much Boston had grown in the in-
tervening seventeen years.

7. Justin Winsor, ed., The Memorial History of Boston,
I (Boston, 1881), 535.

8. Bulletin of the Boston Public Library, new ser., IV,
no. 4 (Jan. 1894), unpaged facsimile, fol. 305. Compare with
the often-quoted resolution passed by the Boston Town Meeting of July 20, 1660 (Boston Record Commissioners, II [Boston,
1877], Pt. 1, 156-57). Although in essence a reiteration of the
former statement, the 1677 petition emphasizes unfair competition rather than proper training. Both statements recognize
one aspect of the breakdown of the apprentice system in
America: the fact that demand for skilled labor tended to short-
en the length of time an apprentice was willing to serve. See
also Carl Bridenbaugh, Cities in the Wilderness (New York,
1938), p. 138.

9. (Portland, Maine, 1944), pp. 29-34. This chest, with
a mahogany date panel, is now in the collection of the Antiquarian Society, Concord, Massachusetts. The panel has different dates carved on either side. At present it is displayed
with the date 1701 facing out. The date, 1700, is on the reverse, facing inward.

10. See the author's "Account Book of John Gould, Weaver
of Topsfield, Massachusetts, 1697-1724, "Essex Institute
Historical Collections, CV (Jan. 1969), 44-45.

11. See Parke-Bernet Gallery, Stuart and Georgian Furniture
Sale Catalog (Feb. 28-March 1, 1958), p. 27, item 134.

12. Suffolk County Registry of Probate, Boston, Mass., V,
340 (hereafter Suffolk Probate Records).

13. Ibid., XVII, 58.

14. Furniture of the Pilgrim Century (New York, 1965),
I, fig. 218.

15. Essex County, Registry of Probate, Salem, Mass.
XXXVI, 217 (hereafter Essex Probate Records).

16. See Patricia E. Kane, "The Seventeenth Century Case
Furniture of Hartford County, Connecticut, and Its Makers"
(master's thesis, University of Delaware, 1968), p. 57.

17. Edwards, p. 331.

18. Ralph Mason, a joiner, emigrated 1635, died 1679. His
sons all joiners, were: Richard, working 1651, died 1674;
Samuel, working 1652, died 1691; John, working 1661, died
1696; and Jacob, working 1665, died 1695. Henry Messenger
emigrated before 1640, died 1682. His sons were: John, working 1661, left Boston ca. 1686; Simeon, working 1666, died
1695 (?); Henry II, working 1678, died 1687; and Thomas, working 1682, died after 1705. Henry I's grandsons were: Thomas
II, a turner, working 1713-20, probably later, and Ebenezer,
working 1718. All were joiners except Thomas II. See the
unpub. MS by the author, "Boston Furniture Makers, 1635-
1726."

19. The joiners are: John Cunnable, emigrated from London,
ca. 1674; Obadiah Wakefield, Sr., working 1674; Ralph Carter,
working 1676; William Smith, admitted as a resident of Boston,
1680; John Blake, the same; Robert Hilliard [alias Holland],
admitted 1681; and John Mulligan, admitted 1685.

The upholsterers are: Edward Tyng, Jr., John Wolfinden,
Alexander More, Jonathan Everard, Joseph Juet, and Harry
Clarke. Wolfinden, More, and Clarke were probably im-
migrants, the others were second-generation New Englanders.
See my "Boston Furniture Makers."

20. While the term "cabinetmaker" might have carried some
overtone of fashionableness about it in Boston, the distinction
in terms of craftsmanship did not necessarily reflect the quality
of workmanship. Batty Langley wrote in 1740 that "it is difficult to find one cabinetmaker in Fifty . . . that can make a
book-case, & c. indispensibly true . . . without being
obliged to a Joiner, for to set out the work." Quoted by
Ralph Fastnedge in English Furniture Styles, 1500-1840
(Harmondsworth, Eng., 1964), p. 132.

21. See Suffolk [County Mass.] Deeds, XIV (Boston, 1906),
267. Brocas was entertained at dinner by Samuel Sewall in
November of that year. See The Diary of Samuel Sewall, I,
in Collections of the Massachusetts Historical Society,

5th ser., V (Boston, 1878), 438.

22. See "Boston Furniture Makers," chap. 8.

23. "An Unpublished Letter of Samuel Sewall," New England Historical and Genealogical Register, XXIX (July, 1870), 291.

24. Suffolk Probate Records, XXVI, 33-34.

25. Mable M. Swan, "Boston's Carvers and Joiners, Pt. I, Pre-Revolutionary," Antiques, LIII (March, 1948), 198-201.

26. Burghers of New Amsterdam and Freeman of New York, 1675-1866, in New York Historical Society Collections, XVIII (New York, 1885), 139, 163.

27. See the unpub. MS by the author, "Salem Craftsmen in 1760: A Contemporary Document," to appear in Essex Institute Historical Collections in 1970.

28. William M. Hornor, The Blue Book of Philadelphia Furniture (Philadelphia, 1935), pp. 317-20.

29. Suffolk Probate Records, X, 412.

30. A Genealogical Dictionary of the First Settlers of New England (Baltimore, 1965), III, 170.

31. Suffolk Probate Records, X 412.

32. Ibid., VIII, 179. Ragland does not appear on the tax list of 1687, nor does his widow, Mary, appear on the tax list of 1695.

33. Ibid., XIII, 304-5.

34. Ibid., pp. 303,492. It is, of course, conjectural if any of these earliest cane chairs were made in New England. Indeed, there is a good possibility that most of them were not. R. W. Symonds, "The Export Trade of Furniture to Colonial America," Burlington Magazine, LXX (Nov. 1940), 152-61, points out that in the year 1697, for example, 1,041 chairs, valued at a first cost of 3 to 10 shillings, were shipped to America. His tables of valuations (p.160) suggest that perhaps 38 percent of these chairs found their way to New England.

35. Suffolk Probate Records, XIII, 683.

36. Ibid., XI, 343.

37. Ibid., p. 165.

38. Dow, p. 62.

39. Essex Probate Records, VIII, 213.

40. Diary, I, 213.

41. Sidney Perley, "Marblehead in 1700," Essex
Institute Historical Collections, XLVII (Jan. 1911), 82-83.

42. Essex Probate Records, CCCVI, 86-88.

43. Ibid., 76-78.

44. "A Round table of black walnut . . . 45s.;
1 [olivewood] looking glass . . . 30s.; 1 pair of
virginalls . . . 60s.," etc., ibid., CCCII, 198-199.

45. Savage, I, 289.

46. Essex Probate Records, CDVIII, 442-43.

47. Ibid., file docket no. 18026. For an insight into
Quaker attitudes when a dominant rather than a minority
group, see Alice Morse Earle, Home Life in Colonial Days
(Boston, 1898), p. 160.

48. "The American Highboy: William and Mary--Queen
Anne," Antiquarian, XVI. Titcomb (born 1682) probably
was not working before 1703. The place of his apprenticeship is not known.

49. It is always possible that the somewhat finer
example in cherry wood illustrated as fig. XII in Luke
Vincent Lockwood, Colonial Furniture in America (New York,
1926), I, 345, was made by a Boston craftsman and is the
prototype of the entire group. Its present location is
unknown to the author.

50. Essex Probate Records, file docket no. 22733.

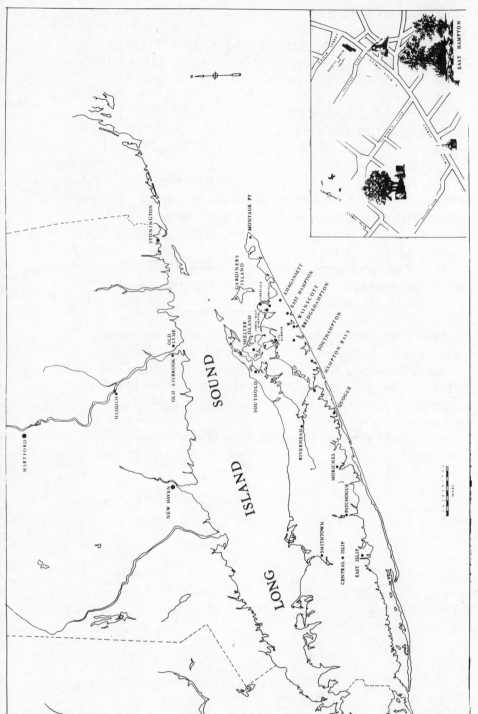

Fig. 1. Long Island and Connecticut towns and villages served by the Dominy craftsmen, with an inset of East Hampton, New York.

THE DOMINYS OF EAST HAMPTON, LONG ISLAND, AND THEIR FURNITURE

Charles F. Hummel

THE Dominy family of East Hampton, New York, produced three generations of artisans who made furniture and clocks during the late eighteenth and early nineteenth centuries. Five questions are of central concern: who were the Dominy craftsmen and what was the nature of their training; where did they perform their work and what area did they serve; what kind of clocks and furniture did they make; who purchased these objects; and, finally, what conclusions may be drawn?

Three members of the Dominy family deserve the name of craftsmen. They are Nathaniel Dominy IV (1737-1812), Nathaniel Dominy V (1770-1852), and Felix Dominy (1800-1868), father, son, and grandson. Their active careers extended from about 1760 to about 1840, or from the height of the handcraft system into the era of its rapid decline. Their legacy of over two hundred manuscript items, most of which are housed in the Joseph Downs Manuscript and Microfilm Collection of The Henry Francis du Pont Winterthur Museum, includes accounts from the 1760s through the 1840s. Also preserved are approximately eleven hundred of their tools, all in Winterthur's collection, and almost one hundred objects made by the Dominys, several of which belong to Winterthur.

It is almost certain that each of these craftsmen received his training as part of a family apprenticeship system. Unlike the city craftsman, who was apprenticed to a specialist, the rural craftsman usually received his training from his father or another closely related member of the family. Unfortunately, almost no documents survive to prove exactly where or how each of the Dominys was trained. Surviving

members of the Dominy family have stated that Nathaniel
Dominy IV received his training from his father, Nathaniel
III (1714-1778). Cited as evidence is the fact that Nathaniel
III is twice described as a "carponder [carpenter]" in land-
sale deeds, which would account for Nathaniel IV's skill as
a woodworker.[1] Another suggestion is that Nathaniel IV may
have learned the "art and mystery" of the clockmaker from
his mother's family: Nathaniel Dominy III married Elizabeth
Eyres in 1736, and there were a number of English clockmakers of that name.[2] Nathaniel IV's grandfather, Nathaniel
Dominy II (1684-1768), possessed surveyor's skills, and it
is recorded that he "looked after" the town clock in 1735.[3]
However, no clocks are known to have been made by him,
and it is likely that the service he performed for the town
was that of a caretaker. Another possible clue to Nathaniel
IV's training as a clockmaker is an inscription inside the
cover of his copy of Nathaniel Colson's The Mariner's New
Calendar, published in London in 1761. In this book the
craftsman wrote that he had purchased it from the shop of
Mr. Bird at Newport on June 29, 1762. As a matter of fact,
however, neither the works nor the cases of clocks produced
by the Dominys resemble Newport, Rhode Island, examples.
It is clear, however, that Nathaniel Dominy IV preferred to
be called a clockmaker rather than a carpenter or cabinetmaker, as his watchpaper proclaims "Watches / Repaired /
By / Nathaniel Dominy / Clockmaker / E[ast]. Hampton,"
and the few advertisements of his business activity refer
only to his work with clocks.

Nathaniel IV's emphasis on clockmaking may have led
to the intensive training in woodworking he provided for
his son Nathaniel Dominy V. Nathaniel V concentrated
his activities in house and mill carpentry, wheelwrighting,
cabinetmaking, and turning from the time that he was nineteen until about 1844 when he was seventy-four. The large
account book kept by the Dominys has an increasing number
of entries "From Nat's book" after 1789.[4] A number of furniture forms not previously entered into the ledger appear
after 1789 or 1790, providing additional evidence of Nathaniel
Dominy V's training as a woodworker. The family apprentice

system, then, allowed Nathaniel IV to concentrate on
clockmaking and the repair of watches and clocks while
his son performed the tasks necessary for their woodworking
business.

Some evidence does exist that Nathaniel V was given
training in clockwork by his father. Between Nathaniel
Dominy IV's death in October 1812 and the making of Felix
Dominy's first clock in December 1817, four clocks are entered into Nathaniel V's accounts. They were made in 1813
and 1814.[5] Unfortunately, none of these four clocks has
survived. This training could not have been very extensive,
for the last of the craftsmen, Felix Dominy, was given no
training in clock- or watchmaking by his father, Nathaniel
V, but was instead apprenticed to a craftsman in New York
City. A notation in Felix's hand states: "Had this in
[. . . 18]15 / Name in my first Watch J Day [. . .L]ondon.
Owned three other watches while working in N York."[6]
Again, although Felix apparently preferred to do metalwork,
and his father, woodwork, these roles were occasionally
switched. In 1832, for example, James C. Horton (Norton)
wrote from Quogue, New York, asking Felix to make him a
"3 ft 6 in--in the clear" gunbox of "oak stuff" and Nathaniel
V to prepare some "good stuff . . . 7 ft 6 in long" for some
wagon shafts.[7]

The family apprenticeship training system was important
to rural craftsmen because the more varied their products and
craft activities, the greater would be the potential number of
customers to serve. It was logical and practical, therefore,
for the Dominys to train their children in a number of different craft skills. Because of the artificial separation of
crafts, primarily economic in origin in most colonial American
cities, the basic relationship and overlapping of tools and
techniques needed to perform adequately in various craft
pursuits is frequently overlooked. Because of their varied
training, the Dominys could complete skillfully almost any
tasks they were asked to perform by their neighbors. Clockmaking, watch and clock repair, gunsmithing, coppersmithing,
and blacksmithing are all functions within the broad category
of metalwork. The woodworking field, similarly, encompasses

cabinetwork, carpentry, and turner's and wheelwright's
work. To determine what single craft practice or activity
provided the most income for the Dominys is not easy and
could be misleading. Any separation or classification of
their work would be arbitrary, because almost everything
they produced involved more than one craft. For example, a
clock was made in their clock shop, and its case prepared
in the woodworking shop. An order for a "woolen" wheel
would require the production of metal parts in the clock
shop forge and the turning and joining of parts of the wheel
in the woodworking shop. There is no evidence in the vast
number of documents that have survived to show that any of
the Dominy craftsmen ever thought, "Now I am a cabinetmaker," "Now I am a carpenter," or "Now I am a wheelwright."

During the years when the Dominy craftsmen were active,
East Hampton Village was the center of the predominantly
agricultural community of East Hampton Township. Located
near the easternmost tip of Long Island, it was described in
1813 as "a Post-Township of Suffolk County, 35 E. of
Riverhead, 112 miles E. of New York, and 272 S. of Albany."[8]
These were forbidding distances by land transportation, and
even with improved roads in the late 1820s it took six days
for a letter sent from Islip to reach East Hampton.[9] As late
as 1840, there were almost five times as many farmers as
craftsmen in this township.[10] Even the Dominys were a
perfect example of the rural artisans described by Tench
Coxe between 1787 and 1794 as men "who live in the country,
generally reside on small lots and farms, of one acre to
twenty, and not a few upon farms of twenty to one hundred
and fifty acres, which they cultivate at leisure times, with
their own hands . . . or by letting out fields, for part of
the produce."[11] East Hampton tax records show that in 1814,
two years after his father's death, Nathaniel Dominy V and
his son Felix were living on a 100-acre property.[12]

In analyzing the products of the Dominy craftsmen, these
two factors--an isolated community and a predominantly
agricultural one--must be kept in the foreground. At least
two prominent figures of the late eighteenth and early

nineteenth century emphasized the isolation of East Hampton.
The comments of Lyman Beecher and Timothy Dwight give
us a picture of the physical setting in which the Dominys
worked.[13] At the same time, their comments provide a
measure of insight into the character of the people whom
these artisans served. From 1799 to 1810 Lyman Beecher
served as pastor of the Presbyterian church in East Hampton.
According to Beecher, the village consisted of "the plainest
farm houses" standing on its main street. Wood was piled
near the front door of all houses, and the barns were close
by, also standing on the street. Beecher commented further
that:

> There was so little traveling that the road consisted
> of two ruts worn through the green turf for the wheels,
> and two narrow paths for the horses. The wide green
> street was generally covered with flocks of white
> geese. On Sunday, all the families from the villages
> . . . came riding to meeting in great two-horse,
> uncovered wagons, with three seats, carrying nine
> persons. It is probable that more than half the
> inhabitants of these retired villages made no other
> journey during their whole lives. There was not a
> store in town and all our purchases were made in
> New York by a small schooner that ran once a week.[14]

About 1811, Timothy Dwight visited East Hampton while on
a tour of Long Island. His incisive description reveals mixed
feelings:

> The town of East Hampton . . . is compactly built,
> and contains an ancient Presbyterian church, an
> academy, and about one hundred dwelling houses
> . . . . The houses are generally of long standing
> [the Dominy House, built in 1715, was almost one
> hundred years old at the time of Dwight's visit].
> I saw but a single new one, and that was erected
> where another had been lately pulled down. Scarcely
> any of them are painted. In other respects they are
> generally in a tolerable state of repair. The passion
> for appearance, so far at least as building is concerned,
> seems hitherto to have fastened very little on the

inhabitants of East Hampton. A general air of equality,
simplicity, and quiet, is visible here in a degree perhaps singular.[15]

Dwight dwelled at length upon the isolation of East Hampton
and the sense of "stillness and sequestration from the world."
The rural character of East Hampton helped to preserve conservative traditions with a consequent demand for conservative-
ly styled products. Dwight's observations on the old traditions prevalent in East Hampton are important in analyzing
products made by the Dominy craftsmen:

> There is . . . no want of the social character; but it is
> regulated rather by the long-continued customs of this
> single spot, than by the mutable fashions of a great
> city, or the powerful influence of an extensive coun-
> try, intimately connected in all its parts, and con-
> trolling, by the general opinion and practice, the
> personal conduct of every inhabitant. Living by
> themselves more than the people of most other
> places, they became more attentive to whatever is
> their own, and less to the concern of others. Hence
> their own customs, especially those which have come
> down from their ancestors (and these are about all
> that exist among them), have a commanding influence
> on their conduct.[16]

Although there is much evidence that the Dominys' outlook
was considerably broader than that of their fellow townsmen,
they were born into this group of people, understood their
preferences, and always remained part of them.

The communities within the area served by the Dominy
craftsmen extended well beyond the confines of East Hampton
Township, as can be seen on the map (fig. 1). Islip,
Moriches, Quogue, Smithtown, and even Flushing were some
of the Long Island villages and towns in which the Dominys
had customers. They served people living a short sail across
Gardiner's Bay and Long Island Sound in Hartford, Haddam,
New Haven, Lyme, and Stonington, Connecticut. Most of
their cabinetwork and clocks, however, were produced for
customers in the immediate vicinity. Of 433 transactions

for furniture recorded in their accounts (see Appendix A),
only 10 were clearly with customers who were nonresidents.
Of 56 transactions for clocks (see Appendix B), only 5 were
with people not living in, or near, East Hampton. Much of
their work outside the township was in the nature of repairs.

Between 1768, when Aaron Isaacs was billed ten shillings
for a "trundle" bedstead, and 1840, when Isaac Van Scoy,
Jr., was charged 2s. 4d. for two "chairs" (see Appendix A),
the Dominys produced at least 890 pieces of finished woodwork. This figure includes a few items like buttons and
trenchers, but a substantial amount of furniture did come
from their shop. From 1768 to about 1828 approximately 90
clocks were produced in their shop although only 54 are recorded in their accounts (see Appendix B). Clearly, production of an average of 12 1/3 pieces of furniture per year and
1 1/2 clocks per year was not enough to support these craftsmen. Those who have read With Hammer in Hand will recall
that cabinetmaking and clockmaking were supplemented by
agricultural labor, house and mill carpentry, production of
domestic equipment, gun repairing, the sale of produce and
merchandise, toolmaking, wheelwrighting, watch and clock
repairs, metalworking, and whatever else would produce a
shilling or a dollar.[17]

Lists of the furniture and clocks produced by the Dominys
are included in Appendixes A and B. Each customer's rank,
taken from the tax lists of real and personal property owned
in East Hampton between 1802 and 1816, appears by his
name.[18] Space does not permit inclusion of every surviving
piece of furniture or clock made by these men; the guiding
principle in selection for the lists has been to show a variety
of forms and to illustrate them in descending order of cost.

The most expensive clock made by Nathaniel Dominy IV
cost ₤38, almost twice as much as the costliest piece of
furniture. It was made in 1797 for Miller Dayton, whose
average ranking on the tax lists was ninth. The example
illustrated (fig. 2) was made two years later for David
Gardiner of Flushing, Long Island, whose average tax list
ranking was sixteenth although he was a nonresident with
landholdings and had no personal property to be taxed. It

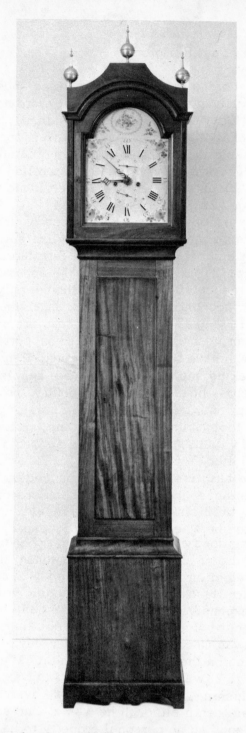

Fig. 2. Eight-day, strike, repeater, alarm clock.
Made by Nathaniel Dominy IV for David Gardiner,
East Hampton, New York, 1799. Mahogany case, white
pine and cherry secondary woods, enameled sheet-iron
dial, brass works. H. 92"; W. 17"; D. 9". Winterthur Museum (57.34.1)

is owned by Winterthur and is displayed in the Dominy clock
shop. Only seven clocks of this type--featuring an eight-
day and striking movement, repeater mechanism, and an
alarm--were made. They were produced between 1791 and
1799 and ranged in price from Ł38 to Ł20 8s. None of the
purchasers of these clocks ranked lower than twenty-eighth
on the tax lists.

David Gardiner paid Ł36, or $90, for his clock, which is
described in an original bill as an "Horologiographical,
Repeating, Alarm, Monition" clock. The mahogany used by
Nathaniel Dominy V to make the case for this clock has a
rich, handsome grain, but with two exceptions the case is a
little different from others made by him in this period. Cyma-
recta amd reversa curves were cut on the applied molding
to form a skirt and bracket feet for the clock. This is one
of the few examples in which the case does not run behind
this bracket to rest on the floor. Its pagoda-shaped
pediment was copied from an earlier one on a clock made
by the Dominys for David's brother, John Lyon Gardiner, in
1791. Nathaniel IV engraved his signature on the brass
alarm dial, as he usually did for his most expensive clocks.

Two very informative letters relating to this clock have
survived. One, from his brother, informed Gardiner that the
clock was ready and that Nathaniel Dominy IV had stated
that it could be put into a case to be shipped "safe by water."
Gardiner was also advised to go to Yules Air Furnace in New
York City for two cast-iron weights, each from twelve to
fourteen pounds. The second letter, from Nathaniel Dominy
IV, gave Gardiner detailed instructions for setting up the
clock on its arrival in Flushing, New York, including the way
the case was to be secured to the wall through the back and
steadied at the base by the use of cleats on the floor.[19]

The Dominys' most elaborate clocks had enamel dials
made in the Birmingham, England, "manufactory" of Thomas
Osborne, and all of the surviving examples bear the firm's
imprint on the back of the dial plate. These dials were often
bought in New York City by the purchaser of a particular
Dominy clock, who was then credited for its expense toward

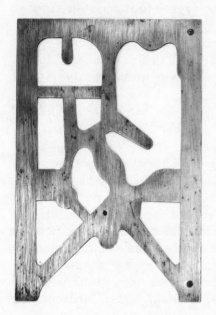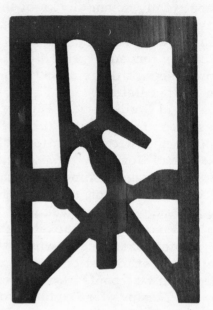

Fig. 3. Clock plate and wood-casting pattern,
Nathaniel Dominy IV, East Hampton, New York, ca.
1785. Tulip wood, brass. H. 7 11/16", 7 13/16";
W. 5 1/4", 5 5/16"; D. 1/8", 1/8". Winterthur
Museum (57.26.502; 57.26.524)

the total cost of the clock. Both David and John Lyon
Gardiner purchased the dials for their clocks in New York
City.[20] This practice presents a concrete example of customer preference, rather than a craftsman's own choice,
entering into the design of a clock.

A significant development in the production of Dominy
clocks occurred in 1783. In that year, Nathaniel IV first
made use of the intricately pierced plates shown in figure 3
to support his clock movements. They are as distinctive and
reliable an identification of a Dominy clock as fingerprints
would be. It may be that he developed these plates because
of the extreme shortage of metal caused by the Revolutionary
War. At any rate, no other clockmaker uses them, and they
must be considered an example of Dominy ingenuity.

Another of the seven elaborate clocks made by the Dominys
illustrates other characteristics of their work. This clock,
purchased in 1791 by John Lyon Gardiner, cost him Ł28, or
$70. This was Ł8, or $20, less than the sum paid by his
brother David. However, the case of this clock had only a
mahogany facing, its sides being constructed of cherry.
Moreover, the bottom part of the case was not shaped like
that of David's clock, and the sawed profile of the applied
molding bracket at the base was much simpler. The design
of its turned wooden ball and steeple finials (imitating the
more common brass examples) was probably used for those
now missing from David Gardiner's clock. John Lyon
Gardiner, seventh proprietor of Gardiner's Island, always
ranked first on the East Hampton tax lists. Between 1802
and 1815 his real and personal wealth increased from a value
of $52,110 to $128,400. His financial worth was always six
to eight times greater than that of Huntting Miller, for example, who consistently ranked second, and eighty times
greater than the value of Nathaniel Dominy IV's property.
It comes as no surprise, then, to find that John Lyon
Gardiner is the only one of the Dominys' customers who purchased more than one clock (see Appendix B). Both were
bought in the same year, 1791, and both were eight-day,
strike, repeater, alarm clocks.

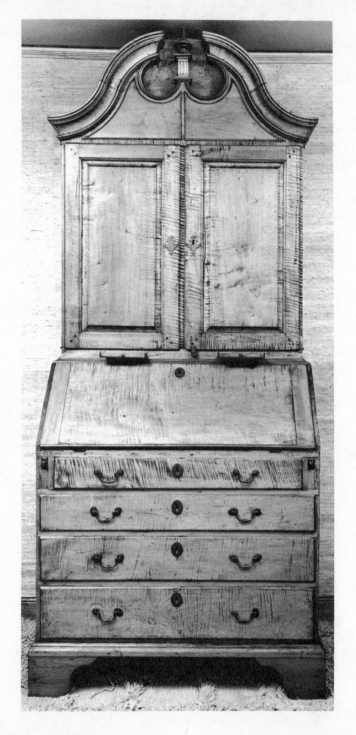

Fig. 4. Desk and bookcase. Made by Nathaniel
Dominy V for John Lyon Gardiner, East Hampton, New
York, 1800. Maple; cherry and white pine secondary
woods. H. 87 1/4"; W. 37 3/4"; D. 20 5/8".
Winthrop Gardiner, Jr., Collection

In order to determine how long it took the Dominys to make their most expensive clocks, one can use a formula which gives equal weight to labor, materials, and profit.[21] That formula produces an allocation of £12, or $30, for the labor involved in the clock made for David Gardiner and slightly more than £9, or $23.33, for producing one of John Lyon Gardiner's clocks. Nathaniel Dominy IV consistently valued his daily labor at 7s. 6d., or about $1.00, in this period. Therefore, it can be estimated that about 30 days' labor went into the making of David Gardiner's clock and approximately 23 1/3 days' work was needed to make John Lyon Gardiner's. The Dominy accounts, however, indicate that the latter transaction continued over a period of ten months. From February to November 1791, when the clock was finally delivered, John Lyon Gardiner was credited toward the purchase price with two clock faces "got at N. York," glass for the hoods, a small bed bought at a vendue sale, twenty feet of mahogany, cash, and a 33 1/2 pound cheese.[22]

Although the dials of their clocks are frequently well marked, only three pieces of surviving cabinetwork made by the Dominys bear some indication of their authorship. The back of the pendulum case door of John Lyon Gardiner's clock bears the inscription "N. Dominie fecit 1791 Novr for John Lyon Gardiner $70."

The most expensive piece of furniture produced by Nathaniel Dominy V was probably his most ambitious example of cabinetmaking (fig. 4). On May 5, 1800, he billed John Lyon Gardiner £20 8s. for making a "desk-bookcase" and for carting it to Fireplace, just opposite Gardiner's Island. There it was undoubtedly loaded aboard a sloop and carried over the water to the island. The present owner, Winthrop Gardiner, Jr., inherited the desk about 1933 and brought it back to the mainland village where it was originally made.

Only one desk and bookcase is listed in the Dominy accounts, but three other examples, one more for John Lyon Gardiner and two made for Dominy family use, have survived. That only four of these pieces were made and that they were produced for their wealthiest customer or for the craftsmen's

personal use are indications of the expense involved in production. About twenty days' labor was required to make this
desk and bookcase, with much of the time spent on its thirteen drawers.

The desk is of maple, with cherry drawer sides and white
pine drawer bottoms and backboards. It provides a fair summary of the Dominys' talent for design--a curious mixture of
sophistication and naiveté--and their unquestionable skill in
handling materials. Its bonnet top has a broken-arch pediment with applied strips of bold and handsome curved molding.
Fielded panels under its pediment repeat its shape in a
technique similar to that of eastern Connecticut or Rhode
Island cabinetmakers. The pediment of the Dominy desk may
have been copied from a handsome Rhode Island high chest of
drawers that once belonged to John Lyon Gardiner and is now
owned by Robert Gardiner. The sliding shelves provided for
candles are an indication of unusual quality. Another detail
that shows Nathaniel V's careful planning is the use of a
nicely shaped bracket applied to the rear of the desk. This
enabled the piece to be pushed flush against a chair rail so
that both bookcase and desk sections fit snugly against the
wall.

The turned finial was thought to be a replacement until a
similar turning, used as a drop under the shaft of a candle-
stand made by Nathaniel V, was discovered. All but one of
the cyma-curved dividers in the bookcase section are missing.
Many of the decorative patterns used for dividers or valances
in this bookcase can be found on three other Dominy desk and
bookcases that have survived. Its bracket feet are replace-
ments.

As ambitious an undertaking as this piece is, it exhibits
the use of tools on which rural craftsmen placed great re-
liance for their decorative techniques--molding planes and
saws. Carving was not used to any great degree on the
Dominys' cabinetwork or, to my knowledge, on other country
furniture. When carving was used to decorate a surface, it
was usually done without skill. Moldings and sawed ornament, however, provided beautiful decoration for furniture
made in rural areas. An unresolved question is why John

Lyon Gardiner would accept this old-fashioned bookcase in
1800 when he could have purchased an up-to-date, fashionable piece of furniture.

In contrast, a desk and bookcase made for family use by
Nathaniel V was evidently designed to handle the needs of
a flourishing family business. Its plain interior in the desk
section contains a number of cabinetmaking tricks. A sliding
panel in front of the drawers gives access to a hidden well.
At the center is a locked door, which pivots on pintle hinges
at its base and falls forward when unlocked. Behind it is a
series of three drawers, one of which conceals a secret
drawer at the rear. The lower left- and right-hand drawers
also conceal secret drawers. Four more drawers are located
in the lower part of the bookcase. Above them, dividers
provide space for eight large ledgers. Sixteen compartments
in the top section give ample storage for bills, receipts, and
correspondence.

The Dominys painted much of their furniture, not having
the respect for a natural cherry or maple wood finish that
people have today. Their own cherry desk and bookcase was
covered with black paint, which is being removed by its
present owner, W. Tyson Dominy. From 1765 to 1818, Dominy
accounts list purchases of "linseed oil, Rosin, Coperas,
bees-wax, chalk, Varnish, lacker, White lead, red lead,
Lamp Black, [and] Spanish Brown."[23] Two alterations have
changed the appearance of the family desk and bookcase.
Originally its bookcase doors consisted of large, individual
recessed panels outlined by heavy quarter-round molding.
In an effort to repair large cracks in the panels, stiles and
rails apparently were added in this century as reinforcement.
A heavy rail with a molded edge was tacked to the front edge
of the bottom of the bookcase section probably at the same
time.

Between 1770 and 1811 at least six "desks" were entered
into the Dominy accounts at prices ranging from £5 10s. to
£11. John Lyon Gardiner paid the latter price for the mahogany
example in figure 5, the only one of its type known to the
author to have survived.[24] Its large drawers are made of
white pine, while the smaller drawers are made of cherry.

The surface of this desk is almost undecorated. A strip of ogee molding is applied to the base, and each of the drawer edges is finished with a slight thumbnail molding. On the drawer fronts are the original post-and-bail handles with circular backplates. The absence of sliding rests for the fall-front lid is explained when the lid is opened. It is supported by iron rods and chain links, a construction technique used on another case piece made by Nathaniel V.[25] The desk's interior is also plain, relieved only by the valance inserts in the letter holes, a double-bead molding on the edge of vertical dividers, and the brass ring-and-screw drawer pulls. The template used to produce the bracket feet that support this desk, and those on other case pieces made by the Dominys, has survived in the Tool Collection. The desk is now owned by Winthrop Gardiner, Sr.

This desk is well documented. On the back of the upper left-hand drawer in the lower section is a pencil inscription that reads "Nathaniel Domine Junr fecit Jany-1802 / For John Lyon Gardiner Esqr - Price 27 $ - 50 cts." It has been noted above that Nathaniel V's ledger book records a billing of Ł11 to John Lyon Gardiner for a desk. Throughout their account books, a constant exchange rate of $2.50 to Ł1 was used after 1790. Perhaps the cost of this desk is a reflection of the slightly less than ten days spent in making it.

The survival of Dominy furniture and clocks among descendants of the Gardiner family can be misleading. It would be natural to suppose that only the wealthiest individual in East Hampton could afford to buy these expensive pieces of furniture in a wide variety of forms. Indeed, this writer made the flat statement in With Hammer in Hand that "affluence could be assumed in a purchaser [of furniture] when the wood used bore the notation 'mahogany.'"[26] On the basis of the list of furniture in descending order of cost, compared with the customer's tax list ranking, it is now possible to make a contradiction of that statement. For example, the only other purchaser of an Ł11 desk was Mulford Hand, who also bought his mahogany one in 1802 (see Appendix A). His average rank on the East Hampton Tax lists was 132. Further, although ranked first, John Lyon Gardiner bought twenty-one different

Fig. 5. Desk. Made by Nathaniel Dominy V for
John Lyon Gardiner, East Hampton, New York, 1802.
Mahogany; white pine and cherry secondary woods.
H. 41"; W. 37 1/4"; D. 19 7/8". Winthrop Gardiner,
Sr., Collection

furniture items from the Dominys; Thomas Baker, ranked
eighty-fourth, purchased twenty different items. Baker's
ranking was quite close to that of the Dominys.

The fact that affluence, or lack of it, did not always influence the selection of furniture or clocks is well illustrated
by the only survival among twelve chest-on-chests made by
Nathaniel Dominy V between 1791 and 1806 (fig. 6). It was
made for family use in April 1796 at a cost of ₤10.[27] This
may have been his standard price for a double chest made of
cherry, because in 1793 a similar form made for Sineus
Conkling at the same cost has the notation "cherry" in the
Dominy accounts.[28]

It is startling to see a piece in a full-blown Queen Anne
style and realize that it was made in 1796. There is a close
relationship between this chest-on-chest and pieces made
in eastern Connecticut or Rhode Island. Without documentation this chest probably would be described as a "cherry
highboy" of Connecticut origin made about 1750. Indeed, as
a result of an article illustrating the Dominy double chest in
the March 1968 issue of Antiques, a fine chest-on-chest from
eastern Connecticut or Rhode Island has been mistakenly attributed to the Dominys.[29] Surviving examples of Dominy
case pieces indicate that they always used pad feet, claw-
and-ball feet, or bracket feet--never a combination of two
different types, which appears often in Rhode Island or
eastern Connecticut.

At the rear of the base section of the Dominys' chest-on-
chest is an extra-wide stile, a continuation of the rear cabriole leg, a construction technique which can be seen on
other New York pieces.[30] It was employed in order to utilize
the full depth of the chest and to enable the whole piece to
be placed close to a wall without interference from the knees
of the cabriole leg. Bead, ogee, and hollow moldings, all
combined on one large block of wood, provide a decorative
finish to the top section of the double chest. These moldings
were used repeatedly by Nathaniel V, especially the deep
hollow molding made by a round plane, which occurs frequently on his clock cases.

Fig. 6. Chest-on-chest. Made by Nathaniel Dominy
V for family use, East Hampton, New York, 1796.
Cherry; white pine and tulip secondary woods. H.
72 3/8"; W. 40 7/8"; D. 20 1/4". Mrs. George N.
Ray Collection

The back of the double chest reveals problems encountered
by country craftsmen and the ingenuity used to solve them.
The bottom rail tapers from left to right in order to accommodate the uneven edge of the white pine board above it. That
board is tenoned into the leg stiles, but the boards of the
upper section are nailed in place. Although large boards
were available (the uppermost is just over 17 inches wide),
a small piece had to be fitted at the top. A strip of molding
provided a decorative and useful barrier at the top of the
base section.

In 1941 the present owner of this piece accompanied a
dealer to the Dominy house to see a family "highboy" that
Charles M. Dominy wanted to sell. To mark the purchase,
the name DOMINY was stamped on several drawers with an
original script branding iron in the possession of the dealer.
This branding iron is now part of Winterthur's Dominy Tool
Collection (57.26.255). Additional documentation for the
double chest exists in the form of the template used to outline the pad foot, cabriole leg, and stile of the base section,
which is also part of the Dominy Tool Collection.

Equivalent to the chest-on-chest in terms of cost was the
Dominys' "silent clock," which was also referred to in their
accounts as a "Timepiece" (fig. 7). Two of these clocks
cost two members of the Hedges family £10 each although
purchased thirteen years apart. Abraham Hedges,
ranked forty-ninth on the tax lists, was billed for his clock
in 1805, and Jacob Hedges, Jr., whose rank was 116, was
billed in 1818 for his example (see Appendix B). The cases
were made by Nathaniel Dominy V, and they are identical.
The swanneck cresting on the domed pediment of the hood
of Abraham Hedges's clock has been broken and lost, but
it was identical to the cresting used on the one made for
Jacob Hedges, Jr. About the only difference between the
two cases is that a dark brown stain was used on the
earlier case while a dark reddish-brown stain covers the
later one.

The dials and movements of these two clocks reflect
some stylistic differences in the work of Nathaniel Dominy
IV and that of his grandson Felix. Nathaniel IV used an

Fig. 7. Silent clocks. Made by Nathaniel Dominy IV
for Abraham Hedges and by Felix Dominy for Jacob
Hedges, Jr., East Hampton, New York, 1804; 1817-1818.
Pine cases, enameled sheet-iron dial and pine dial,
brass works. H. 83", 85½"; W. 13", 12 7/8"; D. 8",
7 3/4". Charles D. Talmage and Mrs. John D. Flannery
Collection.

enameled sheet-iron dial for his clock, while Felix used a
pine dial painted white. Nathaniel IV used a wood dial only
occasionally, but, perhaps because of economic necessity,
Felix Dominy used them on all but one of his surviving clocks.
Arabic numerals appear on the earlier clock, but Roman
numerals were used on the later one; this was probably an instance of customer preference as both clockmakers used both
types of numerals on their dials. There are obvious differences in the pattern used for the hour and minute hands of
both clocks. Nathaniel Dominy placed his name on the front
of the dial, but Felix preferred to sign the back of his clock
dials.

The movement of both clocks is again almost identical--
an indication of the practicality of the design in use for almost twenty years when Abraham Hedges's clock was made in
1804, as well as the indebtedness of Felix to his grandfather
for training in clockmaking. These simple movements consisted of andiron-shaped plates to hold six gear wheels and
an anchor escapement. Felix made one innovation in the design of this clock movement. He eliminated the connecting
section of the arms projecting from the right side of the plate,
effecting a further saving of brass. Beautifully simple mech-
anisms, these clocks had a remarkable low repair rate.

One of the best examples of the lack of direct correlation
between wealth and the purchase of certain types of objects
from the Dominys is a timepiece made for Captain David
Fithian in 1789 at a cost of ₤6 (fig. 8). Fithian ranked
fifteenth on the East Hampton tax lists, but he chose to purchase one of the simplest and least expensive clocks made
by Nathaniel Dominy IV. Other residents of East Hampton who
ranked lower than Fithian purchased much more expensive
clocks. It is difficult to conceive of a simpler tall-case
clock. Its pine case is just under seven feet tall, a fraction
over one foot wide, and less than a foot deep. Only an applied arched molding board on the base, a small thumbnail
molding on the pendulum case door, a bold cove, rabbet,
half-round, and cove molding finishing the case, and a flat-
topped hood with dome-shaped glass panel provide decoration
for the case.

Nathaniel IV used a single hand on the dial to indicate the passage of time. Between each Roman numeral engraved on the pewter dial are eleven marks to note five-minute intervals. The engraved motto on the dial, a distinctive feature of a number of Nathaniel IV's clocks, must have had a humbling effect, not only upon its original purchaser but on subsequent owners: "HARK! / WHAT'S THE CRY. / PREPARE, / TO MEET THY GOD, TO-DAY." It was an apt phrase for people familiar with death. Three of Captain Fithian's nine children died before the age of five.[31] As simple as this clock appears, it is difficult to believe that it was made in slightly more than five days.

From 1794 to 1823 Nathaniel Dominy V recorded a total of 13 "breakfast" tables in his accounts. I saw several breakfast tables during the course of research, but in the absence of family histories substantiated by Dominy accounts, and without patterns, it was impossible to link the tables definitely to the Dominys. If members of the Dominy family had not rescued the table shown in figure 9 from the Dominy house in East Hampton, no example could be illustrated.

This table was probably made for family use and its late-Sheraton design indicates that it must have been produced in the 1820s. It might have been a gift from Nathaniel IV to Felix Dominy for his marriage to Phebe Miller in 1826. It comes about as close to city-oriented furniture as anything the Dominys made and could easily pass for a breakfast table made by a New York City craftsman. It betrays its country origin, however, in the multiplicity of woods used in its construction. Mahogany was used for the table top, leaves, and ring-and-disc-turned legs. The table's apron and frame are made of white pine, the leaf supports are cherry, and the drawer is made of tulipwood.

The table is another example of the "good" furniture these craftsmen made for their own use because the usual charge for a breakfast table in their accounts is £1 10s. or £1 12s. (see Appendix A). In at least one instance a breakfast table sold at the latter price is designated as "cherry." The only mahogany breakfast table listed was sold in 1803 to Abraham Hand, ranked 116 on the tax lists, for £2 16s. Its cost

Fig. 8. Timepiece. Made by Nathaniel Dominy IV for
Captain David Fithian, East Hampton, New York, 1789.
Pine, pewter dial, brass works. H. 79 1/2"; W.
12 1/8"; D. 7 1/2". Frederick M. Selchow Collection

Fig. 9. Breakfast table. Made by Nathaniel Dominy
V, probably for family use, East Hampton, New York,
1815-1830. Mahogany veneer on white pine frame;
white pine, cherry, and tulip secondary woods.
H. 27 7/8"; W. (closed) 18 11/16"; W. (open) 40 1/4";
D. 35 9/16". Winterthur Museum (68.16)

indicates a manufacturing time of 2 1/2 days. This time
is made more plausible by the fact that the legs of the
Dominys' table have been turned. Turned work could be
made more quickly and cheaply than almost anything else
produced in the shop.

Tables and stands of every variety formed a large part of
the Dominys' furniture production (see Appendix A). Between
1770 and 1833, 169 such pieces are listed in their accounts.
Only three tea tables, however, are noted, and they were all
made in 1792 at a cost of Ł1 4s. or Ł1 14s. for individuals
with ranks of 102 and 77, respectively.

A dished, tilt-top, mahogany tea table is visible in an old
photograph of the living room of the Dominy house.[32] This
table was purchased by Winterthur from direct descendants of
the Dominy craftsmen, and it is probably one of two tables
made for family use by Nathaniel V in 1796. Valued at Ł1 16s.,
it took just under two days to complete, which seems incredible
to modern observers. However, only the legs needed sawing
and shaping. The top was turned on a special lathe arbor and
puppet (which has survived in the Dominy Tool Collection)
from a one-inch-thick board down to a thickness of 7/8 inch.
After the top was dished, enough mahogany was removed from
the edge to give the appearance of a half-round molding or
bead. Its sturdy Doric column, decorated with circular rings,
was also turned.

All of the circular-top tables and stands made in the Dominy
shop were dished. A good example is the mahogany stand made
for John Lyon Gardiner in 1799. The diameter of the tea table
is about eight inches wider than that of the stand. At a cost
of Ł1, this was the most expensive stand made by the Dominys,
and only one other like it is entered into Dominy accounts.
The other example was made for Abraham Baker, who ranked
seventy-ninth on the tax lists. The Gardiner stand was brought
to the mainland from Gardiner's Island by the present owner,
Winthrop Gardiner, Sr., in 1936. Another stand was made of
cherry for the same purchaser in 1809, and it cost only
12 shillings.[33] As can be seen in Appendix A, many of the
stands made at a cost of 12 shillings bear the designation
"cherry," but the larger number of stands made at a price of

ten shillings are not described. They were probably of maple,
because a number of stands of that wood made by Nathaniel V
have survived.

Chairs were by far the most common product of the Dominy
woodworking shop. Between 1766 and 1840, their accounts
list 1 closestool chair, 1 easy chair, 31 fiddleback chairs, 8
"great" chairs, 12 rocking chairs, 61 slat chairs, 29 small
chairs, and 206 pieces simply described as "chairs," a total
of 349 pieces. This is more than one-third the total output
of their cabinetwork.

The Dominys' most expensive chair was an easy chair made,
not for John Lyon Gardiner, as one might have expected, but
for Thomas Baker, who ranked eighty-fourth on the tax lists
(see Appendix A). The first reference to rocking chair manufacture by the Dominys was in 1804, when John Lyon Gardiner
was billed sixteen shillings for each of two rocking chairs.
Between that date and 1830, a total of twelve chairs were
produced. Significantly, none of the entries refer to "attaching"
rockers, indicating that the form illustrated (fig. 10) was
originally intended as a rocking chair. This form was among
the most expensive chairs produced by the Dominys and cost
as much as a closestool chair or a "great" chair (see
Appendix A).

On March 2, 1809, Nathaniel V billed Thomas Baker fourteen
shillings for the rocking chair shown in figure 10. Made of
hickory, oak, and maple, this chair would appear at first to
be an early-eighteenth-century slat-back armchair with
rockers added at a later date. But the urn-shaped, curved
arched slats, and armrests with small turned tenons joining
them to the post are all signs of late-eighteenth- and early-
nineteenth-century chair design. The slats are made from a
surviving pattern, and the armrests are similar to a template
that is in the Dominy Tool Collection. It is the turning that
provides excitement and movement for the ornamentation of
this chair. Ball-and-disc turnings interrupt the plain
cylindrical posts. An elongated baluster and a disc-turned
stretcher help to strengthen the front posts of the chair.
Double baluster and disc turnings support the plain

Fig. 10. Armchair with rockers, slat back. Made by Nathaniel Dominy V for Thomas Baker, East Hampton, New York, 1809. Hickory, oak, and maple. H. 41 3/8"; W. 24 1/2"; D. 16". Edward Mulford Baker Strong Collection

Fig. 11. Detail of Fig. 10

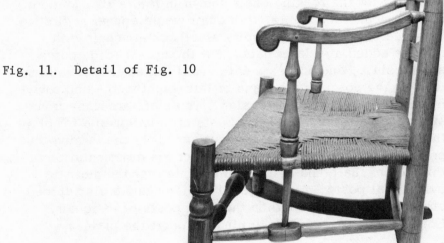

chamfered-edge armrests. It is obvious from a profile view
of the chair that, while turning the posts, the craftsman carefully made incised lines wherever tenons were to join a mortise
or drilled hole. Traces of the original dark green or black paint
can still be found. The only color designation for chairs listed
in the accounts is green.

"Great" chairs and rocking chairs were the only chair forms
more expensive than a mahogany Windsor armchair made in
1794 for Captain William J. Rysam, who is consistently ranked
sixth on local tax lists. A retired master mariner, by 1799 he
had acquired a ropewalk, shipyard, and pier at the foot of Bay
Street in Sag Harbor. In 1804 he signed an affidavit that he
was sole owner of the 202-ton brig <u>Merchant</u>. Mahogany is
not normally used for Windsor furniture, but a clue to its use
here is found in the East Hampton Trustees' journals, where
it was noted in 1807 that "great quanities of mahogany were
brought from Capt. Rysam's Honduras grove."[34]

Under the seat of the chair a chisled inscription offers
proof of Nathaniel's production. It reads "NAT Dominy
(script)/ making (script) 10 [shillings]/ Novr (script) 11
1794/WR." This chair's simple turnings and heavy, thick seat
are similar to other chairs of this type made in the late
eighteenth century. Some attempt was made to lighten the
appearance of the chair by scooping the seat, chamfering its
lower front edge, and using a quarter-round molding to outline
the sides and back. The cost of this chair may have been as
low as 10 shillings because of the likelihood that Rysam
supplied the material for its construction. Family history
says that Nathaniel V made a set of nine similar chairs for
Captain Rysam, but only this example has been located. The
craftsmen's accounts list Rysam as a customer, but not for
chairs--a warning to researchers to avoid relying solely on
ledgers and day books.

Fiddleback chairs are entered in Dominy accounts at a price
of eight shillings. It is likely that "splat-back" chairs of the
type illustrated (fig. 11) cost about the same price. These
chairs are not separated by type in Dominy records, and they
undoubtedly fall into the large category of the 206 "chairs."
Patterns for the splat and cresting rail survive in the Dominy

Tool Collection. They seem to run to a consistent type although the craftsmen occasionally used a Cupid's-bow cresting rail or reversed the position of the splat. Basically, they
are turned chairs, and it is in the turning that Nathaniel V
used imagination and variety, to judge from surviving
examples. Chairs priced from ten shillings or less were
purchased in sets of nine, six, four, three, or two. They were
purchased by clients who ranged in rank from one to 159. (See
Appendix A). This type of chair has come to be known as the
"Hudson Valley side chair." They were made, however, from
eastern Suffolk County, Long Island, to the upper Hudson
River Valley, including sections of New Jersey. A recent
exhibition of New York furniture proved that this type of side
chair was still being made in Albany in the early nineteenth
century. [35]

Slat-back side chairs were among the least expensive
furniture made by the Dominys. Between 1796 and 1818, 61
were entered in Dominy ledgers at prices ranging from four to
six shillings apiece. Because surviving examples indicate
that the craftsmen charged six shillings for a chair with three
slats, it is likely that the chair in figure 12 sold at four or
five shillings. Every part but the slats could be turned out
quickly and easily on the wheel lathe. The slats were made
from templates, some of which survive in the Dominy Tool
Collection. Keeping in mind that the Dominys charged 7s.
6d. per day for their labor, it would seem that a chair of this
kind could be produced in three or four hours. Anyone who has
seen a skilled turner at work would agree that this was quite
possible.

A few further observations are necessary to sum up the
career and the products of this family of country craftsmen.
Most of the objects illustrated, and indeed most of the
Dominys' products, are not classic representatives of fashion
or style. They are, in a very real sense, styleless. One will
look in vain for the sources from which their clocks or furniture were copies. The fact that these craftsmen were able
to make a distillation from the constant repetition of basic
forms and shapes over a long period of time makes their products seem to be timeless. The conservative nature of the

Fig. 11. Side chair, splat back. Nathaniel Dominy V, East Hampton, New York, ca. 1790-1820. Maple, hickory, pine. H: 37"; W: 18"; D: 14½". George V. Schellinger Collection

Fig. 12. Side chair, slat back. Made by Nathaniel Dominy V probably for Captain Ezekiel Mulford, East Hampton, New York, 1790-1820. Maple, hickory, oak. H: 35 5/8"; W: 19½"; D: 13 3/8". Edward Mulford Baker Strong Collection

people they served no doubt contributed to this quality. As
George Kubler has pointed out in The Shape of Time, it is extremely difficult to introduce a new design or plan when people derive satisfaction from the forms they already possess.[36]

The Dominys and their customers must have been satisfied
with the furniture and clocks produced in East Hampton because, if not, they easily could have introduced ideas from
Rhode Island and New York. As noted above, a schooner
provided contact with New York at least once a week.
Nathaniel Dominy IV and Nathaniel Dominy V purchased tools
and other objects in New York City. Felix Dominy was trained
in New York City as a watchmaker. John Lyon Gardiner was a
wealthy and presumably sophisticated man--copies of German
glass catalogues that he owned about 1800 are in Winterthur's
library. As a former mariner and merchant, William Rysam
certainly was aware of events outside of East Hampton or Sag
Harbor. Because the opportunity for cultural contact was present, one must conclude that the furniture and clocks accepted from the Dominys' shops represent cultural choice and a
rejection of values, ideas, and fashions in existence outside
East Hampton.

It is clear that in East Hampton individual wealth had little
correlation to the cost of objects purchased from the Dominys.
Ranking on the tax lists (a reflection of real and personal property) meant very little in terms of the purchase of an object
of quality. Ezekiel Mulford, ranked fifth on the tax list,
bought a clock for Ł10 3s., while Jared Hand, ranked 99,
purchased one for Ł20. Thomas Baker, ranked 84, is
the only customer to have bought three chest-on-chests.
Mulford Hand, whose rank was 132, purchased a mahogany
desk at Ł11 that was probably identical to one bought at the
same price in the same year by John Lyon Gardiner. One of
the reasons for this circumstance should be obvious. The
Dominys operated in a barter economy, and the only way they
could pay for goods and services they obtained was to re-
ciprocate with goods and services in a like amount. It is
entirely possible that in order to pay off a debt, they had to
talk Mulford Hand into accepting an Ł11 mahogany desk.

Finally, it must be noted that the kind of in-depth study

made possible by the wealth of material available about the
Dominys has not been done for enough other craftsmen to
generalize about how typical or untypical they were. It does
give me some hope and satisfaction, however, to envision a
day when we will be able to reply with conviction to those
critics who assail museum collections as not representing the
objects owned by a cross section of earlier Americans, by
stating that "indeed they do."

Appendix A

FURNITURE MADE BY THE DOMINYS IN DESCENDING ORDER OF COST

Brackets enclose woods known from examination of surviving pieces but
not described in the accounts. Letters NR denote nonresident. Letters
NRWL denote nonresident with land.

Form	Cost	Description	Owner and date	Rank on tax list
Desk and bookcase	£20-8-0	Maple	John Lyon Gardiner May 5, 1800	1
		Cherry	Nathaniel Dominy	89
Chest of drawers	£18	Mahogany	Huntting Miller June 9, 1800	2
			Jemima Pain June 1770	–
Wardrobe	£13		Nathaniel Hand April 12, 1798	32
Chest-on-chest	£11		Nathaniel Baker (2) April 8, 1805 April 12, 1806	28
			John Havens Oct. 19, 1803	–
			Deacon David Hedges Oct. 11, 1800	10
Desk	£11	[Mahogany & cherry]	John Lyon Gardiner Jan. 15, 1802	1
		Mahogany	Mulford Hand June 26, 1802	132

Form	Cost	Description	Owner and date	Rank on tax list
Chest-on-chest	Ł10-16-0		Thomas Baker Oct. 1, 1799	84
	Ł0-10-0		Thomas Baker Feb. 26, 1798	84
Bureau	Ł10		Abigail Parsons March 11, 1802	–
Chest-on-chest	Ł10		Nathaniel Baker April 25, 1799	28
			Thomas Baker Sept. 12, 1795	84
		Cherry	Sineus Conkling Oct. 1793	–
			Joseph Dimon Jan. 7, 1801	98
		[Cherry]	Nathaniel Dominy V April 1796	108
Desk	Ł10		Jared Hand Jan. 3, 1810	99
Coffin	Ł10	Mahogany & pine	John Lyon Gardiner Nov. 23, 1816	1
Desk	Ł8		Nathaniel Hand Oct. 1811	32
Chest-on-chest	Ł7-12-6		John Parsons III Nov. 24, 1791	16
Desk	Ł6-16-0		David Rose Oct. 11, 1771	–

Form	Cost	Description	Owner and date	Rank on tax list
Bureau	Ł6		Abraham Edwards March 20, 1807	76
			John Edwards Dec. 12, 1804	54
			Jacob Hedges, Jr. March 22, 1817	116
		Cherry	Joel Miller May 17, 1816	100
			John Parsons Nov. 3, 1803	16
			Charles R. Hand April 14, 1818	–
Clockcase	Ł6		John White Nov. 25, 1806	NR
Bureau	Ł5-10-0		Mary Parsons Dec. 12, 1799	43
Desk	Ł5-10-0		Dr. Samuel Hutchinson May 1770	–
Bookcase	Ł5-0-0		Jonathan Dayton, Esq. Aug. 2, 1814	55
Bureau	Ł5-0-0		Thomas Baker June 3, 1807	84
			Joseph Dimon Nov. 3, 1804	98

Form	Cost	Description	Owner and date	Rank on tax list
Bureau (cont.)	Ɫ5-0-0	Cherry	Joel Miller March 20, 1813	100
			Jonathan Osborn Feb. 20, 1809	79
			Jonathan Stratton Dec. 14, 1809	64
			Thomas Tillinghast June 1807	133
Clockcase	Ɫ5		Henry Dominy 1796	-
Bureau	Ɫ4-10-0		Thomas Baker May 1794	84
			Elnathan Parsons Oct. 1793	6
Table, dining	Ɫ4-8-0	Mahogany, large	David Baker July 16, 1800	50
Case with drawers	Ɫ4		Jacob Conkling	-
Table	Ɫ4	Mahogany 2 at Ɫ4 each	William Huntting May 1, 1810	23
Table	Ɫ3	Mahogany	Mulford Hand August 18, 1803	132
Bedstead, and "teasters"	Ɫ2-16-0		Jonathan B. Mulford Sept. 10, 1819	33
Press, clothes	Ɫ2-16-0		[Rev.] Lyman Beecher May 14, 1806 April 20, 1809	-

Form	Cost	Description	Owner and date	Rank on tax list
Table, breakfast	Ł2-16-0	Mahogany	Abraham Hand March 11, 1803	116
Chest, two-drawer	Ł2-12-0		Elizabeth King Feb. 28, 1807	133
Chest, two-drawer	Ł2-10-6		Mary Field Feb. 28, 1807	131
Bedsteads	Ł2-8-0		John Lyon Gardiner Jan. 1, 1799	1
		"teasters"	John Mulford May 1817	63
		"long, reeded posts & Teasters"	John Parsons March 16, 1818	16
			David Sherril Nov. 29, 1809	107
Table	Ł2-8-0		Jared Hand Sept. 6, 1779	99
			Nathaniel Baker April 25, 1799	28
Table, dining	Ł2-8-0	Cherry	Benjamin Miller April 3, 1819	42
		"teasters"	Jonathan Fithian August 13, 1818	70
		Cherry	Jonathan Osborn March 2, 1809	79
		Cherry	Elnathan Parsons Jan. 22, 1819	6

Form	Cost	Description	Owner and date	Rank on tax list
Table	Ł2-6-0		John Miller Oct. 26, 1793	28
Bedstead	Ł2-4-0		David Miller May 23, 1811	25
		"teasters"	Benjamin Miller Sept. 2, 1824	42
Bedstead	Ł2	"fluted posts"	Thomas Baker April 21, 1809	84
		"long posts"	May 16, 1816	
		"teasters"	Huntting Miller Sept. 8, 1809	2
		"teasters"	Recompense Sherril Oct. 4, 1809	40
Chest, two-drawer	Ł2		Puah Cuff March 27, 1798	–
			Abraham Edwards Feb. 3, 1800	76
			John Huntting June 26, 1812	52
			Stephen Stratton Sept. 12, 1793	38
Table	Ł2		Thomas Baker May, 1794	84
			Sylvester Dearing July 9, 1792	–

Form	Cost	Description	Owner and date	Rank on tax list
Table (cont.)	₤2	"cherry trees"	John Huntting March 31, 1792	52
		cherry	Elnathan Parsons Dec. 12, 1793	6
			John Miller Oct. 26, 1793	28
Table, breakfast	₤2		Abraham Edwards July 2, 1812	76
		cherry	Abraham Huntting March 7, 1810	100
Table, dining	₤2		Abraham Baker August 14, 1794	79
			Deacon William Barnes August 14, 1792	29
		cherry	Nathan Mulford March 12, 1796	–
Table, large	₤2		Nathaniel Baker Dec. 26, 1797	28
Table, round	₤2	"large, maple"	John Lyon Gardiner Sept. 7, 1791	1
Table, dining	₤1-18-0	"large"	Elisha Osborn August 23, 1792	77
Chest	₤1-16-0		Thomas Filer Dec. 20, 1792	102

Form	Cost	Description	Owner and date	Rank on tax list
Chest (cont.)	Ł1-16-0		John Lyon Gardiner Jan. 12, 1817	
Table	Ł1-16-0		Nathaniel Dominy family April 1796	108
Table, breakfast	Ł1-16-0		Jeremiah Dayton July 1, 1812	36
		"part of his stuff"	Jonathan Fithian Oct. 1, 1823	70
Table, oval	Ł1-16-0		John Dominy Sept. 14, 1792	-
Bedstead	Ł1-14-0	"part of his timber"	Joseph Barnes Nov. 12, 1821	88
Chest, one-drawer	Ł1-14-0		Abraham Edwards June 11, 1799	76
			Nathan Miller Feb. 3, 1800	139
Chest, two-drawer	Ł1-14-0		Dr. Samuel Hutchinson April 19, 1786	-
Table, breakfast	Ł1-14-0		Miller Dayton Nov. 8, 1804	9
Table, tea	Ł1-14-0		Elisha Osborn August 23, 1792	77

Form	Cost	Description	Owner and date	Rank on tax list
Chest	Ⅼ1-12-0		David Talmage, Jr. Dec. 20, 1794	60
Chest, one-drawer	Ⅼ1-12-0	"you found brasses"	David Talmage, Jr. Sept. 1790	60
Table	Ⅼ1-12-0		John Havens Oct. 19, 1803	-
			Abraham Parsons July 1, 1809	95
Table, breakfast	Ⅼ1-12-0		Thomas Baker Sept. 12, 1795	84
			Samuel Dayton May 25, 1804	41
		cherry	Samuel Stratton Dec. 20, 1794	NR
Table	Ⅼ1-10-0		Thomas Baker May 1794	84
		"of his boards"	Jonathan Fithian May 1, 1815	70
			Jacob Sherril Oct. 15, 1789	[128]
			David Talmage, Jr. March 17, 1788	60
Table, breakfast	Ⅼ1-10-0		Nathaniel Baker Jan. 8, 1799	28
			Thomas Baker Sept. 12, 1795	84
			Sineus Conkling March 11, 1795	-

Form	Cost	Description	Owner and date	Rank on tax list
Table, oval	Ł1-10-0		Cloe Loper Dec. 1791	-
Table, round	Ł1-10-0		Uriah Miller May 7, 1778	-
Bedsteads	Ł1-8-0	"part of his timber"	Jonathan Baker Nov. 12, 1824	79
		"all long posts"	Joseph Edwards Jan. 6, 1812	152
		"bedstead with a joint to turn up"	Abraham Sherril, Jr. June 1, 1818	42
Table	Ł1-8-0		John Lyon Gardiner July 2, 1803	1
		"part his stock"	Abraham Mulford Dec. 3, 1796	NR
			Josiah Mulford August 9, 1794	44
		"pine with 1 leaf"	Abraham Sherril, Jr. Jan. 4, 1819	42
Table, round	Ł1-8-0		Uriah Miller Dec. 13, 1773	-
Chest	Ł1-6-0	"a complicated chest"	John Parsons III Oct. 1792	16
Bedsteads	Ł1-4-0	"4 long posts"	Thomas Baker Dec. 11, 1801	84

Form	Cost	Description	Owner and date	Rank on tax list
Bedsteads (cont.)	Ł1-4-0		Betsey Burnham July 25, 1807	NR
		"4 long posts"	Nathaniel Hand Dec. 11, 1801	32
			Nathaniel Hand June 17, 1812	32
		"long posts"	Abraham Huntting June 5, 1811	100
		"teasters"	Huntting Miller June 7, 1800	2
		"2 long posts"	Thomas Tillinghast Nov. 14, 1810	133
Chair, easy	Ł1-4-0		Thomas Baker March 4, 1808	84
Chest	Ł1-4-0		Samuel Stratton Jan. 19, 1811	NR
			Benjamin Miller April 18, 1808	42
			Benjamin Miller June 1809	42
			Benjamin Miller May 28, 1813	42
			Abraham Mulford April 12, 1803	NR
			Edward Conkling April 8, 1802	76

Form	Cost	Description	Owner and date	Rank on tax list
Chest (cont.)	Ł1-4-0		Henry Conkling April 8, 1802	78
			Jonathan Edwards March 3, 1812	35
			Benjamin Miller March 20, 1807	42
			Ebenezer Hedges March 8, 1810	76
Clockcase	Ł1-4-0		William Parsons August 8, 1800	96
Desk, writing	Ł1-4-0	"bench"	Isaac Edwards Feb. 20, 1808	34
Frames, looking-glass	Ł1-4-0		N. Dominy family April 1796	108
Table	Ł1-4-0		Bethiah Hiks June 1770	-
Table, oval	Ł1-4-0		Henry Conkling Jan. 29, 1766	-
Table, tea	Ł1-4-0	"mahogany"	Sylvester Dearing July 9, 1792	NR
			Thomas Filer Dec. 20, 1792	102
Chest	Ł1-2-0		John Edwards Oct. 9, 1806	54
		"for Solon-- his lock and hinges"	Elnathan Parsons March 1814	6

Form	Cost	Description	Owner and date	Rank on tax list
Chest (cont.)	£1-2-0	"for Jonah-- he found lock"	Phebe Terbil March 28, 1822	-
Desk, writing	£1-2-0	"bench"	Joseph Edwards Feb. 13, 1808	152
Bedstead	£1-1-6		Lyman Beecher Jan. 15, 1806	-
Bedstead	£1-0-0	"teasters"	Thomas Baker April 26, 1809	84
			Nathan Dayton April 9, 1798	NR
			Archibald Gracy Dec. 17, 1801	38
			Dr. Huntington Feb. 17, 1806	138
			Mary Parsons Dec. 12, 1799	43
			Robert Parsons Sept. 22, 1806	88
			Dr. Ebenezer Sage July 15, 1793	-
Chest	£1-0-0	"you found lock & hinges"	Nathaniel Baker Jan. 18, 1817	28
			Elnathan Parsons Sept. 27, 1802	6
Desk, writing	£1-0-0		Elnathan Parsons Dec. 10, 1795	6

Form	Cost	Description	Owner and date	Rank on tax list
Stand	₤1-0-0	[mahogany]	John Lyon Gardiner March 30, 1799	1
			Abraham Baker Feb. 3, 1810	79
Desk, writing	₤0-19-0	"his hinges"	Jeremiah Dayton Jan. 13, 1801	36
		"bench, screws & hinges found by you"	Timothy Miller Feb. 20, 1808	38
Bedstead	₤0-18-0		Abraham Baker July 26, 1792	79
			Abraham Baker Feb. 3, 1810	79
		"2 long posts"	N. Dominy family April 1796	108
			Daniel Hedges July 11, 1792	15
		"2 long posts & painted"	Jeremiah Miller, Jr. May 9, 1792	49
			Amilia Parsons Sept. 22, 1806	-
			John Gardiner Dec. 8, 1789	1
Chest	₤0-18-0		David Leek Jan. 30, 1788	-

Form	Cost	Description	Owner and date	Rank on tax list
Chest (cont.)			Collins Parsons April 25, 1799	-
Desk, writing	Ł0-18-0		Jonathan Osborn August 8, 1801	79
Table, kitchen	Ł0-18-0	"large"	Jonathan Tuthill Sept. 28, 1817	110
			Jonathan Mulford Jan. 16, 1804	82 [10]
Chest	Ł0-17-0		(2) Elnathan Parsons May 22, 1792 August 5, 1790	6
Bedstead	Ł0-16-0		David Hedges Sept. 29, 1801	10
		"short posts"	David Miller Dec. 24, 1804	25
			Elnathan Parsons May 2, 1799	6
			Dering Ranger Sept. 11, 1810	89
Chair, closestool	Ł0-16-0		John L. Gardiner March 29, 1809	1
Chair, great	Ł0-16-0		Elnathan Parsons August 1, 1793	6
Chairs, rocking	Ł0-16-0	[2]	John L. Gardiner June 8, 1804	1

Form	Cost	Description	Owner and date	Rank on tax list
Chest	Ł0-16-0		David Miller Oct. 3, 1796	25
			Thomas Owen Nov. 10, 1790	-
		"your stock"	Abraham Parsons, Jr. March 16, 1822	90
Coffin	Ł0-16-0	"brother Isaacs corps - his stuff--my lining"	Abraham Hedges Dec. 3, 1814	49
Cradle, child's	Ł0-16-0		David Edwards Oct. 17, 1814	106
			John Mulford May 25, 1813	63
			Ambrose Parsons April 23, 1803	16
			Elnathan Parsons Jan. 8, 1824	6
			Jonathan Stratton Oct. 1803	64
			Thomas Tillinghast Jan. 4, 1806	133
Stand	Ł0-16-0	mahogany	Huntting Miller June 9, 1800	2
			Isaac Scoy, Jr. May 4, 1831	92

Charles F. Hummel

Form	Cost	Description	Owner and date	Rank on tax list
Table	Ł0-16-0	"with drawer"	David Miller Dec. 23, 1805	25
Table, kitchen	Ł0-16-0		Jonathan Tuthill June 6, 1814	110
Stand	Ł0-15-0		Eli Parsons May 25, 1802	24
Stand	Ł0-14-6	"mahogany top"	Thomas Baker April 1, 1807	84
Bedstead	Ł0-14-0		John Lyon Gardiner May 4, 1807	1
		"trundle bed-stead"	Jonathan Mulford April 22, 1802	82 [10]
		"painted"	William Mulford May 29, 1794	41
		"short posts & painted"	Elnathan Parsons Nov. 1794	6
		"bedstead painted"	Isaac Payne May 1792	128
		"short posts"	David Talmage II April 3, 1810	62
Chair, great	Ł0-14-0		Abraham Sherril, Jr. Nov. 2, 1822	42
Chairs, rocking	Ł0-14-0		Abraham Baker April 28, 1817	79

Form	Cost	Description	Owner and date	Rank on tax list
Chairs, rocking (cont.)	Ŀ0-14-0		Thomas Baker March 2, 1809	84
			David Conkling Nov. 15, 1809	75
			Nathaniel Hand April 20, 1811	32
			Dr. Abel Huntington May 1811	138
			William Huntting March 25, 1810	23
			Jonathan B. Mulford 1830	–
			Eli Parsons July 7, 1817	24
			Elnathan Parsons April 1, 1823	6
Chest	Ŀ0-14-0		David Leek Jan. 30, 1788	–
Stand, candle	Ŀ0-14-0		Jonathan Osborn 3d Feb. 1833	107
Table, kitchen	Ŀ0-14-0	"part his stuff"	Jonathan Fithian Oct. 1, 1823	70
Bedsteads	Ŀ0-13-0	"trundle"	John Dominy Oct. 13, 1792	–

Form	Cost	Description	Owner and date	Rank on tax list
Bedsteads (cont.)	Ł0-13-0	"trundle"	Abraham Parsons August 30, 1807	90
		"trundle bed- stead"	Isaac Payne Oct. 13, 1790	128
Chairs, great	Ł0-13-0		Schoolhouse Jan. 23, 1804	-
Chest	Ł0-13-0		Abigail Baker Dec. 24, 1791	[28]
			Jeremiah Gardiner Jan. 9, 1790	57
			Timothy Miller Jan. 30, 1818	38
Bedsteads	Ł0-12-0	"short posts"	Puah Cuff Jan. 5, 1796	-
			John L. Gardiner July 2, 1793	1
			David Leek Nov. 28, 1792	-
Bottle case	Ł0-12-0		Abraham Sherril, Jr. April 27, 1802	42
Chairs, great	Ł0-12-0	[2]	Thomas Baker Nov. 8, 1792	84
			John Dominy August 7, 1790	-
			Elnathan Parsons August 5, 1790	6
			David Talmage, Jr. Dec. 7, 1805	60

Form	Cost	Description	Owner and date	Rank on tax list
Chairs, rocking	Ł0-12-0	"great"	Abraham Edwards March 15, 1809	76
Chest	Ł0-12-0		John Hunting June 1795	52
		"for Dan'l Conkling"	Nathan Dayton 1786	-
		"your boards"	Jonathan Osborn March 7, 1810	79
			Benjamin Parsons Dec. 7, 1792	137
			Elnathan Parsons August 22, 1792	6
Chest, plain	Ł0-12-0		Abraham Baker, Jr. May 30, 1792	79
			Thomas Baker July 1792	84
Coffin	Ł0-12-0		Nathan Conkling, Junr. Dec. 30, 1788	-
Reel	Ł0-12-0		Sylvester Field Oct. 2, 1818	-
			Jacob Hedges, Jr. Dec. 4, 1816	116
Stands	Ł0-12-0		Thomas Baker Dec. 25, 1813	84
		cherry	Isaac Barnes Feb. 21, 1818 July 20, 1818	130

Form	Cost	Description	Owner and date	Rank on tax list
Stands (cont.)	Ł0-12-0		Edward Conkling · March 24, 1804	76
			Harvey Conkling July 3, 1816	100
			Zebulon Conkling 1820	-
			Miller Dayton Jan. 21, 1801	9
		[2]	Jeremiah Miller Dec. 20, 1796	48
		cherry	John Mulford May 1817	63
		cherry	Sylvester Field Nov. 27, 1818	-
			Jonathan Fithian Dec. 11, 1811	70
			Jonathan Fithian Oct. 1, 1823	70
		cherry	John L. Gardiner Oct. 25, 1809	1
			Samuel Mulford April 29, 1818	16
		cherry	Jonathan Osborn July 18, 1818	79
		cherry	Philetus Osborn Oct. 22, 1821	68

Form	Cost	Description	Owner and date	Rank on tax list
Stands (cont.)		cherry	Abraham Parsons June 1829	90
		cherry	Abraham Parsons, Jr. Jan. 25, 1820	90
			Isaac Plato Oct. 16, 1813	120
			Samuel Russell Dec. 18, 1817	-
			Samuel Stratton March 13, 1828	-
		cherry	Jonathan Tuthill May 21, 1814	110
Table	£0-12-0		Joseph & Isaac Dimon June 13, 1804	98
			Benjamin Miller March 4, 1807	42
			Mary Parsons Dec. 12, 1799	43
Table, kitchen	£0-12-0		Ambrose Parsons Nov. 4, 1802	16
Chest	£0-11-0	"for Joel"	Daniel Loper Sept. 30, 1788	-
Chest, plain	£0-11-0		Thomas Baker Dec. 21, 1793	84
Stands	£0-11-0		Jonathan Conkling Jan. 26, 1804	68

Form	Cost	Description	Owner and date	Rank on tax list
Chest	Ł0-10-6	"Luthur"	Jacob Conkling April 2, 1792	-
Bedsteads	Ł0-10-0		Nathaniel Baker June 21, 1768	28
		"trundle"	Henry Dayton July 2, 1784	-
		"trundle"	Aaron Isaacs August 17, 1768	91
		"trundle"	Abraham Miller Dec. 23, 1768	-
Chairs	Ł0-10-0	"6 green"	Elnathan Parsons Nov. 29, 1800	6
		"6 @ 10"	Nathan Miller Dec. 1802	139
		[6]	Nathaniel Dominy family April 1796	108
		"6 green chairs"	John L. Gardiner April 18, 1803	1
		"6 green"	Abraham Mulford April 14, 1801	NR
		[4]	John Huntting Nov. 24, 1803	52
Chest	Ł0-10-0	"Israel"	Jacob Conkling April 5, 1788	-
		"Isaac"	Jan. 3, 1791	
		"long"	N. Dominy family April 1796	108

Form	Cost	Description	Owner and date	Rank on tax list
Chest (cont.)	₤0-10-0		David Hedges April 24, 1799	10
		"large, his stock"	Stephen Hedges July 2, 1799	NRWL
		"for an Indian"	Aaron Isaacs March 15, 1760	91
Clotheshorse	₤0-10-0		John L. Gardiner April 18, 1803	1
Reel	₤0-10-0		Sineus Conkling Oct. 1793	-
			N. Dominy family April 1796	108
			Mary Parsons Dec. 12, 1799	43
			David Dimon June 8, 1795	-
Stands	₤0-10-0		N. Dominy family April 1796	108
			Nathan Dayton April 9, 1798	-
			David Dimon March 18, 1802	-
			Nathaniel Baker Dec. 30, 1812	28
			Thomas Baker Sept. 12, 1795	84
			Abraham Bennet April 7, 1807	159

Form	Cost	Description	Owner and date	Rank on tax list
Stands (cont.)	Ł0-10-0		Henry Conkling March 13, 1813	78
			Benjamin Miller March 4, 1807	42
			Joel Miller July 26, 1803 May 26, 1812	100
			Timothy Miller Feb. 18, 1803 March 21, 1806	38
		"for your daughter Mary"	July 1811	
			Abraham Mulford April 11, 1807	–
			Daniel Hedges July 11, 1792	15
			John Huntting July 14, 1810	52
			Jonathan Mulford Jan. 2, 1809	82
			Jonathan Osborn Dec. 16, 1808	79
			Chloe Parsons Sept. 19, 1801	67
			David Scoy June 11, 1800	98
			Isaac Scoy June 11, 1800	20

Form	Cost	Description	Owner and date	Rank on tax list
Stands (cont.)	Ł0-10-0		David Talmage 3d Nov. 14, 1802	84
		"turned leaf stand"	John Terry April 25, 1793	-
Stand, candle	Ł0-10-0		Thomas Baker Oct. 1, 1799	84
			David Hedges Oct. 11, 1800	10
Table	Ł0-10-0	"plain"	Daniel Hedges Dec. 6, 1790	15
Stands	Ł0-9-0		Nathaniel Lester May 25, 1802	-
Bedsteads	Ł0-9-0	"small bed-stead"	Joel Miller June 6, 1797	100
Chairs	Ł0-9-0	[6]	John L. Gardiner August 27, 1811	1
		[6]	Benjamin Miller June 14, 1810	42
		[6]	Joel Miller Sept. 2, 1811	100
		"6 for your mother"	Timothy Miller June 1, 1814	38
		[6]	Abraham Parsons, Jr. April 6, 1814	90
		[6]	David Talmage II August 28, 1811	62

Form	Cost	Description	Owner and date	Rank on tax list
Stands	Ł0-9-0		Matthew Stratton June 8, 1793	-
Stand, candle	Ł0-9-0		John Gan Jan. 8, 1796	139
		"for George"	Dr. Abel Huntington Feb. 20, 1819	138
Chairs	Ł0-8-0	[4]	Elnathan Parsons August 5, 1790	6
		[2]	David Talmage Jr. Dec. 3, 1790	60
		[4]	March 31, 1791	
Chairs, fiddleback	Ł0-8-0	[6]	Nathaniel Baker Nov. 2, 1797	84
		[6]	Edward Conkling March 24, 1804	76
		[4]	Nathaniel Dominy family April 1796	108
		[9]	Abraham Mulford Dec. 14, 1796	-
Chairs, small	Ł0-8-0		Dr. Abel Huntington April 8, 1802	138
Coffin	Ł0-8-0	"for Widow Russels Corps"	East Hampton May 24, 1789	-

Form	Cost	Description	Owner and date	Rank on tax list
Mortar & pestle (salt)	Ł0-8-0	"Lignum Vitae"	John L. Gardiner Sept. 22, 1814	1
		"Lignum Vitae"	Eli Parsons Dec. 21, 1809	24
Stands	Ł0-8-0		Thomas Baker Oct. 17, 1799	84
			David Dimon June 8, 1795	-
			Daniel Hedges Dec. 6, 1790	-
			Elnathan Parsons Dec. 12, 1793	6
Chairs, fiddleback	Ł0-7-9		Jonathan Stratton Nov. 18, 1808	64
Stand	Ł0-7-6		Jacob Sherril Oct. 15, 1789	-
Footstool	Ł0-7-0	[2]	Sarah Gardiner Jan. 1820	1
Platter	Ł0-6-6		John L. Gardiner April 19, 1806	1
Bedstead	Ł0-6-0	"cot"	Jonathan Osborn March 8, 1833	80
Chairs	Ł0-6-0	[3]	Abraham Bennet March 4, 1808	159
		[2]	Martha Bennet Sept. 10, 1803	-

Form	Cost	Description	Owner and date	Rank on tax list
Chairs (cont.)		[2]	Josiah Dayton Jan. 3, 1804	95
		[3]	Jonathan Fithian Oct. 1, 1823	70
		[6]	Aaron Isaacs August 17, 1768	91
		[6]	June 14, 1770	
		[6]	David Miller April 21, 1772	-
		[6]	Uriah Miller June 13, 1770	-
			Elnathan Parsons June 16, 1800	6
Chairs, slat	Ł0-6-0	[2]	Elisha Payne Dec. 17, 1808	148
Chairs, small	Ł0-6-0	"little chair for Jonathan"	Capt. David Nov. 1790	15
Knife box	Ł0-6-0		Jeremiah Miller Feb. 24, 1807	48
Chairs, small	Ł0-5-6		Jacob Conkling Nov. 11, 1789	-
Chairs	Ł0-5-0	[4]	Capt. Jonathan Barnes August 23, 1804	86
		[4]	Joseph and Isaac Dimon June 13, 1804	98

Form	Cost	Description	Owner and date	Rank on tax list
Chairs (cont.)	Ł0-5-0	[3]	David Miller April 9, 1805	25
		"4 plain"	John Miller June 13, 1798	28
		[4]	William Mulford Jan. 30, 1805	41
		[6]	Ambrose Parsons Nov. 4, 1802	16
		[6]	William Parsons April 7, 1806	96
		[6]	Isaac Payne July 27, 1801	128
		[3]	David Talmage, Jr. June 3, 1806	60
Chairs, slat	Ł0-5-0	[4]	Jonathan Stratton May 25, 1818	64
		[6]	Jeremiah Talmage Dec. 12, 1809	139
Chairs, small	Ł0-5-0		John Hunting Jan. 26, 1796	52
		"little"	David Miller Dec. 28, 1793	25
Chairs, small	Ł0-4-6		John L. Gardiner Feb. 22, 1805	1
Cupboard	Ł0-4-6		Abraham Sherril June 19, 1800	112

Form	Cost	Description	Owner and date	Rank on tax list
Chairs	Ł0-4-0	[6]	Henry Conkling Jan. 29, 1766	-
Chairs, small	Ł0-4-0		Stafford Hedges April 20, 1815	-
			David Miller Dec. 23, 1805	25
			Ambrose Parsons Dec. 17, 1803	16
			Elnathan Parsons Feb. 19, 1824	6
			Nathaniel Sands April 1, 1807	-
			Joseph Barnes Feb. 17, 1832	88
		"little"	Deacon William Barnes Dec. 11, 1795	29
		[6]	Elnathan Parsons Feb. 1789	6
			Parker Bennett 1833	-
			William Bennett Dec. 19, 1806	118
			William Campbell [NR] Dec. 17, 1803	119
			Harvey Conkling Nov. 17, 1816	100

Form	Cost	Description	Owner and date	Rank on tax list
Chairs, small (cont.)	Ŀ0-4-0		Josiah Dayton Nov. 15, 1830	95
			David Edwards April 5, 1815	106
			Joseph Edwards August 6, 1817	152
			Jeremiah Gardiner July 29, 1817	-
			Abraham Sherril, Jr. April 25, 1801 Dec. 29, 1829	42
Coffin	Ŀ0-4-0	"for a Negro child"	Aaron Isaacs May 12, 1768	91
Frame, looking-glass	Ŀ0-4-0		Philetus Osborn 1820	68
Server	Ŀ0-4-0		William Rysam Oct. 26, 1796	6
Chairs	Ŀ0-3-6	[4]	Jonathan Osborn June 14, 1802	80
		"6 plain"	John Parsons June 1, 1787	16
Chairs, small	Ŀ0-3-6	"little"	David Edwards Jan. 18, 1773	-
		"little"	Joel Miller Feb. 14, 1794	100
Chairs	Ŀ0-3-0	[4]	Josiah Dayton Jan. 3, 1804	95
		[2]	Thomas Filer 1792	102

Form	Cost	Description	Owner and date	Rank on tax list
Chairs, small	Ł0-3-0		David Conkling Feb. 19, 1803	73
			Philetus Osborn Jan. 28, 1806	68
			Hedges Parsons Oct. 22, 1812	120
Footstool	Ł0-3-0	[2]	John L. Gardiner May 18, 1804	1
		"plain"	Sarah Gardiner July 24, 1820	1
Frames, picture	Ł0-3-0	[2]	John L. Gardiner May 18, 1804	1
Footstool	Ł0-2-6	[2]	(2) Samuel Ranger July 28, 1825	46
Frame, looking-glass	Ł0-2-6	"small looking-glass"	Recompense Sherril Sept. 15, 1815	40
Frames, picture	Ł0-2-4	[3]	Daniel Dayton Feb. 18, 1767	–
Footstool	Ł0-2-0	[2]	Dr. Abel Huntington July 28, 1819	138
		[2]	Phebe Terbil Sept. 1825	–
Frames, looking-glass	Ł0-2-0		Abraham Parsons, Jr. Jan. 27, 1820	90
Frames, picture	Ł0-2-0	"Glass & ring to Do"	Elnathan Parsons Jan. 22, 1819	6

Form	Cost	Description	Owner and date	Rank on tax list
Candle box	Ł0-1-9		Joseph Robbins Sept. 16, 1790	-
Frames, looking-glass	Ł0-1-9		Uriah Miller Dec. 1790	-
Frames, looking-glass	Ł0-1-6		Isaac [Van] Scoy May 24, 1774	20
Frames, picture	Ł0-1-6	[2]	Abraham Parsons Dec. 15, 1809	90
Chairs	Ł0-1-3	[2]	Isaac [Van] Scoy, Jr. Nov. 14, 1840	92
Chairs	Ł0-1-2	[2]	Isaac [Van] Scoy, Jr. Nov. 18, 1840	92

CLOCKS MADE BY THE DOMINYS IN DESCENDING ORDER OF COST

Brackets indicate ranking is not certain.   Letters NR denote non-resident.   Letters NRWL denote nonresident with land.

Cost	Description	Owner and date	Rank on tax list
Ł38	"To a Repeating-Alarm Telltale Clock"	Miller Dayton June 8, 1797	9
	"To a Repeating, Alarm, Tell-tale Clock"	Joseph Hedges Oct. 5, 1797	NRWL
Ł36	"Horologiographical, Repeating, Alarm, Monition Clock"	David Gardiner Nov. 7, 1799	NR-16
Ł28	"To 1 Clock 70 Dolls" [repeating, alarm clock]	John L. Gardiner Nov. 1, 1791	1
Ł26-16-0	"To an Alarm, Repeating, Telltale Clock"	Abraham Gardiner July 7, 1792	13
Ł23	"To a repeating alarm clock"	John Gardiner April 5, 1791	1
Ł20-8-0	"To a Repeating, Alarm, Telltale Clock"	John Miller Sept. 28, 1792	28
Ł20	"To a Clock"	Thomas Baker Jan. 5, 1788	84
	"To a Clock"	Aaron Isaacs March 27, 1790	91

Cost	Description	Owner and date	Rank on tax list
£20	"To 1 Clock at £20-0-0 old way"	Jared Hand Oct. 21, 1808	99
£14	"To a clock put into an old case repaired"	Matthew Barnes Nov. 2, 1786	52 [heirs]
£11	"To a clock or Timepiece"	Abraham Edwards April 20, 1809	76
	"1 Timepiece"	Joseph Osborn May 26, 1812	85
	"To Timepiece with a Bell"	Jonathan Osborn March 13, 1813	79
£10-16-0	"To a one Stroke Clock"	Jeremiah Bennet, Jr. Oct. 15, 1807	62
$26 [£10-8-0]	"To an eight day repeating Clock, 3 months credit, then Intrest at 6 per cent"	Samuel Ranger Dec. 21, 1818	46
£10-3-0	"to a clock"	Ezekial Mulford Feb. 14, 1772	5
£10-0-0	"To a Time Piece"	Nathan Mulford Jan. 9, 1785	-
	"To 1 Clock or Timepiece"	Dr. Ebenezer Sage Feb. 9, 1796	-
	"To 1 Time Piece or Small Clock"	Abraham Hedges April 24, 1805	49
	"To 1 Timepiece"	Josiah Dayton Jan. 30, 1806	95

Cost	Description	Owner and date	Rank on tax list
£10-0-0	"To 1 timepiece"	Deacon Silas Corwin Feb. 12, 1806	-
	"to 1 silent clock ready cash"	Jonathan Tuthill April 25, 1808	110
	"Timepiece"	Isaac Miller May 26, 1813	-
	"To a Timepiece with Minute Hand"	Jeremiah Dayton Oct. 18, 1814	36
[$25]	"To Timepiece"	Jacob Hedges, Jr. August 8, 1818	116 [61]
[$25]	"To Timepiece"	Mulford Parsons Nov. 1818	61
		Jonathan Osborn 3rd Oct. 8, 1825	80
£9-12-0	"To Silent Clock"	Mary Hopping August 9, 1800	-
£8-12-0	"To a one Stroak Clock (2 handed)"	Seth Parsons Feb. 28, 1793	[64]
£8-6-0	"To a Silent Clock"	Isaac Scallinger Dec. 1787	-
£8-0-0	"To a small Clock or Timepiece 20 Dollars"	Samuel H. Pierson April 21, 1798	92 [NRWL]
	"To 1 Silent Clock"	Dr. Ebenezer Sage June 11, 1803	-
£7-10-0	"To a clock"	John Davis Jr. 1768-1772	-

Cost	Description	Owner and date	Rank on tax list
Ł7-10-0	"to a clock"	William Hedges June 23, 1778	-
	"To a clock"	David Sayre August 7, 1779	-
	"To a Timepiece"	Matthew Osborn August 10, 1786	-
Ł7-0-0	"To a Small Clock"	Isaac Edwards Feb. 3, 1809	34
Ł6-10-0	"Two timepieces" Ł13	James Hazelton May 20, 1783	-
Ł6-5-0	"to a clock"	David Edwards July 4, 1775	-
	"To a Clock"	Jacob Conkling April 17, 1779	-
	"to Clock (in produce at cash price AD 1773)"	May 20, 1780	
Ł6-0-0	"To a clock"	Henry Dayton August 12, 1769	-
	"To a Timepiece"	William Hunting Jan. 19, 1788	23
	"To a Small Clock or Timepiece"	Cap't. David Fithian July 1, 1789	15
	"To a Timepiece"	Isaac [Van] Scoy Feb. 17, 1792	20
	"To 1 small clock or Time Piece"	Joel Miller August 26, 1794	100

Cost	Description	Owner and date	Rank on tax list
Ł6-0-0	"To 1 Timepiece"	Bethuel Edwards August 24, 1814	81
	"A Timepiece with hour hand"	Elisha Osborn Jun Dec. 19, 1817	74
Ł5-8-0	"to a timepiece which you got made for Sarah"	Abigail Baker Sept. 29, 1792	[28]
Ł5-0-0	"to a Clock"	Jacob Sheril Sept. 23, 1775	[128]
Ł4-16-0	"To a Timepiece"	Abraham Mulford Dec. 17, 1783	-
Ł4-8-0	"to a Clock"	Elisha Treet April 4, 1777	NR
Ł3-15-0	"to a Clock"	Cap't. Levi Riley [of Hartford] March 15, 1777	NR
Ł3-5-0	"To Repairing or, rather Remaking 1 Clock"	Payne & Ripley August 21, 1799	-
[Ł3-4-0] $8.00	"To Timepiece To be paid in 6 months"	Matthew T. Hunting 1821	-

Notes

1. Book B, Index of Grantors, Suffolk County Clerk's Office, Riverhead, N.Y. See also East Hampton Free Library (hereafter EHFL), MS (x) FH/117.

2. Newton J. Dominy, Genealogical History of the Dominy's Family (Dublin, Ohio, 1956), p. 82.

3. Records of the Town of East Hampton, Long Island, Suffolk County, New York (Sag Harbor, N.Y., 1889), III, 265-266, 460. See also Jeannette E. Rattray, East Hampton History (Garden City, N.Y., 1953), p. 289.

4. Nathaniel Dominy IV and V, Account Book B, 1762-1844, Joseph Downs Manuscript and Microfilm Collection (hereafter DMMC), MS 59x9a, Winterthur Museum.

5. Account Book and Day Book, Nathaniel Dominy V, 1798-1847, DMMC, MS 59x6, pp. 66, 114, 123. See also DMMC, M 310, p. 23.

6. Account Book, Felix Dominy, 1818-1827, DMMC, MS 59x9.21, p. 35.

7. Letter from James C. Horton, Quogue, N.Y., to Felix Dominy, East Hampton, Oct. 18, 1832, DMMC, MS 59x9.66.

8. Horatio G. Spafford, A Gazetteer of the State of New York (Albany, 1813), p. 180.

9. Letters from Sarah Nicoll, Islip, N.Y., to Felix Dominy, East Hampton, Sept. 22, 1828, and Nov. 3, 1828, DMMC, MSS 59x9.34, 59x9.35.

10. John Disturnell, A Gazetteer of the State of New York (Albany, 1842), p. 468.

11. Tench Coxe, A View of the United States of America (Philadelphia, 1794), p. 443.

12. "Assessment Roll of the Town of East Hampton. . .", EHFL, MS (x) KH18.

13. Lyman Beecher was the progenitor of the family that included Henry Ward Beecher and Harriet Beecher Stowe. Timothy Dwight served as a president of Yale College.

14. Barbara M. Cross, ed., The Autobiography of Lyman Beecher (Cambridge, Mass., 1961), I, 65-66, 86.

15. Travels in New England and New York (London, 1823), III, 297.

16. _Ibid_.

17. Charles F. Hummel, With Hammer in Hand (Charlottesville, Va., 1968), pp. 351–406.

18. Tax lists were used for the years 1802–3, 1805, 1806, 1810, 1814–16. These are located in EHFL, MSS (x) FH17, (x) KH18.

19. DMMC, MSS 57.34.2, 59x9a, p. 131.

20. DMMC, MS 57.34.2.

21. Charles F. Montgomery, American Furniture: The Federal Period (New York, 1966), pp. 23, 26.

22. DMMC, MS 59x9a, p. 131.

23. _Ibid_., pp. 100–01.   See also DMMC, M 310, pp. 33, 38.

24. DMMC, MS 59x6, p. 27.

25. See No. 245 in Hummel, pp. 330–32.

26. _Ibid_., p. 235.

27. DMMC, MS 59x9.1.

28. DMMC, MS 59x9a, p. 57.

29. East Side Settlement House, Catalogue, Winter Antiques Show (New York, 1968), p. 62.

30. See Antiques, XC (July 1966), p. 25.

31. Rattray, pp. 331–32.

32. Newton J. Dominy, p. 64.

33. DMMC, MS 59x6, pp. 8, 147.

34. Rattray, pp. 113–14.

35. Norman S. Rice, New York Furniture before 1840 in the Collection of the Albany Institute of History and Art (Albany, 1962), p. 38.

36. (New Haven, 1962), p. 116.

THE DUNLAPS OF NEW HAMPSHIRE AND THEIR FURNITURE

Charles S. Parsons

ABOUT three hundred joiner-cabinetmakers worked in New Hampshire before 1825. Some of these men, who were engaged primarily in building construction, may have made only a few pieces of furniture. The work of approximately thirty men, or only 10 percent of the total, can be identified today.

Of New Hampshire furniture makers, the name Dunlap is best known, but members of two other well-known families of joiners, the Dennises and the Gaineses, worked in the state prior to the Dunlaps. Thomas Dennis, born in England about 1638, arrived in Portsmouth about 1663, remained there for several years, and moved on to Ipswich. Many pieces made in Ipswich at the time of his residence there have been attributed to him, but none in Portsmouth have been identified as his. John Gaines III, born in Ipswich, moved to Portsmouth in 1724, when he was twenty years old. He died in 1743, before the earliest of the Dunlap cabinetmakers was born. Several chairs in the Gaines family, and others of distinctive design and carving, have been attributed to him and to his son, George. Robert E. P. Hendrick wrote a thesis about their work, that with the Gaines account book is in the Joseph Downs Manuscript and Microfilm Collection at Winterthur.[1]

Joseph Downs, in American Furniture: Queen Anne and Chippendale Periods, said in part:

> Among the joiners in New Hampshire John Gaines and
> Samuel Dunlap II are recognized for their individuality
> . . . .Dunlap created a style of maple high chests,
> chairs and desks unique in their combination of
> carved intaglio fans, scrolls, and open interlaced

pediments . . . . Sometimes one family, by the impress
of its creative ability, established a style of
furniture that became an individual school within a
period. The Dunlaps . . . carved on woodwork and
furniture concaved fans, S-scrolls, and interlaced straps,
which are unmistakably their own choice . . . . The
wide, molded stretchers and elongated back [of the
side chair at Winterthur] further indicate the Dunlap's
personal touch . . . . One of the most distinctive
regional designs evolved in American furniture is the
work of Samuel Dunlap, and his brother John.[2]

Downs's book was published in 1952, when the Dunlap room
(fig. 1) was installed at the Winterthur Museum and before the
addition of more of this New Hampshire furniture. In the past
seven years three account books previously unavailable for
study, examination of family heirlooms, and a photographic
survey of 150 Dunlap pieces have supplied additional information.

New Hampshire Towns

Villages in which cabinetmakers lived greatly influenced
their work. The life span of a village, its type of trade, the
wealth and ancestry of its population, and its proximity to
larger centers, all had a bearing on the furniture styles in
demand. Prosperous and growing settlements supported
several cabinetmakers, and competition among them affected
the design, quality, and price, as well as the opportunity to
learn the trade through the apprenticeship system.

Joiner-cabinetmakers worked in about sixty towns, or one-
third of the places now established. In 1800 Portsmouth was
the only town of 5,000 inhabitants, and there were about
eight locations of one-half that number. The Dunlaps worked
in towns of 1,200 to 1,700 population, or those with fewer
than 200 houses. However, they were all growing communities
located at least fifty miles from Portsmouth or Boston. Amherst,
located close to Bedford (population 898), was the sixth
largest settlement in New Hampshire in 1790 with a population

Fig. 1. The Dunlap Room at Winterthur, as it was
arranged in 1955

of 2,369. Antrim (population 1,059) became the home of John
Dunlap II about 1805.

Seventy-five joiner-cabinetmakers are known to have worked in Portsmouth before 1825. The town directory of 1821, the
first in the state, contains the names of other men who
probably were engaged in work on ships and buildings.

The Dunlap Family of Cabinetmakers

Archibald Dunlap, a weaver from Ireland, was married in
1741 in Chester, a village of 117 houses, located eighteen
miles from Exeter and thirty-two from Portsmouth. He died
in 1754, leaving five sons from two to twelve years old.
Three of them eventually became farmers, and two were
cabinetmakers. It is not known where or from whom the two
cabinetmaker sons, John and Samuel, learned their trade, but
evidence points to apprenticeship. It has been said that
their father was a cabinetmaker, but this is not substantiated
either in provincial deeds or by the inventory of his estate.
In any event, the boys were too young at the time of his death
to have been taught by their father.

Major John was born in Chester in 1746. He worked in
Goffstown as a joiner and cabinetmaker from 1769 to 1777 and
then in Bedford until his death in 1792. Lieutenant Samuel
worked later with his brother in Henniker, before moving to
Salisbury. Four of Major John's five sons followed his
occupation, but they were mere boys when he died, and must
have learned the trade elsewhere. Robert, the eldest, was
only thirteen at the time.

Robert's name appears in his uncle's account book in 1796
and two years later in his ciphering book; he is called a
cabinetmaker in deeds. He lived in Bedford, building about
1830 a house that is still occupied by the family. Archibald,
the second son, called Samuel in some records, moved to
Hartland, Vermont, about 1818. John II, the Major's third
son, spent four years learning the trade from David McAfee,
(1770-1809), according to a Dunlap descendant, Mrs. Kate
B. Andrews Swain. McAfee's name does not appear in Dunlap
accounts, but he is called a cabinetmaker in a deed for the

purchase of the Dunlap pew. When he was working in Antrim, John II made a card table, dated 1807, and chairs, stamped 1830. In 1815 he went briefly to the Mohawk Valley, New York, where he learned to make knitting looms for manufacturing underclothing. Returning to Antrim, he carried on both businesses for twenty years. Less is known of Whitfield Dunlap. He was taxed in Henniker in 1808, and in Bedford in 1810 before going west. One piece in the Garven Collection at Yale University is attributed to him.

John II had a son, Robert N., who helped to turn chairs and to do other work for his father, but none of his work has been identified.

Major John's grandson of the same name, a son of Robert, was a carpenter and builder; he erected a sawmill after retiring to Bedford. He left plans for a house of his own design in Lowell, records of work in Maine, and plans for a church in Virginia. His books included Civil Architecture (1836) by Edward Shaw and Practice of Architecture (1833) by Asher Benjamin.

Lieutenant Samuel, six years younger than his brother Major John, has been referred to as Samuel II, although he was actually the first of that name. His four sons, Samuel II, John IV, James, and Daniel, were all listed in deeds both as "joiners" and as "yeomen."

The will of Lieutenant Samuel, made ten years before his death in 1820, bequeathed to James, the second son, all of his personal property, including a clock, household furniture, joiners tools, and stock; it stipulated that James was to pay each of his brothers and sisters one dollar. James was the administrator and signed as a yeoman. James had a farm in Salisbury where two of his nephews and his brothers helped with the work. His account book records the making of some furniture between 1815 and 1840.

Samuel II (1783-1853) built a grist mill in Salisbury but sold it in 1834 before moving permanently to Andover, Maine.

Daniel Dunlap (1800-1875) worked for his brother James but after his marriage moved to Concord and entered the sash business under his own name.

Little is known about Daniel Dunlap (1792-1866). A cousin

to the Dunlaps of Bedford, he was listed as a cabinetmaker
in Antrim deeds of 1813 to 1847. A kitchen table "signed" by
him was illustrated in Antiques (July 1964), and is now owned
by the New Hampshire Historical Society.

John's army rank came from activity in the militia rather
than from Revolutionary service. Raising and training men
for service, he was commissioned a captain in 1781 and a
major in 1786. From 1788 he frequently acted as highway
surveyor and raised money or services for the building and
maintaining of roads. Other civic duties, including those of
selectman of Bedford (1783-1784), constable, and juror,
rounded out his life as cabinetmaker and farmer.

Books once owned by Major John Dunlap reveal his education, interests, and a few places he had visited. His ciphering book, similar to one written by his son Robert, contains
examples ranging from simple arithmetic, including fractions,
to practical geometry and plain trigonometry. The last example illustrates the use of logarithms and gives directions
on "How to make a Dialling," a horizontal sundial for the
latitude 43° 20". On one page, borders drawn around examples
bear resemblance to the furniture moldings he frequently made.
Other drawings--a peacock, animals, and birds--also hint at
his artistic talent. Other handwritten records include an
account book (which does not cover the last five years of his
life), a time or daybook for the year 1786, and a pocket-sized
book containing tables for converting linear to board feet.

The Practice of Piety contains the signature of his
father "archibald Dunlap." A New History of China (1688);
a copy of the Bible bought in Haverhill in 1771; Hymns and
Spiritual Songs (1772), bought on Christmas Day, 1777, in
Boston; A New and Complete System of Arithmetic by
Nicholas Pike, purchased in 1788, the year of its publication;[3]
and Regulations for the Order and Discipline of the Troops of
the United States,[4] all bear the Major's signature. There was
a circulating library in Bedford as early as May 28, 1789, and
although the list of original subscribers had been lost, a
Dunlap inventory item, "Part in Bedford Library, ten shillings,"
indicates that Major John was one of them. His son Robert
was one of the incorporators of the town library in 1802.

Six years younger than the Major, Lieutenant Samuel
started to work for his brother in 1773, at the age of twenty-
one. Presumably he had completed his apprenticeship,
although we have no record of it. Major John's account book
shows charges to Samuel as follows: "three plane oirns
[irons], one Moyter [miter] gauge, one pair of Compasses,
one Hamer, Cash and other things." We do not have complete
records of Samuel's activities for the next six years, but his
army enlistments were in the years 1775, 1776, and 1777. He
was a taxpayer in Bedford during the next two years, a surveyor in Henniker in 1781, and a selectman from 1783 to 1786.
Samuel returned a number of times to work briefly with John
before settling in Salisbury in 1797. His account book shows
that he made furniture from 1778 to 1821, continuing to do
cabinetwork after purchase of a saw- and gristmill. The sawmill was acquired in two installments: on December 30, 1806,
and during the following March. He sold this property to his
sons John and James in 1811, and John acquired complete control in 1826.

Because of the complexity of family and working relationships, the furniture made by the various Dunlaps is not easy
to identify. The heads of the two branches of the family,
Major John and Lieutenant Samuel, often worked together in
the same shop, and their sons appear occasionally to have
done the same.

Men Who Worked for the Dunlaps

The three known account books contain the names of
fifty-two men who may have worked in the Dunlap shops,
although they do not always specify the type of work done.
Eighteen worked for Major John, twenty-three for Lieutenant
Samuel, and eleven for James. In most cases they were
employed for short periods and did not become independent
joiners.

Neighbors also helped on various projects, as shown by
the ciphering book of Major John: "the Accompt of the (15)
Men that Halled wood for me May the 12, 1773." Seven of
them are listed as having used one or "two pair of Catle."

In the same book are twenty-nine "names of them that Chopt
for me May the 22, 1776." A number of them later received
furniture, although two entries read, "to one day chop
2Ł-0-0." This may have been for clearing land for John's
house in Bedford. Other men hauled boards from the saw
mills and did various other kinds of work.

Of the names listed in the 1790 census of Bedford as part
of Major John's household, those of two males over sixteen
and two nonfamily members under sixteen may have belonged
to apprentices. One blank apprenticeship form, another dated
1785 and marked for five years' service "satisfied," and three
forms for men whose terms were unfinished are on record.

Because numerous men worked for the Dunlaps, and like
the Dunlaps, did not identify their work by labels or by names,
some pieces of furniture can be classified only as from the
"Dunlap circle." Having become independent, an apprentice
may have used tools and materials similar to those of his
former master. It is assumed that one trained through
apprenticeship would have produced well-constructed, useful,
attractive pieces, closely related in design to those previously
worked on, and would have sold them at competitive prices.

An abbreviated, handwritten indenture of apprenticeship of
William Houston to Major John Dunlap, made in Goffstown in
1775, identifies the maker of a high chest with basket-weave
top (fig. 2) that is now at Winterthur and is inscribed
"William Houston." Indicating a period of two years, the
form stipulates that Dunlap was "to help him to make the
wooden part of a set of tools fit for the trade." It was
witnessed by the Reverend John Houston, his uncle, a man
so unpopular because of his Tory sentiments that he was
tried in Goffstown and "placed upon a wooden-horse and
transported back to Bedford." William's father and a
brother were blacksmiths. According to Major John,
William worked briefly before "reaping" and "quit work with
me July 13, 1776." With coworkers Samuel Remick and
Samuel Dunlap, he then fought under General Stark at
Bennington. Upon his return the following year, he again
worked briefly for the Major, but his name does not appear
in Samuel's account book. It is more likely that the piece

Fig. 2. High chest of drawers. Shop of Major John
Dunlap, Goffstown, New Hampshire, 1780, chalk inscription "William Houston," apprentice. Maple and
pine. H. 6' 11"; W. 42"; D. 20 3/4". Winterthur
Museum (57.1391)

at Winterthur was made while Houston was working in the
shop of Major John than at a later date. His activities
after leaving the Major the second time are unknown. It
seems doubtful that he acquired the skill to make this piece
of furniture in such a short apprenticeship, but it was not
made by Samuel II as previously believed.

The apprenticeship system was important to all New
Hampshire craftsmen until at least the 1820s. Craftsmen
advertised for journeymen as well as for boys to serve
apprenticeships. In 1805 the New Hampshire Legislature
passed regulations for the protection of both master and
apprentice. Some of the schoolbooks used by Major John's
boys have names and dates relating to apprentices. Among
them The Scholar's Arithmetic, owned by young John in 1813,
has "forms of Notes, Deeds, Bonds and other instruments of
writing," including a form entitled, "Of an Indenture, A
Common Indenture to bind an Apprentice," which is more
specific than those written by the Major.

Competition

Major John Dunlap apparently had no competition in the
towns surrounding Bedford. He and his brother Samuel, who
worked with him until he was twenty-seven years old, could
supply the large pieces that were not easily transported.
After 1779 Samuel lived in the fast-growing town of Henniker
for eighteen years. David McAfee of Bedford is said to have
taught the Major's son of the same given name, but none of
his cabinet pieces have been identified. David Gregg from
New Boston served an apprenticeship under Major John and
continued to work for him afterward. He was one of the
appraisers of the Major's estate and returned to New Boston,
where he may have done some unidentified work before his
move to Deering.

Samuel moved to Salisbury in 1797. The growing community
was attractive to joiners and cabinetmakers, and probably
because of competition he purchased a sawmill nine years
later. Levi Bartlett of Concord opened a store in Salisbury in
1806, boasting that he could meet Boston prices. Two years

later the advertisement of his Concord shop stated that he
had "received from the first furniture ware-houses in New
York and Boston the latest London and Paris Patterns for
cabinet furniture by which he will manufacture and ornament
to any taste which can be described; and will sell 20 percent lower than the Boston prices, warranted good." Stephen
Ross was in Salisbury briefly after 1813, and his advertisement
used the same illustration as Bartlett's--a secretary-desk with
glass doors. Later in 1817 William Parsons, who had moved
from Pittsfield the previous year, also advertised in Salisbury.

It is difficult to learn much about other Dunlap competitors.
Stephen C. Webster is listed, in The History of Salisbury,
as a carpenter and hotel manager.[5] Webster (1779-1850)
kept an account book which lists, as the most elaborate
piece made in 1808, "one circular mahogany front bureau,
$14." He also made twenty-nine sleighs.

The Dunlap Customers

The earliest record in Major John's account book is dated
1768, when he was twenty-two years old, but for several
years entries were not complete. The ciphering book contains "the work done by J. D. in the year 1770" (which may
not be complete), "60 common chairs and 12 fore backs, 6
grate on[e]s; 2 Low ons and 2 Little ons." Another page of
this book is headed "A Copy of the accompt of the goods
Sold at Vendue at the house of Thomas Shirla on May the 23,
1771 by John Dunlap." Forty-two lots were sold to twenty-
seven customers for a total of ninety-six pieces, including
chair frames, chairs, tables, bedsteads, chests, and two
cases of drawers. The Shirla house bordered on Dunlap's
property and was about halfway between the villages of
Goffstown and Bedford.

A small piece of paper is headed "Vendue held at Chester,
March 8, 1791 at Mr. William Bell's by John Dunlap."
Fourteen lots of chairs for a total of twenty-two pieces were
auctioned to a colonel, two captains, a doctor, a storekeeper,
an owner of a tavern and his brother, and seven others.

It is not known whether there were other auctions.

Church Interiors

The church in Chester was built in 1739, and some of the materials were reused for the new building in 1793, a year after John died. A picture in the town history shows a pulpit similar to those made by the Dunlaps.[6] In these early church interiors a sounding board was "hung over the minister's head, and small children for years, were informed that if the minister told a lie, God would drop it and kill him dead."[7]

In Bedford a meetinghouse was started in 1755; its pulpit was built in 1766; and the construction was finished twenty years later. The 1903 town history states that Captain John Dunlap purchased one of the pews and that Major John Dunlap finished them.[8] This interior was modernized in 1838.

The most complete description of any work of the Dunlaps is contained on two loose leaves of paper owned by descendants, describing the building of the pulpits in Londonderry and Temple, New Hampshire, churches, neither of which is now standing. These towns were both over twenty miles from Bedford. Samuel was established in Henniker about thirty miles from John, and they worked on these projects with two or three helpers. According to these Dunlap papers, the pulpit at Londonderry took 151 man-days in July 1783, and that at Temple only 99.

John Dunlap	40 1/2 Days	£8- 2-0
Samll Dunlap	32 1/2	6-10-0
Samll Gregg	41	8- 4-0
Aron Astens	21	2- 2-0
Robt. McKeen	16	0-16-0
To taking down the old pulpit		0-12-0
The Wole		26- 6-6
		July 9, 1783

The Dunlaps and Gregg received four shillings per day; Astens, who according to the account book was from Henniker, was paid at the rate of two shillings per day; and McKeen, one shilling.

The drawings for a molding have notations, among them:

under the Canepy--Cornish
2 inches
Eags and Ankers (egg and dart)
Dentels
OG [ogee]

Further descriptions introduce the "flowered OG," probably referring to the Dunlap molding, which seems a more appropriate term for this distinctive carving than "dog's tooth." This design closely resembles one in Isaac Ware's 1738 edition of The Four Books of Architecture by Andrea Palladio.

Other notations were "square," "hollow," "round," "beed," "keystone," and the like, indicating that these cabinetmakers had received training in cabinetwork.

Identification of Dunlap Work

Comparison with distinctive details on pieces owned by Dunlap descendants is an aid to identifying other Dunlap work. A photographic survey of 150 examples, half of which are high chests, shows that no two are exactly alike.

The most distinguishing features are the Dunlap flowered ogee molding, as seen on The Currier Gallery of Art desk (fig. 2), the claw-and-ball foot with reverse taper in its ankle, and the S-scroll brackets.

The pair of horizontal S-scrolls vary in detail right from the start of a pair of curves to the full outline of carved edges with raised surfaces. They are generally separated by a heart-shape cutout. The remainder of the skirt is frequently in an inverted arch. The pad feet may stand on small or large, deep discs. The chest-on-chest-on-frames usually have very deep pendants.

A number of types of fans or shells are used alone or in combination on the same object. One type frequently used might be called a spoon-handle motif. In one example, still bearing the original red paint, the spoon handles are finished in gold. Beneath is the start of a pair of S-scrolls, which

Fig. 3. Slant-top desk. Shop of Major John Dunlap,
1780-1800. Birch. This desk was found in Goffstown
and could have been made there or Bedford. H.
45 3/8"; W. 38"; D. 19 3/4". The Currier Gallery of
Art, Manchester, New Hampshire

also appear elsewhere. All of these were laid out on the wood with dividers, and the markings can usually be seen. The number of rays vary slightly according to location, size, and available space.

The basket-weave or lattice tops of high chests, flanked by ninety-degree shells, are shown in Wallace Nutting's Volume III as the work of an unidentified maker.[9] A pair of scrolls terminating in circles is found in the central upper portion and in an inverted position on the skirts of other pieces.

Many drawer fronts are paneled to give the appearance of more than one drawer, such as three in a row or double depth.

The tops of most chests have deep moldings which help to balance the extra decoration of the skirts.

Dunlap Furniture

Country joiner-cabinetmakers apparently did a great variety of work. Three Dunlap account books include items relating to the making and repairing of furniture, household and farm articles, and joiner work. Descriptions are brief. Chairs were made in the greatest quantity. The Major sold 172 rakes and repaired many more. Squares of sash were sold with and without glass. The number of squares for one person varied from 2 to 185, with 12 or 15 or their multiples most common. Joinery by the Dunlaps included laying floors, making doors and cupboards, and "finishing a room." They also did other work that later would be done by specialists, such as painting interiors, coopering, and working as wheelwrights and millers.

A summary of the number of articles made by periods shows the volume and the variation in design and construction. Major John's account book lists eleven desks made in the seventeen years beginning in 1769, with a maximum of three in any one year. After the first year, none were made in the next four years, three were made in the following two years, and none for the succeeding five years.

Values

Major John made twenty-nine high chests, each listed
as "one case of Drawers," between 1773 and 1786, with
the first and last valued at ₤54. Prices of the other
pieces varied, probably due to the value of the pound
rather than the construction or decoration. Three of these
sales were for two high chests made at the same time, and
two of his customers made repeat purchases. Some sales
were to various members of a family such as the Moore
family. Deacon William Moore, a customer sixty-eight
years of age, had been a constable and a selectman.
He was a very religious man and the "owner of several
colored persons called servants." William Moore was
born in Ireland. A brother, who was a prominent resident
of Bedford, served as a selectman and a colonel.
William's son James was a lieutenant in the war and
obtained his Dunlap piece when twenty-three years old.
Job Dow of Goffstown was the owner of a sawmill and a
leading citizen. One high chest that sold for ₤90 to a
man in Deering, over twenty miles away, was partly
paid for in Indian corn at ₤3 per bushel. In 1779 a case
was valued at $108, or nine dollars' worth of cloth
"the old way." Another entry reads: "to carreing the
drawers to Windham (20 miles) $2 old way or $25 in cash."

A tremendous depreciation occurred in the value of
paper money from 1777 to 1781, when $120 of Continental
paper equaled a pound of silver rather than one paper
dollar per pound of the metal.

Because Major John made occasional notations of "Old
tenor," "Lawful Money," and the like and Lieutenant
Samuel's prices reflected the depreciation of the pound
to one shilling, it is difficult to make comparisons between the two account books. On the basis of the most
frequent daily rates and the prices entered for articles,
the maximum times to make pieces were approximately two
days for a bedstead, one day for a chair, seventeen to
twenty-two days for a case of drawers, and fourteen to
nineteen days for a desk.

Major John's records for October 28, 1782, list "James paterson, Dr. to one Desk. Twenty Seven Bushels of Corn or the Vealue thairof in fish or Eals or money." In 1782 he partially paid with "to one Dollers Worth of Eals"; two years later 138 eals, and in 1786 a single entry "to 247 Eals," and the next year "to 66." The books were balanced, and it appears that John received about 500 eals for the desk.

The Major itemized "The Cost of a House Begun Oct the 8, 1775," where he used eight men and 15 gallons of rum, for a total cost £1,480.

Types of High Chests

For comparative purposes all high chests have been classified as gallery-top high chests, chests-on-chests, chests-on-chests-on-frames, bonnet-top chests, or lowboys (or the lower half of highboys that have been separated from the top section).

In 1928 three publications called attention to the unique chests of an unknown cabinetmaker from New Hampshire. In the January issue of Antiques the frontispiece showed a high chest of drawers now at Winterthur. This was also illustrated in the Antiquarian for May. Nutting in his Furniture Treasury illustrated several Dunlap pieces including drawings of the lattice-weave gallery and distinctive shells, attributing them to an unknown maker from New Hampshire. Paul H. Burroughs in the American Collector of June 1937 was the first to identify the Dunlaps in print, although some of his statements are incorrect.

The high chest at Winterthur (fig. 3) is one of the finer examples among seventeen known of similar design. The top of a bottom board of the upper case is signed "William Houston," as noted earlier.

Minor variations occurred in the construction of these elaborately decorated high chests. Five have the Dunlap molding, thirteen have the double S-scrolls on the skirt, thirteen have basket-weave tops, one has square feet, one has a bracket base, four have claw-and-ball feet, and the remaining thirteen have pad feet. Some have from seven to

twelve drawers, and many appear to have more. All have
ninety-degree fans in the corners and variations in shells,
and many have shells on the skirts.

Twenty chests-on-chests are known. The Winterthur
example (fig. 4) has "Salisbury" written on the back of a
drawer indicating that it was made there. The dentil molding is cut out in the same way as that in the house where
Samuel once lived, although in other pieces the dentils
are solid blocks. The shell on the bottom drawer, the
molding at the base, the S-scroll brackets, and claw-and-
ball feet are all typical of Dunlap craftsmanship.

A double chest found in Hopkinton has, on the bottom
drawer, a fan and pin wheel that resembles the lower half
of a highboy illustrated by Nutting. The upper fan and two
star-shaped carvings on the skirt are different from more
frequently used Dunlap designs, but the S-scrolls and
molding make it attributable to the Dunlap circle.

Only five known examples in the high chest group have
tall legs and two drawers or equivalent spacing in the lower
section. It has been said that Dunlap chests have a "low
center of gravity" since additional drawer space was provided in the lower section. A dark cherry high chest, found
in a barn in 1957, has maple legs, thirty-six inches overall
with the square upper portion forming the corners of the case.
An almost identical piece has three separate drawers across
the bottom rather than a wide single one.

Another cherry chest now at Winterthur (fig. 5) has inlay
on the gallery top, border on the drawers, and a vine inlay
similar to that found on the Dunlap tall clock cases. The
base differs in that a deep drawer is placed over a shallow
one.

Twelve chests-on-chests-on-frames are known. One was
advertised in Antiques in 1922 with no comment. At that time
it had wooden pulls, but they were changed before the chest
was used as a frontispiece on the magazine in 1928 and again
as inspiration for an article by Alice Winchester, "The
Dunlap Dilemma," in December 1944. On the inside of the
backboards the maker scribed a shell similar to that appearing on the top and bottom drawers. The upper drawer in the

Fig. 4. High chest of drawers. Shop of Lt. Samuel
Dunlap I, Salisbury, New Hampshire, 1797-1830.
Maple and pine. H. 81"; W. 42"; D. 21". Winterthur
Museum (56.524)

Fig. 5. High chest of drawers. Attributed to the
Dunlap circle, New Hampshire, 1770-1780. Cherry
and pine with inlay. H. 80 1/8"; W. 37 7/8"; D.
18 3/4". Winterthur Museum (54.101)

lower section has double depth, although paneled as two, and could have been used to store a man's top hat or bed coverings. All of the chests in this grouping have pad feet and very deep pendants surrounding them. Two of the chests never had any hardware, and one at Yale (fig. 6) is painted a faded red or pink. One of these stands in a room of a house near a former Dunlap home that has wall to ceiling molding carved in the flowered ogee.

Three bonnet-top or broken pediment pieces exist. The top of one appears very heavy since the scrolls are almost horizontal with large rosettes on the top.

Fourteen pieces have been classified as bottoms of chests. Not all of these have been examined, and some may have been lowboys.

Chests of Drawers

Sixteen of the twenty low chests of drawers now known have the Dunlap flowered ogee molding. The Winterthur example (fig. 7) and two others have claw-and-ball feet, but most of the others have pad feet. The one at The Currier Gallery of Art closely resembles one at Yale except for the molding on the top. The dimensions of all vary. The inlay on the drawer fronts, the two carved moldings, and the bracket feet of the four-drawer chest in the Charles K. Davis Collection are unique.

Desks

Major John made eleven desks; his brother's account book shows nine. Three additional ones are owned by Salisbury descendants: two with claw-and-ball feet and one with pad. Two others are owned by the Bedford branch of the family. None of those from Samuel have the Dunlap molding or carving in the interior. All have wooden pulls. Major John made two desks that have vertical tongue and groove rather than dovetail joints in the small interior drawers. There is great variety in the layout of the small drawers, filing spaces, and decoration. Some of the interior drawers have

Fig. 6. Chest-on-chest-on-frame. Attributed to the
Dunlap circle, New Hampshire, 1780-1800. Maple and
pine, painted pink. H. 78"; W. 43 3/8"; D. 22 1/2".
Yale University Art Gallery, Mable Brady Garvan
Collection

Fig. 7. Chest of drawers. Attributed to the Dunlap
circle, New Hampshire, 1780-1800. Maple and pine.
H. 38 7/8"; W. 40 3/4"; D. 29 5/8". Winterthur
Museum (56.523)

an overhang on the lower part of the fronts permitting a
larger and more attractive display of the shells. The desk
at The Currier Gallery of Art (fig. 3) is perhaps the finest.

Materials Used

The Dunlaps used native woods exclusively: maple,
birch, and sometimes cherry. There was an abundance of
white pine in Goffstown, and "all white Pine trees fit for
his Majesties use for masting the Royal Navey" were reserved. Local millowners, however, did not always obey
this mandate; in 1772 some seventeen men were named for
having possession of logs from fifteen to thirty-six inches
in diameter. Eleven of these men were suppliers to the
Major. Obtaining wood from such a large number of mills
permitted a choice selection and undoubtedly accounts for
the pronounced grain in much of the maple used by the
Dunlaps.

It is not known how much of their work was "cullered";
not all entries in the account book include the term. The
method of making varnish and three colors was described
by Major John. The varnish was made of rotten stone
paste, and he noted "light rubbings brings it to a smooth
surface." Most shells carved by the Dunlaps still show
construction lines for laying out the design. This may
mean that a colored finish with thick pigment filled these
markings so that they were not noticeable. The account
book shows purchases of Spanish brown, logwood, glue,
and beeswax.

The formulas recorded were "to stain wood green; to
stain wood an orange color and to stain wood to Resemble
Mehogany." The last reads:

Take 2 pounds of Logwood chipd fine put it in a
Clean Brass kettle add 1 Gallon of water Boil this
4 hours then take out your chips--evaporate to 1
quart--strain and brush your maple 3 times over
let it dry between each Brushing--Then take 1 oz.
of Curkmy root--1 Oz. of Dragons Blood--1 Oz.

of logwood all made fine put it in a quart bottle add
to this 1 pint of Spirits of wine let it steep 24
hours--turn it of Clear--brush it once over after
the Logwood is brushed--and so Done.

There are few entries of hardware purchases, or separate
items at the time of the sale. In 1775 John charged
Samuel Ł5 for two pairs of table hinges. In 1784 a pair
of desk hinges and screws was valued at Ł1. In
1774 the Major purchased twelve brasses and six "skuchens"
for Ł2 1s. Nails were made locally from bog iron, and the
state offered a bounty for every pound of nails made.

Tools

Some of the Dunlap tools are in the hands of the family,
but the collection is not as complete as that of the Dominys
at Winterthur. The Bedford descendants have adzes, awls,
broad axes, bitstocks, chisels, turning chisels, clamps,
dividers, dies, gauges, gouges, draw knives, patterns, an
assortment of over twelve types of planes, bow saws, spoke
shaves, and squares. A few of these are die-stamped on the
ends "John Dunlap" and "W.D." Some tools were included
in Major John Dunlap's inventory at the time of his death in
1792 such as a "turning lave, wheel, gauges, etc., scrapers,
vices an anvel and grindstone."
One page of the ciphering book has the Major's "Dementions
for Making a Cradle." Beneath this is a floor plan "for a
Shop . . . thirty feet Long and twenty fore feet Wide," which
was built in Bedford with three doors, six windows, and
center chimney.

Clocks

Only two tall clock cases are known. The one now at
Amherst College (fig. 8) had been kept by the family in
Bedford until 1939. It contains all the Dunlap forms of
decoration except the S-scroll. Major John did not list
any purchases or trade for the movement, although the
ciphering book has dimensions for the boards required.

Fig. 8. Tall clock. Shop of Major John Dunlap,
Bedford, New Hampshire, 1780-1800. Inlaid cherry
and pine. H. 7' 3"; W. 18 1/4"; D. 9". Amherst
College, Amherst, Massachusetts, Bequest of Herbert L.
Pratt

Tables

The number of tables made was exceeded only by the
number of chairs. The records show that Major John made
86, his brother 120, and James 38. Only two are known
today.

Examples of the work of the Major's sons Robert and
John exist in the account book, which gives complete
descriptions and quantities. John made twenty-eight tea
tables and his brother eleven, but none of them are known.
Three inlaid card tables are known, however; one has a
handwritten label "John Dunlap-1807 / Cabinet and Chairmaker Antrim." The inlay is similar to that in a family
piece, and there is a matching tilt-top tripod stand. Two
other pieces from the Salisbury branch of the family include
a plain card table with drawer and a tripod stand in red
paint (fig. 9).

Second generation cabinetmakers from Bedford made a
rule-joint table and a two-drawer stand of rather heavy
proportions.

A drop-leaf, one-drawer kitchen table, with "Dan
Dunlap / Antrim" written in large letters under the top, is
now owned by the New Hampshire Historical Society.

Chairs

Major John's account book lists more than five hundred
chairs in a great variety of types. Of the bannister back
chairs made from 1773 to 1786, one set of eight, ten sets
of six, and other sets of three were valued at £4
each. Two four-back chairs remain with the family in
Bedford; others, together with parts never assembled, are
in Salisbury.

One entry in Lieutenant Samuel's book records "215
chairs bottomed" in 1823 by Enoch Colby, a sixty-four-year-
old carpenter, joiner, and mason.

The upholstered side chair at Winterthur (fig. 10) matches
a pair at the Metropolitan Museum, all found in Goffstown
and probably made in Major John's shop.

Fig. 9. Inlaid tilt-top table. John Dunlap II,
Antrim, New Hampshire, 1810. Inlaid cherry.
H. 27 3/4"; top W. 21"; D. 15 7/16". Still in
Dunlap family

Fig. 10. Side chair. Shop of Major John Dunlap,
Bedford, New Hampshire, 1775-1790. The pair at
The Metropolitan Museum of Art were found in
Goffstown. H. 45"; W. 21 3/4"; D. 15 1/4".
Winterthur Museum (60.1054)

Side chairs and a rocker, still in the family, are die-stamped "Iohn/DUNLAP/1830." They are well made and have good proportions but are not distinctive.

Interiors

In 1797 Lieutenant Samuel Dunlap moved to Salisbury, New Hampshire, where he purchased the Elkins property. He installed paneling in one room which has three windows, two doors, a small upper cupboard, and a fireplace. The deep molding from the ceiling was cut with the following shapes: square, large ogee, a small square, ogee about half the depth of the upper, open dentil on a deep square, flowered ogee, and broken bead on the bottom. The panel above the fireplace has egg and dart with crossettes. Mrs. Austin Palmer, the collector and dealer who first brought attention to the Dunlap work, recognized and identified the distinctive Dunlap molding here as similar to that seen on Dunlap furniture. In 1926 this house was moved to New Boston, New Hampshire.

In a house north of Concord a corner cupboard with a large shell may be attributed to Samuel Dunlap, although there is no identifying molding or paneling. It is the only interior work of the kind known in the area.

Major John's account book shows several entries of "finishing a room" and one of making a cupboard, but the houses in question are no longer standing. In 1777 he and his men worked for Zachariah Chandler in the house pictured in the History of Bedford. Zachariah I was one of the grantees of Bedford, and his son Thomas was among the first settlers of the town, marrying Hannah, daughter of Colonel John Goffe. Zachariah II (1751-1830) spent his youth in Roxbury, Massachusetts, and was owner of the house from which the paneling of a Winterthur room was taken. About 1900 a photograph was taken of this room which was "in the first house of entertainment between Nashua and Concord on this road."[10] Zachariah III (1813-1879) moved to Detroit, Michigan, when twenty years old and became a successful merchant. He became successively, mayor, United States senator from Michigan for eighteen years, and Secretary of the Interior under President Grant, all the while making annual visits to Bedford.

Major John lived next to the Shirlas near Goffstown and undoubtedly finished a room for them. The house was dismantled years ago, and the paneling, fireplace, and cupboard were installed in a new residence.

One of the finest houses in the village of Amherst, New Hampshire, was built May 30, 1785, for Colonel Robert Means, a successful merchant. It is described in The White Pine Series of Monographs (1927) and seems to compare favorably with the mansions of Newburyport and Marblehead. The rooms are paneled, with one exception, and the finest is the parlor, where pilasters flank the fireplace. Dunlap molding surrounds the latter, and crossettes decorate the panel above. The room has window seats and shutters. There are, however, no records of the Dunlaps working there, and the paneling in each of the other rooms has its own design. Means's daughters married well: several married jurists, and in 1800 one married the man who later was president of Bowdoin College. One of the latter's daughters married General Franklin Pierce, later President of the United States.

Conclusion

In 1769, just two hundred years ago, Major John Dunlap started his cabinetwork in Goffstown. His brother Lieutenant Samuel, who has been called Samuel II, has been given greater recognition in print. Examples of their work were first published forty-one years ago. However, they were not identified as by the Dunlaps until 1937. These brothers did a great variety of work in wood, using great skill in original, detailed designs. Shortly after 1800, metropolitan patterns and fashions were introduced to New Hampshire, but they were not adopted by the eleven other Dunlap woodworkers.

The Dunlap collection in the Winterthur Museum is an outstanding representation of this family's work.

Table 1

NEW HAMPSHIRE POPULATION

Town	1775	1790	1800	1810	1820	1960	No. of men
Amherst	1,428	2,369	1,420	1,554	1,622	2,051	3
Antrim	-	528	1,059	1,277	1,330	1,121	3
Bedford	495	898	1,182	1,296	1,375	3,636	10
Chester	1,599	1,902	2,046	2,030	2,262	1,053	7
Concord	1,052	1,747	2,052	2,393	2,383	28,991	19
Dover	1,666	1,993	2,062	2,228	2,871	19,131	2
Exeter	1,741	1,722	1,727	1,759	2,114	7,243	8
Goffstown	831	1,275	1,612	2,000	2,173	7,230	4
Hanniker	367	1,127	1,476	1,608	1,900	1,636	3
Hopkinton	1,085	1,715	2,015	2,216	2,437	2,225	5
Keene	756	1,314	1,645	1,646	1,895	17,562	11
Londonderry	2,590	2,622	2,650	2,766	3,127	2,457	
New Ipswich	960	1,241	1,266	1,345	1,273	1,455	11
Portsmouth	4,590	4,720	5,339	6,934	7,327	25,833	75
Rochester	1,548	2,857	2,646	2,118	2,471	15,927	2
Salisbury	448	1,372	1,767	1,913	2,010	415	15
Sanbornton	459	1,587	2,695	2,884	3,329	855	14
Walpole	658	1,245	1,743	1,894	2,020	2,825	5
Weare	837	1,924	2,517	2,634	2,781	1,420	21

Table 2

THE DUNLAP JOINERS AND CABINETMAKERS

Generation	Name	Title	Born	Died	Places
1	Archibald		1713	1754	Ireland; b. Chester; 1741?; d.
1-3	John *	Major	1746	1792	Chester; b., Acct. book Goffstown ca. 1769 Bedford, 1777; d.
1-3-1	Robert*		1779	1865	Bedford; b. & d.
1-3-1-1	John**		1804	1888	Bedford; b. & d. Lowell
1-3-2	Archibald**		1781		Bedford; b. Hartland, Vt.; 1818; d.
1-3-3	John*		1784	1869	Bedford; b. Antrim; 1805 Zanesville, Ohio; 1844 Nashua; 1864; d.
1-3-4-3	Robert N. **		1813	1861	Antrim Zanesville, Ohio
1-3-?	Whitfield**				Bedford; b. Henniker; 1808 Bedford; 1810 to midwest
1-7	Samuel*	Lieut.	1752	1830	Chester; b. Acct. book Goffstown; 1773 Henniker; 1779 Salisbury; 1797; d.
1-7-3	Samuel II*		1783	1853	Henniker; b. Salisbury; 1797 Andover, Me.; 1834; d.

Generation	Name	Title	Born	Died	Places
1-7-5	James**		1787	1875	Henniker; b.; Acct. book Salisbury; 1797; d.
1-7-6	John**		1788	1838	Henniker; b. Salisbury; 1797; d.
1-7-12	Daniel**		1800	1875	Salisbury; b. Concord
	Dan*		1792	1866	Bedford; b. Antrim; 1812; d.

* - Cabinetmaker   ** - Joiner

Note: "Places" includes places of birth, death; places worked and places
      in which account books were kept.

Table 3

SUMMARY OF THE
VENDUE AT THE HOUSE OF THOMAS SHIRLA
ON
MAY 23, 1771, BY JOHN DUNLAP

Article		No. of items	No. of pieces
Chairs	Chair fraims (lots of 6 each)	8	48
	Low Chair fraim	3	3
	grate Chair fraim	4	4
	Black Chairs	2	6
	Black Chair fraims	1	5
	Black Chair fraims	1	6
	two chair fraims	1	2
	one chair fraim	1	1
Tables	Tea table	10	10
	Square tea table	1	1
	Large Round table	1	1
Bed	a Bedstead	2	2
Chest	a Chest Sold @ Ł6-0; 5-17; 6-6; 6-2; 6-0	5	5
Case of Drawers	Ł62-5; 61-0	2	2
		42	96

Table 4

ITEMS IN NEW HAMPSHIRE CABINETMAKERS' ACCOUNT BOOKS

	Major John DUNLAP	Lieut. Samuel DUNLAP	James DUNLAP	James CHASE	Jacob MERRILL	Stephen C. WEBSTER
Born	1746	1752	1787	1737	1763	1779
Died	1792	1830	1875	1812	1841	1850
Account Book	1769	1780	1815		1784	1804
	1786	1820s	1836	1812	1814	1843
Towns	Goffstown	Bedford		Gilford	Plymouth	
	Bedford	Henniker				
		Salisbury	Salisbury			Salisbury
BEDSTEAD-type	12	43	14	7	30	16
High Post		2		1	4	
Turn Up		2	4	1		
Painted		1	15	1	11	
Trundle		1	1		5	1
CRADLE	5	3		1	8	2
BUREAU		8		4	1	3
CHAIRS -Misc.	154	267	63	22	47	
Frames	196	77				
Bannisters	77			6		
Dining				10	11	6
Fanback				16		3
Great	2		1	1	2	
Four Back	36					
Kitchen		66	3	3		
Little	4		1	1		
Rocking			5		11	1
CLOCK CASES	2	1		4	6	1
COFFINS	6	11		3	37	36
CHESTS	18	5	2	3	7	13
CASE OF DRAW-						
ERS	39	27		1	10	
Low	4	37	6	3		
High			6	5		
DESKS	14	9		3		1
CANDLE-LIGHT						
STANDS	5	16	9	5	1	4
RAKES	172	28	7	3	2	7

	Major John DUNLAP	Lieut. Samuel DUNLAP	James DUNLAP	James CHASE	Jacob MERRILL	Stephen C. WEBSTER
SLEIGHS		2		4		33
TABLES–Misc.	41	41	16	9	47	13
Breakfast		5	11	13		4
Card		13	1	4	2	2
Kitchen		6				1
Rule Joint	5	21		6	7	
Tea	26	9			1	
SQUARES SASH	1269	X		1250	1455	X
SPINNING WHEELS					46	
HOUSE JOINER	X	X	X	X	X	X
PAINTING	X	X			X	X
COOPER			X		X	
WHEELWRIGHT			X		X	X
SAW MILL			X			
NUMBER NAMES IN BOOK	276	231		237		

Table 5

NUMBER OF ARTICLES MADE BY YEAR FROM MAJOR JOHN'S ACCOUNT BOOK

ARTICLE	Year 17–?	68	69	70	71	72	73	74	75	76	77	78	79	80	81	82	83	84	85	86	TOTAL
One case of drawers					1	2	1	4	1				2	1	3	4	2	4	3	1	29
Making a case of drawers			2	1	1	1								1		1		1			8
One chest of drawers				1		1	1			1											4
One chest	1			1				2							1			1	2		8
One chest two drawers																		1			1
One low case of drawers														1	1			1			3
																					53
One desk							1							1			1	3			6
Making a desk	1						1							1							3
One shop desk								1													1
One common desk																	1				1
																					17
One bedstead	1			1	2	1	1					1			1						8
Making a Bedstead															1						1
One low Bedstead	1																				1
One cradle						1						2			1		1				5
																					15
White tables	3	1	1	1	3	1	1	2	1	3				2	1	1		1			22
Tea table			1		3	4	2	1							1	1			4		17
Square, round			1		2	2		1										2			8
Cheretry tea table						3					1						1				5
Other tables							1		1			1	1			3	3	5			15
																					67
Total number of sales (119) of all chairs (500) sold	12	0	2	0	7	2	6	17	7	5	4	6	4	3	2	5	7	19	11		119

Table 6

DUNLAP TABLES AND STANDS

	MAJOR JOHN		LIEUT. SAMUEL	JAMES
	1771 Vendue	1774 1784	1779 1821	1819 1826
Table		5	13	2
Large	1	1	1	
Oval		3	4	
Square	1	1	2	
Round		4		1
Great			1	
White		22	10	
Small			1	
Tea	10	18	11	
Cheretry		5		
Round		1		
Square		2		
Card			11	1
Breakfast			5	11
Kitchen			6	
Chamber		1		
Rule Joint		3	21	
Large		1		
Square		1		
3 Foot			1	
3 1/2 Foot			2	9
4 Foot			6	5
Stand			2	
Candle		5	16	3
Light				6
Square Mapel Leaf			1	

| | MAJOR JOHN | | LIEUT. SAMUEL | JAMES |
	1771 Vendue	1774 1784	1779 1821	1819 1826
Pine Leaf			1	
Work			1	
For Camp		1		
To Set Milk On			1	
Citchen the fraime cullerd			1	
White the fraime cullerd			1	
Cullerd fraim			1	
	—	—	—	—
TOTAL	12	74	120	38

Table 7

NUMBER OF CHAIRS MADE AND LISTED
ACCORDING TO TYPE

Type of chair	Number	Frames	Total
Chairs	44	200	244
Bannester Backt	74	3	77
Common	69	10	79
Fore Backt	36		36
Low Chair	1	3	4
Little Chair	–	4	4
Grate Chair	2	1	3
Large Chair	1	–	1
White Chairs	2	–	2
Black Chair	–	3	3
Colored Chairs	4	6	10
Round Backt	2	–	2
Bow Backt	6	–	6
Bottoming for a			
grate chair	1		1
chairs	2		2
black chairs	5		5
colored chairs			
Bottomed with Bark	6		6
Chair for Camp	6		6
Common chairs slag bottom	6		6
Chairs for the Meetinghouse	2		2
A chair	1	–	1
	270	230	500

Source: Major John's Account Book

Notes

1.   "John Gaines II and Thomas Gaines I, 'Turners' of Ipswich, Mass." (1964).

2.   Joseph Downs, American Furniture: Queen Anne and Chippendale Periods (New York, 1952). p. XV.

3.   (Newbury-Port, 1788).

4.   A Presidential order of Congress, Mar. 29, 1779, approved by the General Assembly of the State of Connecticut (Hartford, no date on title page).

5.   John J. Dearborn, The History of Salisbury, N.H. (Manchester, N.H., 1890).

6.   Benjamin Chase, History of Old Chester (Auburn, N.H., 1869).

7.   William Little, The History of Weare, New Hampshire (1888).

8.   History of Bedford, New Hampshire (Concord, N.H., 1903).

9.   Furniture Treasury: Mostly of American Origin (Framingham, Mass., 1928-33).

10.   Antiques, VIII (Jan. 1928); Antiquarian, X (May 1928).

UNSOPHISTICATED FURNITURE MADE AND USED IN PHILADELPHIA AND ENVIRONS, ca. 1750-1800

Nancy Goyne Evans

METROPOLITAN Philadelphia and the surrounding Pennsylvania, New Jersey, and Delaware countryside enjoyed a greater cultural interchange during the last half of the eighteenth century than one might assume.[1] There was extensive communication between city and rural Quakers on both religious and social levels. Business and commercial exchanges from one area to the other were extensive; craftsmen migrated from one settlement to another. The flow of country products into the city in the form of foodstuffs, wood for fuel and lumber, and grain or flour for transshipment was continuous, and it increased as the city grew in size. Conversely, a sizable portion of the foreign and domestic goods imported into the flourishing port along the Delaware River was destined for delivery to the numerous general stores that dotted the farm lands. Many Philadelphia residents had second homes, or "plantations," in the country that were maintained or operated by local people. The newspapers published in the city enjoyed a substantial circulation, both metropolitan and rural, and provided subscribers in each area with a means of advertising their needs, services, or products.

The close ties between city and country are apparent in manuscripts relating to the purchase and use of furniture in southeastern Pennsylvania and adjacent areas during the last half of the eighteenth century. Ownership of sophisticated furniture was not limited to city residents or to the upper, or "comfortable," classes. Even in households where only the basic needs for living were provided, there often were one or two pieces of furniture made from the finer woods, particularly walnut and cherry, or at least several

lesser pieces with pretensions to sophistication. The form
that demonstrates this point more clearly than any other is
the tea table.

Residents of Philadelphia generally favored mahogany
during this period when ordering a new tea table to comple-
ment the household furnishings, although walnut was a close
competitor. Outside the city, tea tables of walnut were
considerably more common than those fashioned of any other
wood. The adjective "mahogany" conveys a mental impres-
sion of sophisticated objects. Even on this elevated plateau
there are various levels. Perhaps on one of the highest
planes stands the tea table that James Gillingham of Philadelphia made in 1769 for James Bordley of Chestertown,
Maryland. With its scalloped top, claw feet, and leaf-
carved knees, it cost Ł5.[2] Over the years, a piece of this
sort retained a substantial proportion of its original value.
When appraisers drew up an inventory of the estate of
Enoch Hobart of Philadelphia in 1782, they considered his
"scollop'd tea table" to be worth Ł3.[3] This figure is about
double the average evaluation of tea tables found in other
city inventories. On descending planes stand the "Curl'd
mehogony teatable" made by William Robinson for the
merchant Stephen Collins in 1760 and the "Plain mahogany
Tea Table" provided for the Charles Norris family in the same
year by Samuel Matthews.[4] In the shop of David Evans a
table of the latter description cost Ł2 15s. in 1774.[5]

Mahogany tea tables were part of the household furnishings of two Philadelphia furniture craftsmen. Robert
Black of the district of Southwark owned one in 1793;
another was in the home of John Brown in 1801. It appears,
however, that a woodworking craftsman was more likely to
have selected a walnut tea table for use in his home. Fifteen shillings was the average price for such pieces from
about the 1760s until the 1790s. One exception appears in
the estate papers of Joseph Trotter, whose walnut tea table
was valued at Ł1 10s. in 1770. John Gillingham owned two
walnut tea tables at the time of his death in 1794. One of
them must have been quite old, for appraisers judged it to be
worth only five shillings.[6] The term "old" occurs frequently

in inventories. The "2 Old Tea Tables" in the estate of
John Hill, a joiner who died in 1767, were appraised together at only five shillings,[7] while "an old tea table &
2 Stools" belonging to Thomas Green, a carpenter, were
worth only two shillings for the lot in 1753.[8] Regardless of
their form or original cost, it is obvious that these particular
tables were no longer considered sophisticated pieces by
their appraisers. In the Wilmington, Delaware, home of
the merchant James Gilpin an "old Tea table" had already
been relegated to the kitchen when appraisers drew up his
inventory in 1798.[9]

Both round and square tea tables are mentioned in
documents, and descriptions are given of several decorative
treatments. William Lewis of Chester County, Pennsylvania,
owned a "Small painted Tea Table" in 1784.[10] Shortly after
the middle of the century, appraisers in Philadelphia listed
a japanned tea table in the estates of Ann Closson, a widow,
and of John Mifflin, a Quaker merchant. Mifflin kept his
table covered with a "Set of China."[11] The value of "1
Maple tea table" used in a home in Chester County in 1784
was the same as that of a walnut table--fifteen shillings.[12]

New tea tables made in the shops of rural cabinetmakers
during the last half of the eighteenth century seem to have
remained constant in price at £1 10s. or slightly more.[13]
When the need arose, craftsmen produced special pieces
such as the "large tea table" made for Isaac Allen, a tavern
keeper of New Garden Township in Chester County. With a
larger-than-average tea table he could better accommodate
the needs of his guests who wished mild refreshment.[14]

The all-round, utilitarian table used in southeastern
Pennsylvania in the eighteenth century was made of pine or
poplar (fig. 1). It varied in size as well as function. One
type is identified in manuscripts as a "kitchen" table. From
descriptive phrases accompanying account entries it is
possible to determine, in general, the appearance of this
piece. In 1779 David Evans noted in his account book that
he had made "a Large Pine Kitchen Table about 5 foot
Long" for Thomas Lawrance, one of Philadelphia's vendue
masters. It appears to have been common practice for

Fig. 1. Table, maker unknown. Possibly Pennsylvania, 1725-1800. American walnut and tulip. H. 30 1/2"; W. 63"; D. 32 1/2". Winterthur Museum (66.1209)

householders to purchase more than one table for use in the
kitchen. When Robert Underwood, who is identified as a
scrivener in city directories, drew up a list of the furniture
he had purchased for his house in 1795, he included both a
large and a small kitchen table. Evans's accounts show
several customers who purchased two kitchen tables at one
time, among them his brother-in-law, William Gardiner, and
the merchant Tench Coxe. Only a few months after George
Bringhurst purchased "2 pine Kitchen tables" from Evans, he
ordered "a Pine Bench for Kitchen 2 or 3 Seats." Since its
length is expressed in "seats," it appears that the bench was
destined for use with one of the kitchen tables. Two pieces
listed together in the inventory of the personal estate of the
joiner Joseph Trotter are a kitchen table and "one pine Joint
Stool."[15] Even an outmoded form such as a joint stool
might be found in a less formal area of the home if still in
serviceable condition.

The account book of Amos Darlington, Sr., working in
West Goshen Township, Chester County, indicates that this
rural craftsman made at least six kitchen tables in the opening years of the nineteenth century. In price they ranged
from £1 10s. to £1 17s. 6d.[16] In both rural and metropolitan
areas a craftsman sometimes fashioned a piece of furniture
from materials supplied in part by the customer. A record
of such a transaction occurs in Evans's accounts for 1791,
where he notes that he made Joseph Miller "a Pine Kitchen
table the top of his Stuff." Another descriptive entry
indicates that Evans supplied Curtis Clay with a "Large Pine
Kitchen Table with a Drawr" at a cost of £1 17s. 6d. Two
decades earlier William Savery had made "a Kitchen Table
without a Drawer" for John Cadwalader. Within a few months
he had produced for the same customer a table that might be
termed a multipurpose piece. He described it as "a Kitchen
Table 4 foot by 2', 6" with a Drawer." To it he "fixed" an
ironing board.[17] Because of the size of the piece, it seems
reasonable to assume that it functioned in several ways.
Probably the board for ironing could be stored underneath, or
was hinged to lift or drop out of the way when not in use.
The "pine table with a Clampt Sliding top" made for Charles

Norris in 1761 by the cabinetmaker Samuel Matthews seems
closely related. [18]

In city inventories and accounts the ironing board appears
with considerable frequency. A few examples taken from
Philadelphia estate papers will serve to illustrate this point:
"a small table & Ironing board" were part of the personal
estate of John Gillingham, the cabinetmaker, in 1794.
Another cabinetmaker, Thomas Tufft, owned "a Table and
Ironing board" in addition "to Citchen furniture of Sundry
Cinds." [19] As early as 1759 Ruth Webb, a shopkeeper, had
in her possession "1 old Ironing Table." [20] More than
fifty years later the estate of Arthur Howell, a tanner and
currier, included "1 Table & Iron Board." The kitchen of
Joseph Richardson, the silversmith, could boast "2 Ironing
boards," presumably for use with one of the "3 Pine Tables"
also in the same room. [21] In one instance there is record
of an ironing board that was placed on trestle supports
instead of on a table. [22]

As demonstrated, the use of utilitarian furniture and
equipment was not restricted to middle-class households.
Three other prominent members of the merchant class called
upon their cabinetmakers for kitchen pieces。 William Lane
ordered "an Ironing Board & Pine table" at a cost of Ł1 2s.
from David Evans in 1776。 A decade later Daniel Trotter
supplied Stephen Girard with "a pine Kitchen Table" and
"a Large Ironing Board" at the substantial price of Ł2 7s. 6d。 [23]
Similar pieces were made by the cabinetmaker William Wayne
for the land speculator Samuel Wallace (Wallis) in 1770 at a
cost of Ł1 11s.

Many of the pine tables recorded in manuscripts are not
identified in terms of function. Those made in Evans's
shop during the last quarter of the century vary in description from "a Table of Pine 4 foot 6 Inchs Long with Drawer"
to "A Pine Table Lock & Handles on Drawr" and "a Pine
table Covered with Green Cloth." The latter could well
have been a writing table, for green baise was a standard
covering of such pieces. During the last decades of the
century Daniel Trotter produced various "common" tables for
his customers. A large order of furniture for Mordecai Lewis

included "2 pine Tables 1 four feet & 1 three feet, 6 Drawers
in Each." One of Girard's purchases from this shop in 1786
was "a pine Cabbin Table," presumably for use on one of
the ships operating in his extensive mercantile enterprise.
In the account book of the cabinetmaker Samuel Ashton,
the journeyman Samuel Davis received credit in 1795 "for
1 Table for a Grog shop" valued at 11s. 3d. The 1767 inventory of Samuel Austin, a joiner, mentions "1 long Pine Table
& 1 old Do," along with two joint stools.[25] In various
documents the terms "hinged" or "square" also appear in
relation to pine tables. A cost survey using documents
dating between 1750 and 1800 showed that new pine tables
varied in average price from 10s. to ₤1 17s. 6d., with most
falling into the narrower range of 15s. to ₤1 2s. 6d. Prices
remained relatively constant throughout the period, except
during the later years of the Revolutionary War, when currency
was highly inflated. Inventory valuations of pine tables
varied from two to nine shillings, and a few pieces in well-
to-do households exceeded ten shillings.

An interesting purchase from the shop of David Evans on
September 18, 1777, reflects the inflation of the early war
years and the unsettled nature of the times. John Biddle,
proprietor of the Indian King Tavern, took delivery of "2 Large
Pine Dining Tables," which cost him "₤6 per Table." He
paid an additional ₤1 15s. for having the pieces painted. He
could well afford the expense, for business was flourishing.
Military personnel came and went in the city. The inns and
boarding houses were crowded; their sleeping and dining
accommodations, overburdened. The addition of two large
tables to the furnishings of the tavern must have been a
welcome relief to mealtime congestion. Within eight days,
however, the clientele at the tavern changed. On September 26
Evans recorded in his accounts, "The British Army marched in
this City."

The reference to painting the pine tables purchased by
Biddle opens up another avenue of investigation. Apparently,
many pine pieces were "left in the wood"; that is to say,
they were not painted. There are just enough references to
painted pieces, however, to indicate that this method of

finishing was not uncommon.   Ephraim Haines supplied
Girard with two painted pine tables in 1801.   One piece had
a drawer.   In general, householders favored one of three
colors for painted furniture--blue, green, and mahogany.
A "Blew painted Table" valued at 7s. 6d. is mentioned in the
inventory of the chairmaker Daniel Jones, who died in 1766.
In George Flake's bill for painting, delivered to Daniel
Trotter in the early 1790s, many furniture forms and colors
are itemized, among them "6 Tables Green" and one "Table
Moho[gany] Couller."   No doubt the cost of painting
depended on the size of the piece.   Flake's charge for
finishing these tables varied from 2s. 6d. to 3s. 6d.   Another
reference to a "Small pine board table painted a Mohogany
colour" appears in Robert Underwood's account of furniture
purchased for his house in 1795.   Immediately following
this entry is another for "12 Windsor Chairs painted a
Mahogany colour."[26]   It seems reasonable to assume that
these pieces were all for use in the same area.   The table
may also have been in the Windsor style.   In my research
notes are few references to the use of the word "red."   The
inventory of William Lewis, a joiner of Haverford Township,
Chester County, in 1777 included "1 Square table painted
read."[27]   "Read," as used here, probably refers to the
brownish-red color still found today on a number of painted
pieces of the eighteenth and nineteenth centuries.   Even
painted pieces required a certain amount of maintenance
and occasional repainting.   White and Byrnes of Wilmington
mended and painted a table for John Ferris in 1785 at the
cost of 7s. 6d.
     Poplar was second only to pine for use in the construc-
tion of utilitarian tables, although its greatest use seems to
have been in the rural areas surrounding Philadelphia.
Tables made of poplar appear in the inventories of at least
two country craftsmen who are identified as joiners--one in
Chester County and one in Philadelphia County.   These
pieces are often described as being small in size or square
in shape.   They varied in value from one to seven shillings.
From descriptions of new pieces in the account book of Enos
Thomas, who worked in Goshen Township, Chester County,

it is evident that there was as much versatility in the design
and use of poplar tables as there was in those made of pine.
During the 1790s this cabinetmaker produced several poplar
tables that he painted blue.   Another table received a coat
of brown paint.   Prices for the new pieces ranged from
11s. 3d. to 18s. 9d.[28]

Two oval cedar tables, both valued at fifteen shillings,
are itemized in a Philadelphia inventory drawn up by appraisers on April 10, 1766.   They were part of the first-floor
furnishings in the home of George Smith.   Furniture made
primarily of red cedar was seldom recorded either in inventories or craftsmen's accounts.   The principal function of
red cedar was as a secondary furniture wood and a material
for the construction of coffins.   Another unusual piece, "an
Oak Oval Table," appears in the inventory of David George
of Blockley in Philadelphia County in 1759.   The table,
apparently a survival of an earlier period, is listed along
with "old Chairs."   In another place in the inventory the
appraisers listed a joint stool.[29]

Fortunately, many eighteenth-century inventories for
urban areas list household furnishings room by room,
making it possible to pinpoint the rooms where tables of
pine, poplar, and other unsophisticated woods were in
use.   As one would expect, they are found most frequently
in the kitchen, although a few are scattered around in other
downstairs areas, including the parlor and dining room.
Simple tables are found less frequently in upstairs rooms.
The more common practice apparently was to use older, once
fashionable pieces in the bedchambers.   Inventories in rural
areas, however, were less frequently itemized room by room.

Pine stands, some of them painted, probably doubled in
many instances as small tables.   The craftsman George
Claypoole made and painted two such pieces for Samuel
Meredith in 1772 and charged him £1 6d.   "Two pine tables"
made at the same time at a cost of £1 12s. apparently were
left unpainted, for there is no additional charge made in the
account.   John Cadwalader purchased "a green Stand" from
William Savery on two occasions during the early months of
1771, along with several other pieces of unsophisticated

furniture. In the country Enos Thomas made a poplar stand
in 1796 and painted it blue.[30]

The toilet table is an unusual piece of furniture, for it
began life as a simple pine frame and then was elevated to
the ranks of sophistication by the addition of a fabric skirt.
Such elegant dressing tables appear to have been used
almost exclusively in the city and within prosperous households. John Douglass made "2 Toilet Tables" for the
merchant Zaccheus Collins in 1794 at the modest price of
Ł1 10s.[31] The real expense lay in the trimming. Earlier
in the 1770s the price of a frame was slightly cheaper. For
"a Large Tilet Table" Cadwalader paid Savery only twelve
shillings.[32] The cost of a toilet table made by Evans for
Joseph Pemberton, a merchant, was even less--a mere 7s. 6d.
Perhaps this piece replaced an older toilet table in the
Pemberton home whose top had been repaired in the previous
year by Savery.[33] An example of the forerunner of the
toilet table is to be found in a Philadelphia inventory of
1753. Among the furnishings of the widow Closson there
are listed "1 Dressing Table & a painted Cover," together
valued at Ł1.[34]

Other tables worthy of note are the two slate tables used
in bedchambers in the Philadelphia homes of the carpenter,
Thomas Green, and Dr. Lloyd Zachary during the 1750s.[35]
By the last decade of the century ornamental painted furniture had come into vogue. From this period dates the "pine
card Table painted" that Benjamin Thaw purchased from
Daniel Trotter at a cost of Ł1 17s. 6d.[36]

The chair is the most common form appearing in inventories
during the period between 1750 and 1800. First to be considered are the survival pieces--those chairs popular and
fashionable in another era but still in serviceable condition.
Perhaps the oldest of these in stylistic terms is the "Great
Arm Chair and Cushion" valued at fifteen shillings in 1761
in the inventory of Roger Kirk of West Nottingham, Chester
County. Turned chairs were one of the early types made in
America and in one form or another remained popular into
the present century. Another early form, the wooden chair
with board seat, appears in several documents. Upon the

death of Samuel Austin, a joiner of Philadelphia, appraisers
noted that the estate included "5 Old Woden Chairs."[37]
Eight years later the merchant James Pemberton called upon
Savery to make six new "board bottom chairs" for his
daughter. These apparently were for use in her kitchen as
"a Kichen table with a draw"; other related pieces appear
on the bill.[38] Perhaps board-bottomed chairs withstood
the hard usage of the kitchen better than rush-bottomed
pieces, and in the long run were more practical. We can
only speculate on the appearance of "6 Citchin Chairs"
listed in the inventory of the Haverford Township joiner
William Lewis. Perhaps they had board bottoms. A
"wooden Arm Chair" appears in 1760 in the extensive estate
of another nonurban resident, Grace Lloyd of Chester,
a close relative of the Richardsons of Philadelphia.[39]

   By 1750 cane-backed chairs had been out of fashion in
metropolitan areas for almost a decade. Solomon Fussell
had made a few during the 1740s, but, by and large, they
had been replaced by the walnut chair with horseshoe-shaped
seat in the so-called Queen Anne style. Still, the appearance of "6 Cane back'd Chairs" in the 1759 inventory of
William Buckley of Philadelphia is not unusual. They were
in use in a bedroom described as "the first Chamber up two
pair [of] Stairs." Not faring as well and showing definite
signs of age were similar chairs owned by Sarah Lyn in the
same year. The "Six Cane chairs and Arm Chair" left to
her in her husband's estate had "broken bottoms." By 1788
the "Seven Cane back chairs" owned by Mary Richardson of
Philadelphia were considerably out of date.[40] Leather-
covered chairs of the same period are mentioned in inventories. It is necessary to distinguish, though, between
leather-bottomed and leather-backed pieces. The former
are frequently "Queen Anne" style chairs with slip seats,
which were still fashionable during the third quarter of the
eighteenth century. There is no doubt, however, that the
"6 old Lather bottom Chares" valued at five shillings each
in 1759 by appraisers of the estate of Lucey Bowling, a
Philadelphia widow, were of an earlier vintage. Perhaps
the "7 Red Leather chairs and 1 arm Ditto" owned in 1756 by

Dr. Zachary of Philadelphia and valued at about seven
shillings each were survivals of that great influx of leather
chairs from Boston during the 1730s. [41]   Many of these
pieces had red leather coverings. [42]   "Five leather backed
Chairs" were put to good use by the Chester County tavern
keeper Isaac Allen before his death in 1784.   They were
part of a group of thirty-one chairs of various sorts found
in his establishment.   By 1788 Mary Richardson's "Five
Leathern back chairs" valued at fifteen shillings were as
out of date as her cane-backed chairs. [43]   She was a Quaker,
and her reluctance to part with serviceable furniture even
though it was old may have stemmed from the idea of strict
economy held by many of her religion.

Fashions in the mid-eighteenth century were as subject
to change as they are today, and records point out a
parallel change in value.   The early walnut Queen Anne
chairs with their horseshoe-shaped seats eventually gave
way to more modish pieces fashioned of mahogany with
shaped rectangular seats.   By the time the appraisers
listed "6 compass Seat Walnut Chairs" in the estate of
Enoch Flower, a Philadelphia joiner, in 1773, their value was
only ten shillings apiece.   Although the cabinetmaker John
Gillingham owned plate valued at Ł29 in 1794, half of the
formal chairs listed in his inventory had "compass" bottoms,
which were very much out of date, judging by prevailing
trends in cabinetry.   Perhaps as a craftsman he recognized
that good design is never out of style. [44]

The popularity of the rush-bottomed chair during most of
the eighteenth century cannot be overestimated.   It is the
chair most commonly listed in inventories both in the city
and in the surrounding rural areas until the 1780s and 1790s.
It found a place in the households of rich and poor alike.
Cadwalader purchased "6 rush Bottom Chairs" from Savery
in 1770 at a cost of Ł2.   The wealthy Quakeress Grace Lloyd
had four such chairs in "the back room Upstairs" in her
Chester home ten years earlier.   Many craftsmen used rush-
bottomed chairs in their homes.   Among furniture makers,
John Fox and Joseph Trotter each owned six such chairs in
the 1770s.   Another joiner, Samuel Austin, who was a man

Fig. 2. Armchair, maker unknown. Delaware Valley,
1740-1800. Maple. H. 44 5/8"; W. 20 7/8"; D. 22".
Winterthur Museum (67.1725)

Fig. 3. Armchair, maker unknown. Pennsylvania,
1740-1765. Maple. H. 40 7/8"; W. 20 1/16"; D.
22 1/4". Winterthur Museum (67.803)

of comfortable means when he died in 1761, owned a great
many rush-bottomed chairs. Sixteen were found in his
garret, along with eight bedsteads and their bedding. Austin
owned two Negroes and two white male servants, and may
have had journeymen or apprentices; the large garret would
have served well for their accommodation. Downstairs in
the Austin home there were twenty-seven rush chairs in
addition to others of different types. [45]

Two shipwrights of Philadelphia, John Spencer and
Thomas Stewart, who both died in 1753, used rush-bottomed
chairs in their homes. The carpenter Andrew Jolley owned
eleven rush-bottomed chairs in the same year. The home of
Philip Alberti, a pewterer, apparently contained "6 Rush
Bottom Chairs and a Pine Table" as part of the kitchen
furnishings in 1780. Five rush chairs and two tables
belonged in the kitchen of the silversmith Jeremiah Elfreth
in 1765. Occasionally a rush-bottomed chair with arms is
mentioned, as in the 1753 inventory of Joseph Groff, a
yeoman. In two widows' inventories taken during the 1750s,
appraisers recorded "low" rush-bottomed chairs. [46]

Who made these chairs and exactly what did they look
like? As early as 1738 Solomon Fussell of Philadelphia was
engaged in a sizable chairmaking business. Much of his
trade was in rush-bottomed chairs, of which he produced
several styles. Some had plain slats; others had slats
that were arched at the center (fig. 2). Fussell formed most
of his chairs by turning the upright posts, or stiles. It is
apparent from his accounts, however, that there was a
framed type accommodating an encased rush seat, for he
speaks of "crookt feet" (cabriole legs) and "rakt backs"
(fig. 3). The "rakt back" could be the rear stile of the
Queen Anne form, which angles backward at about seat level.
Perhaps the "archd" and "carvd heads" are the contoured
and molded crest rail frequently found on these pieces. [47]
An example of this style of chair, which was made over a
period of several decades, appears in 1765 in the inventory
of silversmith Elfreth, where appraisers listed "6 fram'd
curl'd Maple Rush Chairs" valued at ₤3. [48]

During the 1740s and into the third quarter of the century,
William Savery produced many of the same chair styles as

Fussell, his master.   His keen Quaker sense of business
and skilled mastery of his craft enabled him to build a
successful cabinet trade and to enjoy a comfortable middle-
class life.   A number of chairs exist today that still bear
his label.

Other craftsmen of Philadelphia helped to supply the
need for home furnishings in a city whose population was
increasing sharply each year.   The shop inventories of the
chairmakers Daniel Jones and William Davis, who died in
1766 and 1767 respectively, tell something of the extent of
their trade in rush-bottomed chairs.   There were more than
one hundred and twenty-five finished chairs in Jones's shop
when he died.   The backs had from three to five slats, some
plain, others arched.   A few seats were "cais'd," or
framed.   Several arm chairs were part of the group, but it
is obvious that the side chairs were in greater demand.
Davis had only a few finished chairs on hand.   Both shops,
however, had an extensive number of chair parts made up
and ready for assembling, including lists, slats, rails,
"caisins," and feet.   Also listed in the Jones inventory are
"Croock Backs & Bannesters," very likely the crest rails
and splats for the "cais'd" chairs.   Both craftsmen used
maple plank, and each had a quantity of seating material
on hand.   Davis's inventory included "1000 Bundles of
Rushes," along with "3 Slat Presses" and an assortment of
tools and shop equipment.   Maple was not the only wood
used for making rush-bottomed chairs.   The inventory of
Mary Richardson lists "Six Walnut Rush bottom Chairs"
in 1788.[49]

Throughout this same period rush-bottomed chairs were
in extensive use in the rural areas surrounding the city.
Prior to 1753 Abraham Shoemaker, a yeoman of Bristol
Township, Philadelphia County, used "half a Dozen of Rush
bottom Chairs" in his home.   Both rush-bottomed side
chairs and an arm chair appear in the inventory of Joshua
Pusey of London Grove Township, Chester County, in 1760.
The joiner William Lewis of the same county owned six
rush-bottomed chairs in 1777.[50]   Perhaps he had made them
in his own shop.

From the parlor to the kitchen, from the bedchamber to
the garret, there was no area in the home where a rush-
bottomed chair might not be found.   Many of these were
painted.   Fussell's accounts show that in the 1740s the
colors black and brown enjoyed considerable popularity,
though he finished a few chairs in an "Orange Coular"--
perhaps a stain.   The white chairs mentioned in the account
book might have been pieces whose wood surfaces were left
unfinished.[51]   After the middle of the century black remained
in use, but a new color appeared.   The inventory of Roger
Kirk of West Nottingham, Chester County, records "6 Black
Chairs" at eighteen shillings and "6 Chairs painted Blue"
at £1 7s. in 1761.   Other blue-painted chairs could be found
in Jones's shop in Philadelphia a few years later.   Thomas
Pim, Sr., of East Caln Township, Chester County, furnished
the back room over his parlor with "6 Blue Chairs Rush
Bottoms" before his death in 1786.   In a room over his
kitchen there were "3 Splint Bottom Chairs."   The Chester
County cabinetmaker Enos Thomas owned a rush-bottomed
chair painted blue at the end of the century.[52]

As early as August 23, 1748, David Chambers advertised
in a short announcement in the Pennsylvania Gazette that he
made Windsor chairs in his shop on Society Hill.   This was
a modest beginning for a craft that became extensive in the
city within two decades and spread up and down the eastern
seacoast by the end of the century.   The earliest-known
branded chairs bear the name of the Quaker craftsman
Thomas Gilpin, who was working in a small rented shop in
Philadelphia in the 1750s.[53]   Gilpin was only one of many
artisans in the city who became specialists in the craft.
Josiah Sherald advertised Windsor chairs made in his shop
in the Pennsylvania Gazette of September 5, 1765.   Francis
Trumble produced Windsors before 1760 and was still turning
them out in 1798, the year of his death.   His branded fan-
back chair of the 1770s or 1780s is typical of Philadelphia
styling of the period--sturdy proportions and turnings,
combined with lightness and delicacy (fig. 4).   The Windsor
was a universal chair.   All classes used it in all areas of
the home.   For public houses and buildings, it proved quite

Fig. 4. Side chair. Francis Trumble, Philadelphia,
1775-1795. Probably tulip, maple, and hickory.
H. 35 5/8"; W. (seat) 18 1/2"; D. (seat) 19 1/4".
Mrs. Carter Coleman Curtis Collection

durable and economical. Its great advantage over the rush-bottomed chair was that its seat did not require frequent replacement.

As early as 1756 the inventory of Dr. Zachary's possessions records "Ten Windsor arm chairs" in the parlor of his plantation house outside of Philadelphia. In nearby Darby, John Paschall, "practitioner in Physick," owned at least four Windsor chairs in 1779, including one in the "low back'd" style. Thomas Pim, Sr., of Chester County had a "high Back" Windsor chair in his parlor in 1786. Both John Fox and Samuel Austin, joiners of Philadelphia, used Windsor chairs in their homes. Fox's Windsors evidently were dining side chairs, for the appraisers listed them jointly with his dining table in 1780. John Penn's extensive inventory drawn up in 1795 includes Windsor chairs in several areas of the house: six in the northeast chamber and three in the southeast chamber, nine in the front parlor and five more in the housekeeper's room.[54]

In New Garden Township, Chester County, Isaac Allen found his six Windsor side chairs and one armchair an invaluable supplement to the rush-bottomed and leather-backed chairs used in his tavern. Nearby in Kennett, William Lewis, a miller, used "Six green Winsor chairs" in his best bedroom along with his "Small painted Tea Table." Until the 1790s green was the most widely used color for Windsor chairs. In the last decade of the century craftsmen introduced several additional colors, along with decorative effects produced by striping and two-tone combinations. Perhaps the "Two Arm Chairs Moho[gany] Coull[er]" listed on Flake's bill to Daniel Trotter for painting in 1791 are Windsors.[55] Mahogany became a popular color in this period.

Occasionally appraisers noted a chair for a child in their inventory listings. In the second bedchamber in the home of William Buckley of Philadelphia "1 childs Chair & Pan" shared quarters in 1759 with a dozen old rush-bottomed and cane-backed chairs, indicating that the piece probably had not seen service for some time. Jones's shop contained at his death in 1766 "24 Childrens Chairs," all with rush

bottoms, along with the dozens of side chairs already
enumerated.   Cadwalader looked to Savery to provide him
with "a Culerd Childs Chair" for his small daughter, Anne,
in 1772 at a cost of 4s. 6d.   Later the same year Savery
put a new rush bottom on a child's chair for the same
customer.[56]   Near the end of the century appraisers of the
estate of James Gilpin, a partner in the mercantile firm of
Ferris and Gilpin in Wilmington, indicated that "2 armed
Chairs & 1 childs ditto" were part of the kitchen furnishings.[57]

Like children's chairs, rocking chairs do not appear
frequently in inventories.   One such piece could be found
in Buckley's parlor in 1759.   Enos Thomas made and painted
another, which he sold to a customer in Chester County in
1801 at the low price of 7s. 6d.[58]

Perhaps the settle did not figure in the furnishings of a
metropolitan home during the last half of the eighteenth
century.   The four examples of this form that I have found
are all listed in rural households.   In the home of Jacob
Levering, a joiner of "Roxburrow " Township, Philadelphia
County, "a Walnut Settle" was valued at £1 5s. in 1753.[59]
No exact location is given for the settle owned in the same
year by Benjamin Walton, a yeoman of Byberry Township,
Philadelphia County, but two others are pinpointed to their
area of use.   John Hall of Springfield used his "Suttle, "
valued at fifteen shillings, in his kitchen prior to 1760;[60]
in 1766 a similar piece was in "the frunt Room" of the home
of Edmond Haines of Evesham, Burlington County, New
Jersey.

The joint stool already mentioned in the discussion of
tables enjoyed sufficient use during the third quarter of the
eighteenth century to merit recognition as a household form
of the period.   It appeared both in rural and city homes.
Construction materials are mentioned in several instances:
the Philadelphia joiner Joseph Trotter owned a pine joint
stool in 1770; earlier in the city the merchant Henry Van Aken,
who died in 1753, used "Two walnut Joynt Stools" in his
"Back Garrett"; a year later, in 1754, Jacob Arnatt, a
weaver of Lower Sufford Township, Philadelphia County, left
two similar stools in his estate.   Perhaps Arnatt's stools

served an important function in his trade.[61]

A variety of other stools are mentioned in manuscripts.
Brief descriptions in the account books of David Evans
give some picture of their range of use and function.   Tench
Coxe purchased "2 Stools for Store use" in 1781; George
Bringhurst ordered "2 Benches or Stools to Sute for [a]
wrighting Desk"; and a stool for a similar purpose was made
for Dr. John H. Gibbons in 1790.   A few benches appear in
inventories.   At least two were located in Philadelphia
kitchens.[62]   Others are designated "wash" benches and
served as platforms to hold the cedar tubs in which the
housewife or maid servant did the family laundry.   Craftsmen
made benches for workshop areas.   An artisan who was not
a woodworker might pay for his wooden shop fixtures by
exchanging services with a carpenter or cabinetmaker.

A symbol of status in the eighteenth century was ownership of a high-post bedstead with its complementary suit of
hangings.   The mahogany bedstead was the most elegant.
One made for Jonathan Jones by Evans in 1797 is described
as "A high Post fluted mohogany Bedsted & cornice" and cost
its purchaser Ł12.   Generally, even the most sophisticated
bedsteads had headposts made of a cheaper wood stained to
imitate mahogany, such as the "high Post Bedsted Painted
mohogany Colour with 2 feet Posts of mohogany" made by
Evans for William Powell at a cost of Ł3 17s. 6d.   Since
the headposts were virtually concealed by the long hangings,
there was no need for them to be made of an expensive wood.
If extensive hangings were to be used, it was not unusual
for an entire bedstead to be made of a cheaper wood and then
stained to imitate mahogany, or painted.   Hymner Taylor,
an upholsterer, advertised such a piece in the Pennsylvania
Journal on January 19, 1780; he described it as "a painted
four post bedstead, with calico furniture fringed, and made
to draw in drapery, with cornices."   No one will dispute
that this was an elegant piece of furniture, even though its
frame had been made from an inexpensive wood and painted.

Two other bedstead styles enjoyed eighteenth-century
popularity--the field bedstead and the low-post bedstead.
Like its high-post counterpart, the field bedstead could

accommodate hangings. At times it was a very elegant
piece, such as the "mahogany field Bedstead Caps &
Castors" that Daniel Trotter made for Stephen Girard in
1796 at a cost of £9 10s. or the field bedstead with an
"og[ee] top" that the journeyman Samuel Howel made in the
shop of Samuel Ashton in 1801.[63]   More frequently it was
constructed of a less expensive wood and then stained or
painted. This was also the common mode of finishing the
low-post bedstead.

Occasionally the use of walnut is encountered in the
construction of bedsteads. Arnatt, the Philadelphia
County weaver, owned a "Wallnut Bed-Stead " in 1754.
According to craftsmen's accounts, however, poplar was
the universal material for bedstead construction in Philadelphia and vicinity. Poplar was relatively inexpensive,
it turned well on the lathe, and it took a stain readily.
Because families were large, most households needed
several bedsteads. Illustrative of this is the Philadelphia
inventory of George Wescott, probably a brazier, which
lists "2 Mohogany and 4 Plain Bedsteads." Even the well-
to-do furnished their secondary bedrooms with moderately
priced pieces. When the merchant James Pemberton ordered
a mahogany bedstead with fluted pillars for £6 from Thomas
Affleck in 1775, he also purchased another of poplar, which
was stained and polished, at a total cost of £2 5s. A low-
post bedstead cost him £1 5s. In the same year a nephew
of James was charged £2 5s. by Savery for "Making a Poplar
Bed-stead with Caps & Bases." Staining cost an additional
nine shillings, and "Brass bosses & Screws" raised the price
another six shillings. A "plain Mahogany Bed-Stead"
purchased at the same time cost £5 10s.[64]

Daniel Trotter sold Mordecai Lewis a high-post poplar
bedstead in the 1790s.[65]   Two decades earlier the merchant
Stephen Collins had purchased a similar bedstead from
William Wayne for less than £2.[66]   Evans's account books
show that he made and sold many moderately priced bedsteads of poplar throughout his career. If account books
existed for other city cabinet shops, they probably would
reveal a similar trade. The poplar bedstead was used

widely enough outside the state of Pennsylvania to establish
it as a good risk for venture cargo.   On April 8, 1786, Evans
noted in his accounts that he had "Shipd on Board the Sloop
Betty, Jno Morrison Master, 1 High Post poplar Bedsted
Staind with Sacking Bottom & cornice which Said Master is
to Dispose of to the best advantage for his accounts in
Virginia the Danger of the Sea Excepted & Remit the Neat
[sic] Proceeds to me [per] first safe conveyance."

Mahogany bedsteads were not as common in the country
as in the city, but there was an abundance of painted pieces
in all styles.   In the large back room over his parlor
Thomas Pim, Sr., of Chester County used a "Pair of high
Bedsteads."   A modest room over the kitchen, perhaps used
by hired help, was furnished with two simple chaff beds and
bedsteads.   The account book of Enos Thomas, working in
Goshen Township, reveals a sizable production of bedsteads
during the 1790s.   He specifically identifies some as being
made of poplar.   No doubt most of his painted and stained
pieces were of this material.   Craftsmen's accounts show
that many other country-made pieces were constructed of
poplar, and painted. [67]

Occasionally craftsmen made bedsteads of red cedar,
a durable, rot-resisting material.   In December 1772, John
Elton provided the merchant John Reynell with "a field bedstead of read Sedor with Sacking bottom and cord."   Two
months earlier he had supplied the same customer with a
"high post read sedar bedstead" complete with curtain rods,
hooks, and ferrules obtained from the founder William
Rush. [68]   Two decades later Evans repaired "a red ceader
Bedsted" for the "Spanish Minister" in residence at the
seat of government.

Craftsmen used several other materials for making bedsteads.   One example of beech appears in 1756 in the
account book of William Smedley, working in Middletown
Township, Chester County.   Another made in the same year
by Smedley was fashioned of black walnut.   Pine as a bedstead material appears occasionally.   Only one specific
reference occurs in Evans's account books.   In 1782 the
craftsman made George Bringhurst two low-post bedsteads of

pine.   The inventory of Leonard Kessler, a Philadelphia
cabinetmaker, lists "One high posted pine Bedstead" in
1804.[69]

In still another craftsman's accounts, dating near the
end of the century, one additional bedstead wood is
mentioned.   At the time that Jacob Wayne billed Captain
Joseph De Costa for a high-post bedstead with mahogany
foot posts priced at £6, he charged him £4 10s. for one of
the same style, which he described as being "all Button-
wood."[70]   Further evidence of the use of this wood occurs
in the receipt book of the Philadelphia cabinetmaker
Thomas Williams.   In 1796 Williams paid Benjamin Parker
£53 "for button wood bedstead stuff."[71]

Five or six colors for bedsteads appear in accounts and
inventories during the last half of the eighteenth century
(and particularly the last quarter) in rural and metropolitan
areas of southeastern Pennsylvania.   Mahogany-colored
pieces enjoyed widespread use in both city and country, no
doubt because of their visual similarity to the more expensive
product.   Williams paid John Sims ten shillings "for painting
a bedstead Mahogany Colour" before it was delivered to a
customer in 1796.[72]   Blue-painted pieces also found favor
in both areas.   The inventory of Dr. John Morgan of Philadelphia, ca. 1788–90, lists "3 New blue painted bedsteads."
Evans's shop in Philadelphia and Thomas's in Chester
County also produced pieces painted blue during the 1790s.
Daniel Jones, the chairmaker, had owned a blue bedstead
at his death more than two decades earlier.[73]

Green paint as a bedstead finish appears to have been
almost exclusively a metropolitan choice, according to
manuscript data.   This color was in fashionable use in the
city for a variety of other furnishings, including Windsor
chairs, small tables and stands, and Venetian blinds.   The
accounts of Daniel Trotter for the 1780s and 1790s show
considerable patronage of artisans skilled in the craft of
painting.   John Gardner and George Flake finished a variety
of pieces made in Trotter's shop--many of them bedsteads.
Flake's bill to Trotter records the use of green paint on both
high- and low-post bedsteads.   His price of 7s. 6d. for

materials and labor was the same regardless of the style.
Perhaps one or more of these pieces were destined for
Trotter's customer Stephen Girard, who purchased a number
of painted bedsteads near the end of the century.   Evans
produced "a Field Bedsted painted Green" for his customer
Balthazar Woucher at a cost of Ł2 15s. in 1790.[74]

In Chester County the cost of a "High-post white" bedstead from the shop of Amos Darlington, Sr., was Ł2 8s. 9d.
in 1801.   Whether this was a painted piece or one left in the
wood is uncertain.   Two other bedstead colors are mentioned
in Enos Thomas's account book: brown appears in six entries,
four of them for "short post" bedsteads; red occurs in one
additional listing of a piece with low posts.[75]

Apparently the press bedstead, a folding piece, had
almost entirely slipped from the scene by 1750.   Houses
were larger, and economy of space was not so critical.
Appraisers list one survival piece in the inventory of John
Caldwell, a joiner of Chester, in 1772.   However, demand
continued for the trundle bedstead, a low frame on wheels
that could be rolled, or "trundled," under a larger bed when
not in use.   Two craftsmen's inventories of 1753 illustrate
the use of the trundle bedstead in city and country areas.
Appraisers for the estates of Thomas Stewart, a Philadelphia
shipwright, and Fredrick Ludwick Marsteller, a blacksmith
of Providence Township, Philadelphia County, listed in each
a "Truckle" bedstead.   The extensive personal estate of the
Philadelphian John Mifflin, Esq., appraised six years later,
included a trundle bedstead in the room over the kitchen.
Throughout the last quarter of the century cabinet shops of
Philadelphia produced new trundle bedsteads in considerable
numbers.   In the woodworking establishments of both
Samuel and Isaac Ashton, customers ordered this form.
Evans made a trundle bedstead for Clemment Biddle in 1776
at a cost of Ł1 3s. and another for Leonard Dorsey a few
years later.   The Dorsey piece was stained at a charge of
3s. 9d. above the cost of construction.   A painted trundle
bedstead is one of the items that Evans listed in the account
of William Garrigues for 1790-91.   Garrigues settled part of
his indebtedness to Evans by doing carpentry work.   From

the shop of Daniel Trotter came other trundle bedsteads
expertly painted in green or colored in mahogany by George
Flake.   In Chester County cabinet shops craftsmen produced trundle bedsteads throughout the entire second half
of the eighteenth century.   One piece from Thomas's
establishment is known to have been painted brown.[76]

A simple yet extremely useful piece of furniture found
frequently in eighteenth-century inventories and in use
even today is the cot bedstead.   When not in service it
could be easily folded up and stored away.   References to
this form appear mainly in the city.   As early as 1753
Captain Thomas Laing, a mariner, owned a cot bedstead
valued at ten shillings.   Such pieces were indispensable
during the war years.   Evans's account books are filled
with references to this form.[77]   When George Haughton,
an upholsterer, advertised military equipment in 1777, he
indicated that he could supply gentlemen with "camp stools,
cott bedsteads to fold up, [and] camp tables," all "on the
shortest notice."[78]   Later in the century the Ashtons
supplied their customers with cot bedsteads.   "A Cot
Bedstead new painted and Sacking Bottom" is listed in the
inventory of Dr. Morgan of ca. 1788-90.   Ephraim Haines
in 1802 put "a Bottom on [a] Cott Bedstead" for Stephen
Girard at a replacement charge of 1s. 10 1/2d.[79]

The couch, or day bed, a survival from the William and
Mary and Queen Anne eras, continued to be a useful piece
of furniture during the third quarter of the eighteenth century
in both rural and city households (fig. 5).   Many examples
were equipped with mattresses and bedding over a rush
bottom.   A couch owned in 1760 by Joshua Pusey of Chester
County had a leather bottom.   Another, used in the city a
few years earlier by yeoman Joseph Groff, was furnished
with "One Rugg 2 pillows 2 Sheets and One blanket."
Several areas in the home proved to be suitable locations
for the couch.   Some rural inventories list a couch with
the kitchen furnishings.   Undoubtedly, the best-heated
room in the house was the most suitable place for a busy
farmer to rest briefly after chores.   Parlors were another
favorite location.   In at least two instances a bedchamber

Fig. 5. Couch (day bed), maker unknown. Probably
Coatesville, Pennsylvania, 1725-1750. Tulip.
H. 35 1/2"; W. 30"; D. 75 1/4". Winterthur Museum
(58.2979)

proved suitable for accommodating a couch.   Grace Lloyd
had a "Couch & Bed" in her "Front Room up Stairs."   The
"Front Chamber" in Dr. Zachary's plantation house contained
"a Walnut Couch with Damask Bottom & Pillow" in 1756.[80]
Probably very few couches were as sophisticated as this
one, however.

The crib and cradle were common to eighteenth-century
households.   A sophisticated piece made of mahogany
might be used in a well-to-do residence or in the home of
a furniture craftsman.   Even the "plain" mahogany cradle
that William Robinson made for Cadwalader in 1771 after the
birth of his daughter cost £3.   Less expensive were the
walnut cradle made for Samuel Wallace by Webb & Trotter
in 1771 at a cost of £1 10s. and the "Cherry Tree Cradle"
purchased by Ebenezer McCutchin from Evans in 1806.   In
the country, walnut cradles were produced throughout the
last half of the eighteenth century in Chester County cabinet
shops.   As early as 1756 Smedley's accounts show the sale
of a black walnut cradle for £1 5s.   A walnut piece produced
in the shop of Amos Darlington, Sr., in 1801 sold for £1 17s.
6d.   Poplar continued to be used as one of the cheaper
cabinet woods in country cradles.   In the city there are
references to the use of another wood: Benjamin Saixes was
one of several purchasers of a "Gum Cradle" from Evans's
shop.   Listed in the 1799 inventory of the joiner Thomas
Bryan is a cradle of the same material.   Forty years earlier
appraisers had recorded a "pine Cradle" in the inventory of
William Buckley.   Buckley was a resident of Philadelphia
at the time of his death, but had formerly lived in Bristol,
Bucks County.   Painting and staining were the common
methods of finishing cradles made from the cheaper woods.
Flake painted "a Criab Moho Couller" for one of Daniel
Trotter's customers in 1792 at a cost of four shillings.[81]

Corner cupboards, whether built-in or free-standing,
provided storage area for an array of household wares,
particularly pewter, ceramics, and glassware (fig. 6).
The Philadelphia cabinetmaker Francis Trumble advertised a
variety of furniture forms in 1754, which he constructed of
"mohogany, walnut, cherry-tree, mapple, &c."   His listing

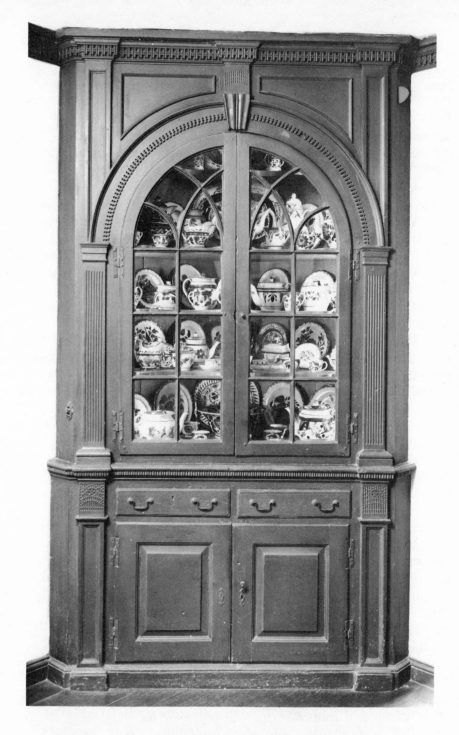

Fig. 6. Corner cupboard, maker unknown. Vicinity of Philadelphia, 1780-1810. White pine. H. 102 7/8"; W. 61 1/8"; D. 29 1/2". Winterthur Museum (59.1126)

included corner cupboards.[82]   At the early date of 1756
Dr. Zachary had "a large Mehogany corner Cupboard" in the
front chamber of his plantation house.   Every bit as pretentious were a "Walnut Corner Cobart about 7 foot high
with Sash doors & Pediment head" from the city shop of
Evans and another of the same wood made with double glass
doors, scroll top, and dentil cornice in the Chester County
shop of Thomas at a cost of £10 in 1800.   Slightly cheaper
was a cherry cupboard from the same rural shop with double
glass doors above, a double panel below, and a rounded
interior.   On a less expensive note, Thomas produced a
pine cupboard having "two pair double panel doors," which
he painted a "poplar" color for a total cost of £3 in 1792.
In Philadelphia, Savery made a pine corner cupboard meas-
uring 5 feet 6 inches by 2 feet for Cadwalader in 1771 at a
cost of £2 10s.   Two small pine cupboards, perhaps not of
the corner variety, are listed in the inventories of two Philadelphia woodworking craftsmen, in areas that appear to be
the kitchen.   The value of the cupboard belonging to George
Shaw, a joiner, was three shillings; that owned by Barney
Schumo, a turner, was worth even less.[83]

Poplar cupboards compared in price with pine pieces.   A
small cupboard of poplar in the Chester County home of
Joshua Pusey was worth five shillings in 1760.   Another in
the rural home of Roger Kirk was evaluated at fifteen shillings
in the following year.   Among new pieces, a pretentious
poplar corner cupboard from Thomas's shop had glass doors
above and double doors below and was painted mahogany
color.   The cost in 1796 was £4 17s. 6d.   Three decades
earlier Daniel Jones, Philadelphia chairmaker, had owned
a "Blue painted Cubbard" valued at ten shillings, probably
made of pine or poplar.   An unusual piece is the "red Cedar
corner Buffett," or cupboard, owned by George Smith of
Philadelphia in 1766.[84]

Corner cupboards described as either being small or having
glass doors were to be found at the end of the eighteenth
century in the homes of several craftsmen, including John
Gillingham and John Brown, cabinetmakers, and Daniel
Fletcher, a gunsmith.   In some households it is possible to

pinpoint the specific location of a corner cupboard: in the
home of Grace Lloyd of Chester such a piece was to be
found in the dining room in 1760; both William Miller of
Chester County and Abraham Shoemaker of Philadelphia
County found a cupboard useful in the kitchen; the furnishings of one of the bedrooms in the home of Mary Richardson
of Philadelphia included a cupboard.[85]

In the bedroom of another Philadelphia home, that of the
merchant Henry Van Aken, a small corner cupboard held
glassware. The chairmaker Daniel Jones provided similar
storage for both his glassware and "Chainey." A corner
cupboard in the home of Enoch Hobart, which appraisers
valued at sixty shillings, held upon its shelves "6 loose
plates" as well as "11 flatt plates & 1 water Do 7 Dishes
& a bason," presumably all of pewter.[86] Across the
Delaware River, in Evesham, New Jersey, the corner cupboard of Edmond Haines held pewter and tin-glazed earthen-
ware (delft), in 1766.[87] A "Caster and Sundries" could be
found in a cupboard in the "new End" of the house of tavern
keeper Allen of Chester County.[88]

Closely related to the cupboard, and performing a similar
function of storage and display, was the dresser. Having
an open top section, it was well suited in the eighteenth
century to hold the family pewter. Without the encumbrance
of doors, the flatware could be reached easily for daily use.
Between meals the shiny surfaces of the plates added a
bright note to the room. "All the pewter upon the dresser"
in the home of Philadelphia County blacksmith Marsteller was
evaluated at £3. The value of the dresser was only a
fraction of that amount. In nearby Byberry Township in the
same year the dresser of yeoman Benjamin Walton held
"puter Dishes Plates and Trenshers." When appraisers
drew up an inventory of the estate of Rees Peters in Chester
County in 1784, his dresser held "12 pewter plates 1 dish"
and "Sundries."[89] New dressers were still being made in
the city and surrounding areas during the third quarter of
the eighteenth century. Robert Parrish made one to be used
in the kitchen of the merchant Stephen Collins in 1769.[90]
In Chester County the cabinetmakers William Smedley and

Thomas Sugar produced dressers for the rural market
between 1753 and 1781.[91]

The bookcase or desk-and-bookcase, ordinarily a formal
and sophisticated piece, was generally made of mahogany
or walnut and occasionally made of cherry.   But there were
a few examples of painted pine produced in Philadelphia
toward the end of the eighteenth century.   Daniel Trotter
constructed "a Large Bookcase painted" for Stephen Girard
in 1796.   Even in pine the price was substantial--Ŀ20 15s.
Less expensive was "a Large Sett of Draws and Bookcase
pine painted" made by Evans in 1789 for Joseph I. Miller at
a cost of Ŀ15.   An individual bookcase "painted with Sash
Doors" cost Benjamin Tucker Ŀ6.   Another piece from the
same shop was "Painted mahogany Color."   Its price was
only Ŀ2 5s., indicating that it was considerably smaller in
size.   At the same time poplar bookcases were being made
in the country at Thomas's shop.   One piece is described
as "double poplar with several drawers & double panel doors,"
and it cost Ŀ3.[92]

Like the bookcase, the desk could be made of inexpensive
woods and then finished by staining or painting (fig. 7).   As
a frame of reference for values, it might be well to note that
two mahogany desks purchased by Cadwalader from Thomas
Affleck in 1770 and 1771 cost Ŀ10 and Ŀ11, respectively.   A
varied and interesting group of more ordinary desks were
made in Evans's shop during the last decade of the century.
In 1790 Joseph I. Miller purchased "a Large Pine wrighting
Desk 10 foot 10 Inches Long with 47 Cullums" costing Ŀ4 10s.
Judging from its size, the piece apparently was destined for
use in a counting house.   Perhaps Dr. Gibbons kept his own
accounts at the "Wrighting Desk & Stool" he bought in the
same year for Ŀ2 12s. 6d.   The firm of Wills and Morris
ordered two pine desks for their business house in 1792--
"one with Pidgeon holes and one with Draws at 52/6 per
Desk."[93]   It seems likely that the "Large Writing Desk &
Stools" made for Girard in the shop of Daniel Trotter in 1782
served a similar purpose.   Many years earlier, in the
inventory of John Mifflin, appraisers recording the contents
of the counting house of Mifflin and Saunders included a

Fig. 7. Desk, maker unknown. Probably Pennsylvania,
1725-1800. Tulip. H. 37 3/16"; W. 36 3/4"; D.
22 1/4". Winterthur Museum (64.1919)

"Counting house Desk covered with Green Cloth, a stool &
steps belonging to the Desk" and valued them at Ł3.[94]

Well-used and outmoded desks are recorded in inventories.
A "Desk old fashioned Vannear'd" was part of the estate of
the widow Lyn of Philadelphia in 1759.   Both an oak and a
pine desk, each valued at 2s. 6d., were in the home of Mary
Richardson in 1788.   Enoch Hobart's possessions included
"a Maple desk" worth Ł3 10s. in 1782.[95]

It cannot always be determined whether the "chests"
listed in inventories are six-sided boxes with hinged lids or
chests of drawers.   In many cases the valuations seem to
indicate the former.   Craftsmen's accounts are more reliable,
for they itemize cases of drawers, chests of drawers, and
bureaus, as well as chests.   Morris Shipple purchased an
interesting piece from Evans's shop in 1777.   It is described
as "a Chest 4 foot Long with 2 Tills & 2 Drawers" and cost
Ł3 10s.   This price may have been somewhat inflated by
the press of the war.   A year earlier a painted chest with
two locks had cost Amos Strettle Ł1 15s. in the same shop.
Pine chests purchased by Girard near the end of the century
from the shops of Daniel Trotter and Ephraim Haines cost
between 15s. and Ł3.   At least one chest made in Trotter's
shop is known to have been painted "Lead Couller"; three
others listed on Flake's bill for painting are identified as
"Moho Couller."[96]

In Chester County during the last half of the eighteenth
century craftsmen made a few chests of walnut or black
walnut.   They constructed others of white pine and poplar
and finished them with stain or paint.   Blue, brown, and
mahogany were the prevailing colors.   Prices ranged from
12s. to Ł1 5s.   A very small or a very simple chest might
cost as little as 7s. 6d.   Some customers ordered pieces
fitted with locks, hinges, and handles; others specified
chests made with drawers or compartments.[97]

Comparable with the data from craftsmen's accounts are
entries for chests in inventories of the period (fig. 8).   In
rural homes walnut, pine, and poplar chests were in use.
In the city appraisers recorded pine pieces.   A small number
of chests were made from other woods.   In 1772 joiner

Fig. 8. Chest, maker unknown. United States, 1800-
1850. White pine. H. 19"; W. 53"; D. 19 3/4".
Winterthur Museum (59.1670)

Caldwell of Chester owned "a wild Cheree Tree Chest"
valued at fifteen shillings. At about the same time
Dr. Paschall of Darby had in his possession a chest of oak.
Other oak chests were in the Chester County homes of the
joiner William Lewis in 1777 and Thomas Pim, Sr., in 1786.
At Lansdowne, the Schuylkill River estate of John Penn,
there was "a large Cedar Chest" in the garret. Two inventories of the 1750s throw some light on what was stored in
these chests. At the home of blacksmith Marsteller in
Philadelphia County, a pine chest in one of the upstairs
rooms contained "6 Yards Linnin 7 Yards stript Linsey."
In Philadelphia, William Buckley stored "printed Books"
in a chest "in the Passage up two pair Stairs." Perhaps
Robert Underwood used the "Large pine board Chest" that
he purchased in 1795 to store some of the tools he also
bought in that year. There is no question about the use of
"a Large close [clothes] Chest" that Benjamin Thaw purchased
from Daniel Trotter in 1785 for Ł1 17s. 6d.[98]

The clothes press, or wardrobe, is another kind of storage
chest that saw considerable use, particularly during the
third quarter of the eighteenth century. This large piece
has double doors at the front, usually over a long drawer or
a bank of drawers. Sometimes the cupboard is fitted with
pegs, other times with adjustable shelves. From the
movable nature of the interior comes the term "sliding-
presses," as used by the cabinetmaker Trumble in an
advertisement in the Pennsylvania Gazette on August 8, 1754.
The craftsman indicated that he was prepared to construct
such pieces from a selection of woods, including mahogany
and walnut. According to the terms of the will of Quakeress
Grace Lloyd of Chester, her mahogany clothes press, still
valued at Ł5 in 1760, was to be given to Mary Norris of
Philadelphia. A mahogany wardrobe at Lansdowne, apparently an elegant piece, was appraised at Ł18 in the late
1780s.[99]

The size and the amount of primary wood needed in construction seem to have made walnut presses more common than
those of more expensive mahogany. The "walnut press"
listed in the inventory of Philadelphia yeoman Groff evidently

was rather old even in 1753, for its value was no more than
Ł1.   Another piece owned by Thomas Willcox of Concord
Township, Chester County, in 1780 must have been more
fashionable; it was considered to be worth Ł2 10s.   The
price of a new walnut clothes press can be determined from
a bill rendered to the young merchant Samuel Meredith by
George Claypoole in 1772, about the time Meredith was
setting up housekeeping.   Claypoole's charge for materials
and labor was Ł11.[100]

Common woods, however, were used in making the
greatest number of clothes presses, with pine predominating.
A simple press of pine at Lansdowne in the 1780s was valued
at Ł1 10s., triple that of the "Pine Cloths press" in the estate
of the widow Lyn in 1759.   Among the furnishings purchased
by Cadwalader from Savery in 1770-71 was "a large Clothes
Press Painted," which cost Ł5.   Its color is not known.
Earlier, Thomas Howell of Chester County owned "one Blew
pine close press."[101]

Clothes presses of poplar were made and used in Chester
County.   One was in the home of Joshua Pusey in 1760.
Cabinetmaker Thomas made another in 1804, which he
painted blue.   A press made of cedar appears in the inventory
of the widow Bowling of Philadelphia in 1759.   Its value was
twenty shillings.[102]   Contrary to twentieth-century ideas
on the storage of clothes, most presses used during the
third quarter of the eighteenth century were located in the
parlor.

Large and small miscellaneous hanging shelves helped
the housewife to solve her storage problems in the home and
the merchant to safekeep his business records in the counting
house.   In the accounts of Isaac Ashton for 1791 there are
several references to shelves.   Cornel Wiles paid 9s. for
"3 Shelves"; a Mr. Fernant ordered "3 Corner Shelves" at
5s. each and "2 Long Shelves" at 7s. 6d. each.   Evans
provided Charles Shoemaker with "4 Shelves for Store
Windows" in the same year.[103]

Ownership of a tall-case clock in the eighteenth century
represented a sizable outlay of cash or a substantial
indebtedness.   Such a piece was obviously more a luxury

than a necessity. The well-to-do, however, did purchase
fine mahogany cases with eight-day movements. The
elegant cabinet ordered by Joseph Pemberton from Savery in
1775, which is described as "a Mahogany Clock case
Scrole head & Cullum Corners," cost Ł10. There was an
extra charge of ten shillings for glazing the door of the
hood.[104] The movement was a separate expenditure.
Merchants with smaller businesses and prosperous shop-
keepers could pay for a tall clock in merchandise. In
December 1805, John Ruckman, who operated a general
store in Lahaska, Bucks County, signed an agreement with
Jonathan Kinsey, a rural cabinetmaker who had trained in
Philadelphia with the firm of Clifton and Gillingham, for
the delivery of "a Compleat Clock & Cas" within two months.
Ruckman supplied Kinsey with two watches in part payment.[105]

Among middle-class craftsmen, the exchange of products
and services enabled them to acquire material objects they
would otherwise have been unable to afford. Joseph
Graisbury, a tailor of Philadelphia, enjoyed a substantial
trade. Several of his customers were cabinetmakers who
purchased articles of clothing both for themselves and for
their apprentices as they reached their time of "freedom."
In return for his work Graisbury received some handsome
furniture for his home, including a mahogany clockcase from
Robert Moore valued at Ł12 10s.[106]

David Evans may have obtained the movement for his
clockcase from the craftsman, Robert Leslie, with whom he
had business connections. The cabinetmaker made a
handsome mahogany case for one of Leslie's customers in
1788. The following year Leslie repaired Evans's tall
timepiece and in exchange received a walnut stand valued
at Ł1 5s. In 1791 the cabinetmaker supplied a semi-
sophisticated case to the Bank of the United States at a
cost of Ł4. He noted in his accounts: "To Making a Clock
Case--Painted & put up in the Directors Room."

Some of the other furniture craftsmen of Philadelphia who
owned timepieces in tall cases, which they apparently had
made, include Thomas Tufft, John Fox, Jacob Martin, and
John Brown. Leonard Kessler, a cabinetmaker who died in

1804, owned an "Eight day Clock mahogany Case" valued
at $25.   John Gillingham's estate included a similar
timepiece in a cherry case at his death in 1794.   Nicholas
Bernard, a carver, owned only one "Clock very old" when
he died in 1789.[107]   Craftsmen in other trades who had
tall clocks in their homes range from John Spencer, a shipwright, and Thomas Green, a carpenter, to Samuel Taylor,
a brushmaker, and Joseph Richardson, a silversmith.   Individuals without craft or mercantile connections might inherit
a timepiece or perhaps could afford to purchase a second-
hand clock at vendue.   Philadelphia widow Sarah Lyn
enjoyed the use of an eight-day clock left to her by her
deceased husband.[108]

Householders usually placed their tall clocks somewhere
in the downstairs area, generally the parlor.   This was the
location of a timepiece owned by Philadelphia merchant
Van Aken in 1753.   In the same decade the parlor furnishings
in the home of John Mifflin included a clock.   Another timepiece described as "old" had been moved to the rear bedchamber on the second floor of the same home.   The
carpenter Green chose to have his tall clock in his dining
room.   At Lansdowne there was an eight-day clock in the
kitchen.   When appraisers valued the estate of William
Miller of New Garden Township in 1768, they noted that
"an Eight Day Clock & Case" located in the hall was worth
£12.   In 1781 an appraisal of the same estate, or that of a
son of the same name, indicated that the clock had been
moved to the dining room.   Its value remained constant.[109]

Craftsmen introduced the Venetian blind to Philadelphians
during the last half of the eighteenth century.   Apparently
these window coverings met with enthusiastic acceptance.
An early advertisement for the "newest. . . Venetian sun
blinds" appeared in the Pennsylvania Journal on August 20,
1767, where John Webster, an upholsterer, described the
operation of the blind in these words: "it moves to any
position, so as to give different lights, screens from the
scorching rays of the sun, draws a cool air in hot weather,
and is the greatest preserver of furniture of anything of the
kind ever invented."   Certainly, this is just what house-

holders needed to protect their furnishings.   Blinds could
be purchased in varying degrees of plainness or elaboration.
The accounts of Evans, who had a substantial trade in
Venetian blinds during the 1790s, shed considerable light
on the appearance, use, and versatility of this window
covering.   Decorative as well as utilitarian were the blinds
that Evans repainted and "new hung with tossils" for Ann
Head; elegant were those with "frett fronts" that he made for
Thomas Robert; sophisticated were the "mahogany" blinds
purchased by Simon Gratz.

Price depended upon size, style, and materials.   Venetian
blinds intended for use in the home, in the front parlor or
the back parlor, usually cost ₤2 5s. apiece.[110]   A cheaper
blind made earlier by Savery for use in the kitchen of Joseph
Pemberton's house probably was constructed of canvas.
The cost for making and hanging it and supplying the plates,
staples, and screws was 16s. 4d.[111]   Custom blinds such
as the three that Evans made for the "octagon Windows
upstairs" in the home of Richard Rundle cost a bit more than
standard-size Venetian blinds.   On the other hand, a
savings could be realized in the purchase of "second hand
venetian blinds" for some areas of the home.

Venetian blinds proved suitable for commercial and public
use also.   William Nichols paid ₤2 5s. for a "Blind for his
office."   The attorney John Wills paid slightly more for his
two blinds.   The firm of Baker and Commegys ordered a
blind for the front window of their store and another for the
circular window in their counting house.   Two Venetian
blinds were installed in the Bank of North America in July
1790.   Six months later Evans made a blind for the office of
the Secretary of Congress, "in the West Wing of the State
house."   He supplied "2 Canvas Blinds" costing fifteen
shillings each at the same time.   Congress also ordered
"6 Venetian Blinds. . .with Plain fronts" for use in the
Senate Chamber and committee rooms and nine additional
blinds "for Arch Windows. . .in the house of Representatives of the United States," all located in the County
Courthouse.   The monthly meeting of Friends of the Middle
District ordered three blinds for the Market Street Meeting

in 1793.   Three years later the Presbyterian Church on
Market Street called upon Evans to make three Venetian
blinds at a discounted price of Ł22 10s.[112]

Without modern conveniences, the eighteenth-century
housewife or maidservant spent long hours in the kitchen
preparing meals and tending to household chores.   A
frequent task was making bread for the family.   After the
ingredients had been mixed, the dough was placed in a
wooden troughlike box near the warmth of the fireplace to
rise (fig. 9).   The cover, or lid, on the top of the box
served as a kneading board to work the dough and finally
form it into loaves.   In city and country houses alike, the
dough trough was an indispensable piece of kitchen equipment at virtually every level of society.

In the Philadelphia inventory of cabinetmaker Kessler,
appraisers described his dough trough as being made of
pine.   Business accounts of city furniture craftsmen provide
more information.   During the early 1750s the Quaker
merchant John Reynell purchased a new top for his dough
trough from the joiner James James.[113]   About 1778 Isaac
Ashton made a "Doe Trough" for Samuel Batterson at a cost
of eleven shillings.   Itemized in the account for painting
that Flake rendered to the cabinetmaker Daniel Trotter in
1793 is "a Doe Troft Lead Couller."   The charge for painting
it was 1s. 3d.   Another essential item in the breadmaking
process, an "oven peal [peel]," was supplied by Trotter to
John Downes in 1789.[114]

Cabinetmakers in rural areas also provided customers with
dough troughs.   In 1752 one from Smedley's shop in Chester
County cost eight shillings.   Thomas Sugar made several
dough troughs during the 1760s for twelve shillings apiece.
Another piece built with a frame cost fourteen shillings in
1777.   By the end of the century Thomas was charging
between 14s. and 18s. 9d. for a dough trough made in his
shop.   The painted pieces were blue or brown in color.[115]

Helpful in preparing other kinds of baked goods were
kitchen tools such as the "past[ry] board" and "roleing pin"
supplied by Savery for the home of James Pemberton in
1775.[116]   Rolling pins could also be purchased at Trumble's

Fig. 9. Dough trough, maker unknown. Probably the
South, 1750-1825. American walnut and magnolia.
H. 25"; W. 38 5/8"; D. 23". Winterthur Museum
(65.2748)

shop.[117]   Useful for serving the baked goods were such
articles as a bread tray from Tufft's shop or a "read Sedar
carrying tray" supplied by Savery.[118]

A variety of specialized boxes were needed in the home.
The watch box served to safeguard the pocket timepiece of
the master of the household at night.   In 1801 William Guier
found that his "watch case" required a new coat of paint
and took it to Evans's shop.   In the country, in particular,
boxes for hat storage were common.   The joiner John
Caldwell of Chester owned a hatbox, or hatcase, in 1772.
He kept it in the "Back Room down Stairs."   The spice box
also seems to appear more frequently in rural inventories
than in city documents.   Grace Lloyd of Chester had two
spice boxes in her house in 1760--one in the "back Room"
and the other in the "Closet Room."[119]   Savery made a salt
box for James Pemberton in 1775 at a cost of 2s. 6d.   In the
same year he turned "2 lids for Shugar jars."[120]   Among the
items which the journeyman George Sower made in the shop
of Samuel Ashton during 1803 were a salt box and a knife box.
From the accounts of Isaac Ashton, it can be seen that
ordinary knife boxes sold for five to seven shillings.[121]
Mahogany boxes cost as much as several pounds.

In counting houses it was necessary to have a box in
which to store the miscellany of loose papers that accumulated
in the course of business.   Young Joseph Shippen ordered
"2 boxes for papers" from George Claypoole in 1767.[122]
During the 1790s Evans made "a Paper Case with Draws &
Doors" for James Thompson at a cost of Ł2 5s. and "a Box
for Papers" to accompany "a Large Pine wrighting Desk" for
Joseph Miller.[123]

Spitting boxes are recorded in both the accounts of David
Evans and those of Isaac Ashton.[124]   Filled with sand,
these containers found use in public places as well as in
private homes.   Dr. Alexander Hamilton mentions such boxes
when speaking of his Tuesday Club in Annapolis, which
required that "each member. . .provide his own sand-box
as a spitoon in order to spare the floors at members'
houses."[125]   In 1790 Evans supplied "50 spitting Boxes for
Congress" at a cost of Ł6 5s.[126]

Various other boxes provided by Philadelphia cabinet-makers include: "a chopping Box for mincing meat" from Evans's shop;[127] coalboxes made both by Evans and Claypoole; "a Box for a gun" from Claypoole's shop; "a box for strays & sundries" made in 1775 by Tufft for Mary Norris, widow of Charles; and "2 wig box tops" supplied to Charles Norris some years earlier by Samuel Matthews.   Robert Kennedy, a gilder and picture-frame maker, advertised in 1767 that he sold boxes "of the neatest Kind" for the "Shell and Wax-Work" made by the ladies.   A kind of multiple box is the "Nest of Drawers" made by William Wayne for Stephen Collins and the "Nest of Seed Draw[er]s [for the] Garden" ordered by Norris in the 1760s from Matthews.[128]

Frames and racks had a variety of uses in the home. George Claypoole, Sr., fashioned a frame for candle molds for merchant Reynell; later he provided the same customer with a "frame with foure Leafs to hang Close on."[129]   The "plate rack" in the kitchen of Lansdowne, John Penn's home, may have been closely related in design to the "Bottel and Plait Drenor" made by the carpenter Robert Mullen for the merchant Stephen Collins in 1789.   "One Quilting Frame & Trussils" was part of the household equipment of Mary Richardson in 1788.[130]   Some years earlier, Tufft had made "a Mahogany frame," probably for needlework, for "Debe" Norris.[131]   Related equipment listed in inventories includes wool cards, spinning wheels, and swifts.

To perform the routine cleaning tasks about the home there were a variety of helpful aids fashioned by the woodworkers: buckets, scrub brushes, washing tubs, clothespins, and clothesbaskets.   To keep the home looking orderly a family could purchase "a cloths horse" such as those sold in Evans's shop.   A chimney board to hide the sootiness of the fireplace in the summertime was available from Isaac Ashton.   Personal cleanliness might be made easier with a "Roller for [a] Towell & 2 wash stands" such as those purchased by the "Spanish Concul" from Evans in 1791 for less than £2 (fig. 10).   Other items included the "Shower Bath" that Evans "Sold. . .for Cash" in 1797, the "Bathing Tub" owned by John Brunstrom, a pewterer, in 1793, and the "Bath" at Lansdowne.[132]

Fig. 10. Towel roller, maker unknown. Probably
Pennsylvania, 1750-1850. American walnut. H.
9 1/4"; W. 19 3/4"; D. 5". Winterthur Museum
(67.667)

In summary, the unsophisticated furniture of Philadelphia
and surrounding rural areas took many forms; the craftsmen
who produced it utilized a variety of materials and employed
a selection of finish colors.   Pine furniture was common to
city and country alike.   Poplar, on the other hand, was
little used by metropolitan craftsmen except for bedstead
construction.   Gum and cedar found some limited use in the
city.   Until near the end of the century cherry furniture was
more common in rural areas, but during the 1790s it became
fashionable in Philadelphia.   In general, painted furniture
was supplemental to sophisticated pieces in city households.
In the country, however, painted furniture frequently pre-
dominated.   Outmoded pieces were found in households in
both areas, but they lingered longer in the country.   Metropolitan appraisers showed a decided consciousness of styles
they considered "old."   In city and country alike, the
furniture that householders used most extensively and found
least dispensable were those pieces that were simple in form
and utilitarian in nature--tables, chairs, and bedsteads.
Once basic needs had been provided, a family might consider
the purchase of "decorative functional" pieces.   To a
country yeoman a plain walnut tea table might symbolize
sophisticated living; to a merchant prince in Philadelphia
sophistication generally took the form of a carved mahogany
tea table.   Although ideas of sophistication varied with
financial circumstances and environment, there was, nevertheless, a consciousness of metropolitan trends and
fashions among country dwellers.   Through normal business
exchanges in commodities and services, and from the
constant migration of craftsmen, the two areas maintained
relatively close contact.

Notes

1.   This study is based on household inventories and
craftsmen's accounts.   I have presented what I consider
the most important data contained in the documents that I
have examined.   The generalizations regarding apparent
trends as well as many of the interpretations are based upon
information in many more documents than I have specifically
quoted or referred to in the text.   Because of the expansive
scope of the study in terms of geographic area and time
period, it must be considered exploratory in nature and only
a first step in developing a total picture.   A definitive
study of this kind should be based upon evidence from
several thousand documents representing a substantial
cross section of society.   More limited studies might be
drawn from fewer documents.   An important tool for further
research of this nature is now available in Philadelphia at
the Office of the Register of Wills in the form of microfilm
copies of Philadelphia County probate records (including
wills, inventories, and administration records) from 1682
onward.

2.   MS material being processed for publication elsewhere.   It will be cited hereafter as Evans, MS notes.

3.   Joseph Downs Manuscript and Microfilm Collection, Henry Francis du Pont Winterthur Museum (hereafter
DMMC MS 56x8.8).

4.   Evans, MS notes.

5.   Account Books of David Evans, 1774-82, 1784-
1806, 1796-1812, microfilm copy, Microfilm no. M-305,
DMMC; originals at Historical Society of Pennsylvania.

6.   DMMC Photostat 71.

7.   City of Philadelphia, Register of Wills, Wills and
Administration Papers, 1682-1900, Will Book H (hereafter
Philadelphia Wills).

8.   Ibid., Microfilm, 1753, reel 1, no. 41.

9.   Evans, MS notes.

10.   DMMC Photostat 557.

11.   Philadelphia Wills, Microfilm, 1753, reel 1,
no. 73; 1759, reel 1, no. 135.

12.   DMMC Photostat 558.
13.   Margaret Berwind Schiffer, Furniture and Its
Makers of Chester County, Pennsylvania (Philadelphia,
1966), pp. 225, 235.
14.   DMMC Photostat 556.
15.   DMMC Photostats 1124, 87.
16.   Schiffer, p. 64.
17.   Nicholas B. Wainwright, Colonial Grandeur in
Philadelphia: The House and Furniture of General John
Cadwalader (Philadelphia, 1964), p. 49.
18.   Evans, MS notes.
19.   DMMC Photostat 81, MS 65x84.
20.   Philadelphia Wills, Microfilm, 1759, reel 1,
no. 175.
21.   DMMC MSS 53x165.642, 53x165.69.
22.   Evans, MS notes.
23.   Girard Papers, American Philosophical Society
(hereafter APS), Microfilm ser. 2, reel 210.
24.   DMMC Photostat 1150.
25.   Evans Account Books, DMMC; DMMC MS
67x89.2; Girard Papers, APS, ser. 2, reel 210; DMMC MS
62x60.2; Philadelphia Wills, Microfilm, 1767, reel 1, no. 121.
26.   Girard Papers, APS, ser. 2, reel 210; Philadelphia
Wills, Will Book J; DMMC MS 67x90.36, Photostat 1124.
27.   DMMC Photostat 390.
28.   Philadelphia Wills, Microfilm, 1753, reel 1;
DMMC Photostat 397; Schiffer, pp. 234-35.
29.   Philadelphia Wills, Microfilm, 1753, reel 1,
no. 37; 1759, reel 1, no. 179.
30.   DMMC MS 55.508; Wainwright, p. 49; Schiffer,
p. 234.
31.   Evans, MS notes.
32.   Wainwright, p. 49; Evans Account Books, DMMC.
33.   Evans, MS notes.
34.   Philadelphia Wills, Microfilm, 1753, reel 1, no. 73.
35.   Ibid., no. 41; DMMC Photostat 209.
36.   DMMC MS 67x90.77.
37.   DMMC Photostat 392; Philadelphia Wills,
Microfilm, 1767, reel 1, no. 121.

38.   Evans, MS notes.

39.   DMMC Photostats 390, 389, MS 53.165.542.

40.   Philadelphia Wills, Microfilm, 1759, reel 1, nos. 149, 180; DMMC MS 53.165.152.

41.   Philadelphia Wills, Microfilm, 1759, reel 1, no. 164; DMMC Photostat 209.

42.   Pennsylvania Gazette (Philadelphia), Sept. 23, 1742, advertisement of Plunket Fleeson.

43.   DMMC Photostat 556, MS 53.165.152.

44.   Philadelphia Wills, Will Book F; DMMC Photostat 81.

45.   Wainwright, p. 49; DMMC Photostat 389; Philadelphia Wills, Will Book F; DMMC Photostat 87; Philadelphia Wills, Microfilm, 1767, reel 1, no. 121.

46.   Philadelphia Wills, Microfilm, 1753, reel 1, nos. 40, 35, 59; DMMC MSS 56x14.1, 62x59; Philadelphia Wills, Microfilm, 1753, reel 1, nos. 29, 73; 1759, reel 1, no. 164.

47.   Arthur Leibundguth, "The Furniture-Making Crafts in Philadelphia, ca. 1730 to ca. 1760" (Master's thesis, University of Delaware, 1964).

48.   DMMC MS 62x59.

49.   Philadelphia Wills, Will Books D, J; DMMC MS 53.165.152.

50.   Philadelphia Wills, Microfilm, 1753, reel 1, no. 72; DMMC Photostats 387, 390.

51.   Evans, MS notes.

52.   DMMC Photostat 392; Philadelphia Wills, Will Book J; DMMC Photostat 560; Schiffer, p. 233.

53.   Evans, MS notes.

54.   DMMC Photostats 209, 553, 560; Philadelphia Wills, Will Book F; ibid., Microfilm, 1767, reel 1, no. 121; DMMC MSS 56x14.2, 55.511.

55.   DMMC Photostats 556, 557, MS 67x90.36.

56.   Philadelphia Wills, Microfilm, 1759, reel 1, no. 149; ibid., Will Book J; Wainwright, p. 62.

57.   Evans, MS notes.

58.   Philadelphia Wills, Microfilm, 1759, reel 1, no. 149; Schiffer, p. 233.

59.   Philadelphia Wills, Microfilm, 1753, reel 1.
60.   Philadelphia Wills, Microfilm, 1753, reel 1,
no. 84; DMMC Photostat 396.
61.   DMMC Photostat 87; Philadelphia Wills,
Microfilm, 1753, reel 1, nos. 39, 89.
62.   Evans Account Books, DMMC; DMMC Photostat 86.
63.   Girard Papers, APS, ser. 2, reel 210; DMMC
MS 62x60.2.
64.   Philadelphia Wills, Microfilm, 1753, reel 1,
no. 89; DMMC MS 56x7.5, Photostats 1127, 141.
65.   DMMC MS 67x89.2.
66.   Evans, MS notes.
67.   DMMC Photostat 560; Schiffer, pp. 64, 225, 233.
68.   Evans, MS notes.
69.   Schiffer, p. 217; Evans Account Books, DMMC;
Philadelphia Wills, Will Book K.
70.   DMMC MS 55.548.
71.   Evans, MS notes.
72.   Ibid.
73.   DMMC Photostat 1078; Evans Account Books,
DMMC; Schiffer, p. 233; Philadelphia Wills, Will Book J.
74.   DMMC MSS 67x90.37, 67x90.36; Evans Account
Books, DMMC.
75.   Schiffer, pp. 64, 233.
76.   DMMC Photostat 397; Philadelphia Wills,
Microfilm, 1753, reel 1, nos. 35, 78; DMMC MSS 62x60.2,
62x60.64; Evans Account Books, DMMC; DMMC MS
67x90.36; Schiffer, pp. 64, 217, 225, 233.
77.   Philadelphia Wills, Microfilm, 1753, reel 1,
no. 49; Evans Account Books, DMMC.
78.   Pennsylvania Journal (Philadelphia), March 12,
1777.
79.   DMMC MSS 62x60.1, 62x60.2, Photostat 1078;
Girard Papers, APS, ser. 2, reel 210.
80.   DMMC Photostat 387; Philadelphia Wills,
Microfilm, 1753, reel 1, no. 29; DMMC Photostats 389, 209.
81.   Wainwright, p. 82; DMMC Photostat 1151; Evans
Account Books, DMMC; Schiffer, pp. 64, 217; Evans
Account Books, DMMC; DMMC Photostat 72; Philadelphia

Wills, Microfilm, 1759, reel 1, no. 149; DMMC MS
67x90.36.

82.   Pennsylvania Gazette, Aug. 8, 1754.

83.   DMMC Photostat 209; Evans Account Books,
DMMC; Schiffer, p. 234; Wainwright, p. 49; DMMC
Photostats 401, 86.

84.   DMMC Photostats 387, 392; Schiffer, p. 234;
Philadelphia Wills, Will Book J; ibid., Microfilm, 1753,
reel 1, no. 37.

85.   DMMC Photostats 81, 73, 78, 389, 551;
Philadelphia Wills, Microfilm, 1753, reel 1, no. 72;
DMMC MS 53.165.152.

86.   Philadelphia Wills, Microfilm, 1753, reel 1,
no. 39; ibid., Will Book J; DMMC MS 56x8.8.

87.   Evans, MS notes.

88.   DMMC Photostat 556.

89.   Philadelphia Wills, Microfilm, 1753, reel 1,
nos. 78, 84; DMMC Photostat 558.

90.   Evans, MS notes.

91.   Schiffer, pp. 217, 225.

92.   Girard Papers, APS, ser. 2, reel 210; Evans
Account Books, DMMC; Schiffer, p. 233.

93.   Wainwright, p. 44; Evans Account Books, DMMC.

94.   Girard Papers, APS, ser. 2, reel 210; Philadelphia
Wills, Microfilm, 1759, reel 1, no. 135.

95.   Philadelphia Wills, Microfilm, 1759, reel 1,
no. 180; DMMC MSS 53.165.152, 56x8.8.

96.   Evans Account Books, DMMC; Girard Papers,
APS, ser. 2, reel 210; DMMC MS 67x90.36.

97.   Schiffer, pp. 217, 225, 233-34.

98.   DMMC Photostats 397, 553, 560, 390, MS 55.513;
Philadelphia Wills, Microfilm, 1753, reel 1, no. 78; 1759,
reel 1, no. 149; DMMC Photostat 1124, MS 67x90.77.

99.   DMMC Photostat 380, MS 55.511.

100.   Philadelphia Wills, Microfilm, 1753, reel 1,
no. 29; DMMC Photostat 554; MS 55.508.

101.   DMMC MS 55.511; Philadelphia Wills, Microfilm,
1759, reel 1, no. 180; Wainwright, p. 49; DMMC Photostat
364.

102.   DMMC Photostat 387; Schiffer, p. 235;
Philadelphia Wills, Microfilm, 1759, reel 1, no. 164.
103.   DMMC MS 62x60.1; Evans Account Books, DMMC.
104.   Evans, MS notes.
105.   Decorative Arts Photographic Collection, File:
Pennsylvania, Jonathan Kinsey, Winterthur Museum.
106.   Evans, MS notes.
107.   Philadelphia Wills, Will Books B, F, M, T;
DMMC Photostat 81; Philadelphia Wills, Will Book B.
108.   Philadelphia Wills, Microfilm, 1759, reel 1,
no. 180.
109.   Ibid., 1753, reel 1, no. 39; 1759, reel 1,
no. 135; 1753, reel 1, no. 41; DMMC MS 55.511,
Photostats 551, 552.
110.   Evans Account Books, DMMC.
111.   Evans, MS notes.
112.   Evans Account Books, DMMC.
113.   Evans, MS notes.
114.   DMMC MSS 62x60.1, 67x90.36, 67x90.59.
115.   Schiffer, pp. 217, 225.
116.   Pennsylvania Gazette, Dec. 27, 1775.
117.   Evans, MS notes.
118.   Ibid.
119.   Evans Account Books, DMMC; DMMC Photostats
397, 389.
120.   Evans, MS notes.
121.   DMMC MSS 62x60.2, 62x60.1.
122.   Evans, MS notes.
123.   Evans Account Books, DMMC.
124.   Ibid., DMMC MS 62x60.1.
125.   Gentleman's Progress: The Itinerarium of
Dr. Alexander Hamilton, 1744, ed. Carl Bridenbaugh
(Chapel Hill, N.C., 1948), p. xvii.
126.   Evans Account Books, DMMC.
127.   Ibid.
128.   Evans, MS notes.
129.   Ibid.
130.   DMMC MS 55.513; Evans, MS notes; DMMC
MS 53.165.152.

131.   Evans, MS notes.
132.   Evans Account Books, DMMC; DMMC MS
62x60.1; Evans Account Books, DMMC; DMMC MSS
56x14.2, 55.511.

No. 2 on the Check List of
Furniture exhibited during
the conference. Joint
stool, probably by Stephen
Jaques, master carpenter,
Newbury, Mass., 1680-1710,
red oak. H. 20 3/4";
W. 17 3/8"; D. 13 3/4".
Winterthur Museum (60.189)

No. 3 on the Check List of
Furniture exhibited during
the conference. Joint
stool, maker unknown, area
of Boston, ca. 1700, walnut.
H. 23"; W. 17 7/8";
D. 13 3/4". Winterthur
Museum (60.189)

No. 31 on the Check List of Furniture exhibited during the conference. Dressing table, maker unknown,
eastern Massachusetts, 1740-1760, maple, birch top.
H. 32"; W. 35"; D. 19¾". Winterthur Museum (59.839)

THE MATTER OF CONSUMERS' TASTE

Wendell D. Garrett

IT IS exceedingly difficult to deal with taste in early
American decorative arts, or the useful arts in contrast to
the fine arts, as they were called at the time. There is no
generally accepted definition of "taste" among scholars.
Certainly that given in the <u>Oxford English Dictionary</u> is too
rigid and formal for our purposes: "Taste, the sense of what
is appropriate, harmonious, or beautiful; especially dis-
cernment and appreciation of the beautiful in nature or art."
(At one time I checked the card catalogue at the New York
Public Library under "taste," to satisfy my curiosity and
possibly to convince myself of the scarcity of books on the
subject, only to discover about a hundred cards, beginning
with <u>On the Delicacy of the Sense of Taste among Indians</u>
and ending with <u>The Taste for Vice</u>--which only goes to prove
that scholarship has its own rewards.) Other slightly--but
only slightly--more relevant titles come to mind, such as
Francis Henry Taylor's <u>The Taste of Angels</u> (1948) and Russell
Lynes's <u>The Tastemakers</u> (1954).
    Every man has had his own views on taste. Lynes said that
"taste is our personal delight, our private dilemma, and our
public facade."[1] Another said more recently in the same vein,
"Display is as much a manifestation of taste as the choice of
objects displayed."[2] To quote Edith Wharton, "the essence
of taste is suitability";[3] Robert Louis Stevenson was more
pessimistic and in 1881 traced the spurious bloodlines of
taste: "I have always suspected public taste to be a
mongrel product, out of affectation by dogmatism."[4] One
could extend this list of observations by lofty and sometimes

ribald annunciators of cultural values who have been
attracted to the formidable artistic energies of American
civilization. Watcher at the gate or cracker-barrel Socrates,
vatic bard or populist sage, monologist in the general store
or humorist in the music hall--there is a distinctive brand
of American writer and talker who carried on the tradition
of the frontier publicist traveling the wide land with his
grammars, recipe books, shreds of the Apocalypse, and
nostrums for spirit and bowels. Yet paradoxically it has
traditionally been the foreign, not native, observers from
Crèvecoeur and Tocqueville to Anthony Trollope and Lord
Bryce who have analyzed American culture in depth more
accurately. It has been the foreigners who have sensed the
anachronisms or bifocal vision in American life and art
which militated against the cultivation of an idiosyncratic
style or a cast or stance of spirit and artistic expression
salient enough to create a recognizable persona. Biformity
characterized the people's personality--their polite rapacity,
their erosive buoyancy, their collective individualism, their
bourgeois aristocracy. The same was true of their arts--as
seen in the Puritan aesthetic, "ostentatious austerity";
the Quaker aesthetic, "of the best sort but Plain"; and the
plain style or "non-style as style."[5] As Americans realized
at the time, a national style was hard to compose within
and ever harder to impress upon a mode of life so diffuse,
so beautifully unresistant to the new.

In American furniture, even though there were many
diverse strains and influences at work, a recognizable,
coherent style did eventually crystallize, I would argue; it
was the local work of craftsmen that combined quality,
utility, and beauty at times to an astonishing degree into
what may be called, for want of a better phrase, artisan
mannerism.

By artisan mannerism I mean a personally conditioned
mode of expression in furniture that was ambivalent in
nature. It was a style, in the widest sense of the word,
of simultaneous imitation and distortion, slavishly aping
high style, yet deliberately exaggerating it. It assumed a
precarious balance between affectation and overcompensation

on the one hand and subtlety and elegance on the other.
Because of the limited training of the craftsmen, artisan
mannerism reflected a feeling of insecurity and individuality,
replacing and deforming harmony and regularity with sub-
jective and evocative features, the bizarre and abstruse.
With the coming of mass production and furniture warerooms
in the nineteenth century, it became a hackneyed style, a
self-conscious style, overstraining its forms and reducible
to certain formulas.

An anonymous writer, presumably of French extraction,
commented on this indigenous style in a New York newspaper
of 1803 as he urged France to export furniture to the United
States in the American taste: "Our first step, therefore,
must be to procure models or patterns of every article of
this nature suitable to the American taste because their
furniture differs much in form from ours, and is framed and
finished in a manner peculiar to the use of Americans, or
suited to their houses."[6] This was the essence of artisan
mannerism in American furniture. Cabinetmakers were less
explicit in their own newspaper advertisements, relying on
catchwords such as "newest fashion," "genteelest taste,"
"best manner," and particularly "neat" and "neatness."[7]
A typical one from the Charleston papers in 1740 was for
cabinetwork made "after the newest and best Fashions,
and with the greatest Neatness and Accuracy."[8] Artisan
mannerism was the expression of a people on the move,
in constant motion, seeking their fortunes in new, upstart
towns; they required arts that were swift, spontaneous,
and direct. As early as 1762 an advertisement appeared in
the Boston Gazette of the "Household Furniture belonging
to a Gentleman about leaving the Province. . .[including] a
Set of great Chairs with strong Cane Bottoms and Backs,
contrived for easy Transportation, as they may be speedily
on-fram'd and fram'd again without Damage."[9] Such util-
ity--chairs which could be knocked down and reassembled
again--was not only a reflection of the mobility of the
American people but also indicated the flexibility of public taste: furniture had to be simple enough to be portable,
yet fashionable enough to be considered permanent.

Finally, a sense of style was to be found in how well
the average citizen lived. When Francis Grund toured this
country in the 1830s, he was much impressed by the
dwellings of the laboring class: "On entering the house
of a respectable mechanic in any one of the large cities of
the United States," he remarked, "one cannot but be as-
tonished at the apparent neatness and comfort of the
apartments, the large airy parlors, the nice carpets and
mahogany furniture."[10] Indeed, it might be said that it
was in the course of the years following the Revolution
that the average citizen came into his own as cultural,
as well as political, arbiter and participant.

Growing out of the colonial culture, artisan mannerism
became a persistent habit and a positive force in American
decorative arts, particularly in rural furniture, for over a
century, until the opening of the Industrial Revolution.

But beyond such a modest and straightforward statement,
how can we delineate and document this style in furniture?
These were artifacts created by an inarticulate class for an
inarticulate class who rarely verbalized their attitudes and
thoughts about furnishings. Moreover, even among cultural historians furniture has persistently suffered from a
"tuck-it-in-the-back" attitude. It has also suffered from
the historians' favorite trope: polarity, or the historical
method of balancing off contrasting opposites. As useful
as it is, it nearly always sacrifices accuracy to neatness.
Ever since Russell Kettell published his Pine Furniture of
Early New England in 1929 and William Hornor his Blue
Book: Philadelphia Furniture, William Penn to George
Washington in 1935, the analysis and interpretation of
American furniture have been consigned to the cursed
limbo of polar pairs: city or country, mahogany or pine,
carved or turned, complex or simple, ornamented or plain,
inlaid or painted, curved or straight, proportioned or dis-
torted. This method is simple enough, and useful to a
point, but when pieces fail to fit neatly into these categories
we then speak about restrained ornamentation or the simple
curve in urban furniture and sophisticated simplicity or
elegant painted graining in country examples. These

phrases expressing a paradoxical aesthetic vision, as I
have suggested earlier, probably come closer to the
reality of American decorative arts.

What marred the published work of the furniture
historians of a generation ago was, it seems to me, the
severe dilemma that emerged out of their simplistic, con-
flicting theories about American society and American
art. They polarized the arts between high style and low
style, the fine and the folk, the city and the country;
their general analyses admitted extremes and dualisms
and paradox; they punctuated their broad assessments of
the arts with illustrative detail of change and upheaval,
transition and conflict in styles. But not in society. Their
historical interpretation remained wedded to a theory of
consensus and classlessness--that is that American
society has always been a middle-class democracy. They
could not admit to struggles between the privileged and
the less privileged, conflicts between rival ideologies,
upheavals between classes and economic interests. Conclusions were drawn about the entire society on the basis
of examination of the minority at the top. In his foreword
to Kettell's Pine Furniture, Edwin J. Hipkiss observed,
"The interesting objects of more or less homespun
variety. . .were personal matters, for they were made by
individuals for individuals, and they smack of the
directness and independence of spirit of those who
honour their own place in life."[11] This was basically a
conservative view that emphasized the homogeneity of
American history; it was curiously lulling, even comfortable, to the susceptible reader. Kettell himself reasoned
that "it is the spirit of frank simplicity that gives this
work its fundamental appeal."[12]

Hornor wrote about furniture at the other end of the
spectrum: "Philadelphia Furniture from William Penn to
George Washington covers the aristocracy of furniture
made prior to the era of mass production." Hence, his
title Blue Book; the furniture was aristocratic, but
artisans and clients are happily lumped together in the
narrative, snugly, maybe even smugly, sharing a common

past. "Woven into the decorative pageant in which the
eighteenth century cabinetmaker, chairmaker, carver,
turner, and upholsterer played important roles, were the
echoes of those seemingly unconnected events," he
wrote, listing the various historical episodes in
Philadelphia's history.[13] "All left their indelible mark
upon the artistic as well as the practical expansion of
furniture-making," Hornor concludes. This is all very
well, but where are the artisans, the common people,
the laborers? An appendix does list them by name with
their taxable property and occupational taxes. We are
never carried into the company of what the Victorian
bourgeoisie would have called, with a curl of the lip,
tradespeople. My quarrel with this genre of furniture
history is that it reads the past in the light of subsequent
preoccupations, and not as in fact it occurred. This form
of elite history imposed on the entire society the characteristics and values of a single stratum; and as a result only
this group is remembered. The blind alleys, the lost causes,
the poor and the foolhardy, the casualties and losers and
dropouts are not recorded in narrative history. Is there not
some way to get down to this level of society and document
the lives of these working men, the inarticulate craftsmen?

This brings me to the central proposition or thesis of my
paper: the study of furniture history has remained fairly
static on a plateau from which it will advance and expand
only by our becoming involved in the history of the working
classes, of the social conditions, and of the theories and
ideologies associated with those who produced and used
this furniture. This is social history of a special sort,
labor history if you like, which makes use of hitherto
neglected sources, not necessarily that social history
defined by Trevelyan as "the history of a people with the
politics left out." This is history from the "bottom up"[14];
this kind of social history looks on historical events from
below and attempts to describe and explain them by search-
ing for their roots in the economic and social substructure.

Two recent books make use of this new methodological
and ideological approach and reveal many insights into

this field. The first is <u>The Making of the English Working Class</u> (1964) by E. P. Thompson; the second is <u>Toward a New Past: Dissenting Essays in American History</u> (1968), edited by Barton J. Bernstein, with particular attention to the opening essay, "The American Revolution Seen from the Bottom Up," by Jesse Lemisch. When one adds to these books some recent articles in the journal <u>Labor History</u> by Staughton Lynd, Alfred Young, Roger J. Champagne, David Montgomery, and Maurice F. Neufeld, their relevance and potentialities for adding insights and new dimensions to our investigations among the decorative arts become at once obvious.[15] And, I am happy to note, these scholars are finding the research done in the Winterthur Program rewarding: the dissertations of Ian Quimby and Morrison Hecksher are cited in an article by David Montgomery in <u>Labor History</u> on "The Working Classes of the Pre-Industrial American City, 1780-1830."

What do we mean by the inarticulate? These were the powerless, the common people, the people on the bottom of society, the submerged working men, "the casualties of history" who suffer "from the enormous condescension of posterity.[16] Some historians felt the inarticulate "lived their lives below the level of historical scrutiny."[17] But did they? To be sure, I know of only three American cabinetmakers and one from England who ever wrote auto-biographies, and they all survey mid-nineteenth-century careers.[18] Artisans rarely talked about themselves and their work. There are therefore methodological and sub-stantive problems in writing their history. But if we begin with the assumption that human actions, even at the bottom of society, are purposeful and related to some pattern of thought, then we are under an obligation to examine by every possible means the thought and conduct of the inarticulate themselves. What this group of young historians is asking for "is nothing less than an attempt to make the inarticulate speak."[19] Thompson said of his approach: "I am seeking to rescue the poor stockinger, the Luddite cropper, the 'obsolete' hand-loom weaver, the 'utopian' artisan, and even the deluded follower of Joanna

Southcott. . . .Their crafts and traditions may have been dying.
Their hostility to the new industrialism may have been
backward-looking. Their communitarian ideals may have
been fantasies. Their insurrectionary conspiracies may
have been foolhardy. But they lived through these times
of acute social disturbance, and we did not. Their
aspirations were valid in terms of their own experience."[20]
In his impressive work of original research, the heroic
culture of the working people can now be seen passing
through the truly catastrophic nature of the Industrial
Revolution: the economic disequilibrium, the intense
human misery and exploitation, the factory system with
its new discipline, political repression and popular
agitation, and finally greater insecurity. On the American
side, Jesse Lemisch's model article, "Jack Tar in the
Streets: Merchant Seamen in the Politics of Revolutionary
America," was published in the William and Mary Quarterly.
The article is an attempt to delineate the "ideological
content" in the conduct and thought at the time of the
Revolutionary War of these men, who were "fugitives
and floaters, powerless in a tough environment."[21]

This digression into the writings of some of the young
historians whose work in labor history has broken with
the earlier consensus has been made in the hope that it
might provide us with new concepts that are useful and
meaningful. For, it seems to me, if we are ever going to
formulate generalizations about cabinetmakers and their
furniture that have more than limited validity, we must
approach the subject with some of the same earnest
imagination and new concepts of these social historians.
Despite our pretensions to using new tools and sources,
we are hardly more genuinely informed about these artisans
as a class than we were thirty or forty years ago. The
conventional approach of treating objects as historical
documents, although useful, has, I fear, tended to distort
our view and, sometimes, to cut us off from past reality.

Let me hasten to add that I do not have complete answers
on cabinetmakers based on the new revisionism, nor am I
prepared to provide a new intellectual synthesis, nor do I

have any suggestions on how to use a fine-meshed
sociological net for capturing a pure specimen of this
class of workers. I do have several questions to ask,
shifting from the conventional emphasis and focus, in
the hope that a series of new approaches and interpretations, if not a new synthesis, will suggest themselves.

The Aesthetics of Taste

One of the questions I would like to raise about the
aesthetics of taste in country furniture concerns period-
ization: even though it is known that shop joiners,
cabinetmakers, and chairmakers worked outside the
coastal seaports and in the hinterland as early as the
seventeenth century, at what point in time did people
distinguish in their own minds between the urban and
rural origins of furniture? And then at what periods or
specific years thereafter did major shifts occur in which
the craft of cabinetmaking was significantly affected and
altered?
There are at least four crucial decades (these are, I
stress, offered tentatively) in which historical and
stylistic change was accelerated to the point that one
can properly call them radical or revolutionary periods.
The first took place sometime between 1710 and 1730. The
documentation for this period is extremely thin, but Hornor
said of Philadelphia: "There was a noticeable decline in
the quality of furniture produced, a decrease in the
number and size of the cabinet shops, and a slight but
none the less general deterioration in workmanship from
1710 onward for about twenty years. . . .Production was
temporarily ahead of the slackening demand. It was not
until the 1730 decade that any revival was manifest."[22]
If this was true of Philadelphia, it was probably true for
the other colonial towns. A search for clues in the
nomenclature of the newspaper advertisements during the
Queen Anne and Chippendale periods is not significantly
revealing or rewarding. A "new Fashioned Bed. . .
new Fashion Chests. . .and Wainscot Desks" were

offered for sale in Boston as early as 1714.[23] By 1732
notices of "all sorts of bespoke work" and that "Chairs
and Couches are made and mended" appeared in
Charleston.[24] "Desk and Book Cases, with Arch'd,
Pediment and O. G. Heads" appeared there by 1740.[25]
A guaranty was included in the same advertisement:
"N. B. He [the cabinetmaker] will warrant his work
for 7 years, the ill usage of careless Servants only excepted." In New York "a good Mahogany Chest of
Drawers, with Eagle's Claw Feet, a Shell on each knee,
and fluted Corners" was offered in 1753;[26] however, Hornor
stated that "the first documentary reference to this foot
was in 1745" in Philadelphia.[27] "Compass Seat Black
Walnut Leather Bottom Chairs" appeared in Boston in 1756.[28]
Two years later in Boston there was "a marble Table supported by Carved Eagles";[29] in New York in 1763: "A neat
mahogany desk and book case, in the Chinese taste";[30]
in Charleston in 1772: "Sophas, with Commode fronts
divided into three sweeps, which give them a noble look."[31]
The last advertisement gave the first evidence I have found
of copying imported furniture: "carved Chairs of the newest
fashion, splat Backs, with hollow slats and commode fronts,
of the same Pattern as those imported by Peter Manigault,
Esq.--He is now making some Hollow-seated Chairs, the
seats to take in and out, and nearly the pattern of another
set of Chairs imported by the same gentleman, which have
a light, airy Look, and make the sitting easy beyond expression."

The second decade of change was during the years 1765
to 1775, when a distinction was drawn in the public mind
between country and city joiners. The third period covers
the decade 1795 to 1805, when journeymen revolted
against master cabinetmakers over wage demands in what
might be called the price book war. And finally the fourth
decade, 1835 to 1845, saw labor unrest generated from
consequences of the spread of the factory system.

The half century between 1725 and 1775 was a crucial
period in the history of American furniture. We know a

great deal about this golden age of the Queen Anne and
Chippendale styles. From newspaper advertisements it
is quite clear that there was a great deal of mobility
among cabinetmakers: not only were many craftsmen
arriving from London to work in coastal seaports, but also
there was, it seems to me, an astonishing movement of
men in the craft and furniture up and down the coast. This
seems to be particularly true of Charleston, where cabinetmakers and imported furniture were arriving all the time.
But I am not so certain this mobility of men and furniture
was present in overland trade between coastal towns and
the hinterland. There were, to be sure, cabinetmakers
working in the country; in fact, one in "the Town of
Dumfries in Virginia, about Twenty miles above Port
Tobacco--near Potowmack River" advertised in an
Annapolis newspaper in 1762 for "Two or Three Journeymen
Cabinet-Makers who are versed in their Business and can
go on with any common Branch in the Cabinet Way."[32]
But transportation over primitive roads into the back
country was difficult. By 1775 a Philadelphia upholsterer
advertised that he "has no objection to serve any lady or
gentleman at a small distance in the country."[33] As late
as 1798 a Wilmington, Delaware, cabinetmaker informed
potential customers: "All work bespoke from said Penny,
will be delivered Gratis at the distance of ten miles."[34]
Until the transportation revolution in the nineteenth
century, this mobility and trade in furniture applied only
to maritime traffic.

I also feel that newspaper advertisements of the
eighteenth century have misled us in another way: namely,
into thinking of cabinetmaking as becoming an increasingly
urban-based craft as a result of the eighteenth century's
spectacular population growth and urban expansion. The
well-known highly skilled craftsmen were indeed in the
cities; and since the newspapers of that era were located
in the larger cities, most of the surviving documentary
evidence relates to them, not their country cousins. Yet
the best evidence indicates that before 1820 America was
becoming more rural, rather than urban, in terms of

the percentage of the total population. Carl Bridenbaugh
pointed out that "in 1690 the combined inhabitants of the
five leading towns numbered but 18,600, and the total for
the twelve colonies only slightly exceeded two hundred
thousand; by 1776 over 108,000 people lived in the principal
urban centers, and the total for the revolting provinces was
about two and one half millions.[35] Significantly, these
figures show that during this period of a little less than a
century the population increased 12.5 times in size, but
the urban population in the five leading towns dropped
from 9.4 percent of the total to 4.3 percent. It is quite
clear that the urban population cannot account for all of
the artisans and craftsmen working in colonial America;
that is, the remaining 95.8 percent were not all farmers.
In fact, the best guess now is that on the eve of the
Revolution husbandmen "made up about eighty per cent of
the people, artisans constituted about eighteen per cent.[36]
David Montgomery found: "By 1820 some 12 percent of the
nation's labor force was engaged in manufacturing and construction, and 28 percent in all non-agricultural occupations,
but at that time the residents of these cities and their con-
tiguous suburbs totalled only 356,452, or 3.7 percent of
the American people."[37] From his study of the working
classes in the nation's four northern cities--Boston, New
York, Philadelphia, and Baltimore--he concluded: "During
the five decades before 1830 these cities were essentially
depots for trans-oceanic shipping, and their labor force
was largely tied to maritime commerce. . . .Most manufacturing, in other words, was carried on outside of the major
cities."[38] In his Report on Manufacture, Alexander
Hamilton noted that surrounding each of these cities was
"a vast scene of household manufacturing" where country
folk produced clothing, shoes, and other necessities, "in
many instances, to an extent not only sufficient for the
supply of the families in which they are made, but for
sale, and even, in some cases, for exportation."[39] As
transportation improved, the circle of trade widened and
encouraged the development of early efforts toward the
factory organization of production. Household industries

and the workshops of mechanics became fewer, and village
monopolies and local self-sufficiency began to yield to
competition from towns and cities.

Although most manufacturing was carried on outside the
great urban centers before the Industrial Revolution, when
did the colonists begin to distinguish, to sense a difference, between city and country furniture? When did they
begin to use "country" as an adjective when they were
speaking of cabinetwork? The earliest use of the word
in this sense that I have been able to find is in a 1773 newspaper advertisement by Thomas Burling, New York cabinetmaker and lumber dealer, where he announced that he "Has
opened a yard of all kinds of stuff suitable for country
Joiners, which he proposes to sell on reasonable terms."[40]
As early as 1732 a Charleston newspaper announced that
"At New-Market Plantation, about a mile from Charlestown,
will continue to be sold all sorts of Cabinet Work, Chest
of Drawers, and Mahogany Tables and Chairs made after the
best manner. . . .Where all sorts of bespoke work is made
at the lowest price."[41] By a strict definition, this plan-
tation-made furniture might be considered country furniture, but it was not until the 1770s that contemporaries
used the adjective themselves to make the distinction.

There is other evidence to substantiate the contention
that this decade in question, 1765 to 1775, was one of
intense intellectual ferment and social change. And if we
accept the proposition that the Revolutionary War was
fought as much as an assertion of cultural independence as
a declaration of political independence, then these
years take on added significance. It was John Adams who
wrote to Thomas Jefferson in 1815: "What do We Mean by
the Revolution? The War? That was no part of the Revolution, It was only an Effect and Consequence of it. The
Revolution was in the Minds of the People, and this was
effected, from 1760 to 1775, in the course of fifteen Years
before a drop of blood was drawn at Lexington."[42]

Bernard Bailyn in his recent book, The Ideological Origins of the American Revolution, drew attention to the
shift in intellectual thought during this decade:

The intellectual history of the years of crisis from
1763 to 1776 is the story of the clarification and
consolidation under the pressure of events of a
view of the world and of America's place in it
only partially seen before. . . .In the intense
political heat of the decade after 1763, these
long popular, though hitherto inconclusive ideas
about the world and America's place in it were
fused into a comprehensive view, unique in its
moral and intellectual appeal.[43]

The "clarification and consolidation" of taste at this
time "under the pressure of events"--the verbalization
of a balanced counterpoise between thought and emotion
within their choices among the arts--when viewed as
intellectual history merits further investigation within
current explanations for this crucial decade of change.

The decade began with the Non-Importation Agreement
of 1765, which dramatically reduced importations from
England, including cabinetwork; in Pennsylvania, for
example, the value of English imports dropped more than
half between the years 1768 and 1769.[44] In May 1765
Captain Samuel Morris wrote his nephew Samuel Powel,
Jr., then in London: "Household goods may be had here
as cheap and as well made from English patterns. In the
humour people are in here, a man is in danger of becoming
Invidiously distinguished, who buys anything in England
which our Tradesmen can furnish. I have heard the joiners
here object this against Dr. Morgan & others who brought
their furnishings with them."[45] As a result of the influx
of English craftsmen, particularly from London, in the
decades prior to 1770, Americans had become preoccupied
with imitating English fashions and taste. "The quick
importation of fashion from the mother country is really
astonishing," wrote William Eddis, collector of customs
in Annapolis, early in the 1770s. "A new fashion is
adopted earlier by the polished and affluent American, than
by many opulent persons in the great metropolis [London]. . . .
Very little difference is, in reality observable in the manners

of the wealthiest colonist and the wealthy Briton."[46] It
was in the coastal seaports that fashionable taste--"the
newest fashion, both elegant and plain"[47]--took root and
flourished among the merchant aristocracy and the
government elite; that taste was shaped and satisfied by
skillful, indigenous craftsmen, as well as by highly
trained competitors from abroad, and by the quantities of
imported furniture, sometimes advertised as "all London
Make."[48]

Another significant event occurred at the end of this
decade: the proposal of "the ingenious John Folwell" of
Philadelphia in 1775 "with the cooperation of merchants
in New York, Baltimore, Annapolis, and Charleston, to
publish an American counterpart of the celebrated English
work [by Chippendale], under the title of 'The Gentleman
and Cabinet-maker's Assistant, Containing A great Variety
of Useful and Ornamental Household Furniture.'"[49] This
edition of Chippendale's designs adapted to America--
"drawings of distinctive Philadelphia patterns that would
be an improvement upon those of contemporary England,"
in Hornor's opinion--was unfortunately a casualty of the
Revolution and was never published. Folwell's ambitious
"Proposals" to publish this "large Folio Volume, containing Two Hundred Designs and Examples, curiously engraved
on Sixty Folio Copper-Plates" engraved by John Norman was
an event, it seems to me, of paramount importance: more
than reflecting that moment when cabinetmaking, particularly
in Philadelphia, had reached a supreme confidence and
maturity, it reveals that stage within a style when it has
been completely rationalized and when all of its inner
tensions have been resolved--that brittle moment just before
it fragments and shatters.[50] This is not to say that the
Chippendale style in American furniture went into sudden
eclipse with the war; on the contrary, the style flourished
longer in time than we have traditionally assumed. An
engraving in the Gentleman's Magazine, October 1814,
provides proof that a London cabinetmaker's shop was
selling furniture in the Queen Anne and Chippendale style
at that late date.[51] But the war did alter the style and

cripple the craft of cabinetmaking in unexpected, permanent
ways. Cabinetmakers' newspaper advertisements support
Hornor's contention that the Revolutionary "War had
caused a tremendous upheaval in the cabinet-making trade,
and among those engaged in it."[52] Trade was cut off, and
Americans suddenly found themselves outsiders in a world
of exclusive trading systems. As the ports were closed
and the colonies drifted into war, the internal problems,
indeed the interior, with its problems of economy and
defense, absorbed the nation's attention as never before.
The English-American axis or polarization in taste, as in
many other shared experiences, shifted in this country to
an urban-rural one. With the opening of western lands
after the Treaty of Peace in 1783, this internal focus of
attention became stronger as the country struggled with
the problems of developing what was predominantly an
agricultural economy, an agrarian polity, and a rural
society. But I would argue that it was not until the
colonies were ready for the parting of the ways with
Britain in a vague cultural sense, when the whole history
of a geographically separate and different people in
America came to a climax-- in this decade immediately
before the war, that Americans differentiated between the
urban and rural characteristics of their own culture.

The pre-Revolutionary mind felt no dualism
between rural and city furniture, no inner contradiction,
no stylistic polarity, no artistic oppositions. Such a
transformation in taste and judgment could only occur
with the coming of the American Revolution, a revolt that
cleanly and definitely cut the cultural, as well as
political, ties connecting two peoples. For what could be
more incomprehensible to an age of unshaken faith in the
cohesive qualities of their culture than that there should
be two different kinds of furniture and two different sources
of design? But the Revolutionary War precipitated just
such changes in thought. Begun for only limited political
and constitutional purposes, it released social forces that
few of the leaders ever anticipated. Thoroughly new conceptions of party and faction emerged in politics, reflecting

the opposing interests of city and country, North and South,
low-country and up-country, merchant and planter, farmer
and artisan-mechanic. And it was indicative of this new
unstable equilibrium in American society in the new nation
that the cleavage between city and country furniture deepen-
ed and hardened.

The third decade of change, 1795 to 1805, was one in
which an intense struggle, if not strictly a class conflict,
took place, in Philadelphia in 1796 and in New York in
1802, when journeymen took economic action against their
employers, the master cabinetmakers. If one reads the
charges and countercharges in the newspapers, the con-
fusion and complexity of the issues become readily
apparent.[53] The immediate cause of the general strike by
the journeymen cabinetmakers in each city was the publication of price books that fixed, and in one instance reduced, wages paid by the masters. As Charles Montgomery
explained in a full account of this literature in America:
"Cabinetmakers' and journeymen's price books are manuscripts or printed lists of prices for the making of furniture
at rates sought by journeymen or agreed upon by masters."[54]
It is hard to determine whether the price books were the
cause or the effect of the labor disturbances. Certainly
behind the unrest was the culmination of numerous postwar
economic and political trends: "the shift from custom-made
to whole-sale order work, the decline of apprenticeship and
indentured servitude, the emergence of a factory district. . .
[which] coincided with the influx of poor immigrants to in-
tensify the conflict between employer and employee, as well
as between the mechanics en masse and the city's merchants."[55]

In the rhetoric and patriotism of "the spirit of '76," the
Philadelphia journeymen cabinetmakers in 1796 looked "to a
generous Public for protection who stand conspicuous in the
civilized world for their zealous support of Independence."
They accused their employers of:

preventing the improvements of Mechanism in

America, by destroying the liberty of its Pro-
fessors. . . .As rapid advances have been made
to introduce into this Free Country that system
of oppression and disorganization which European
mechanics labour under, from the intolerable
avarice of their employers, we would think our-
selves highly criminal, if we did not, at this
important period, step forward in order to preserve
that independence which as active and industrious
citizens we ought to possess.[56]

When the New York master cabinetmakers answered their
journeymen's charges in 1802, they concluded their re-
buttal with a slight touch of condescension: "We have in
the above not been studious to adorn it by an imitation of
the Declaration of Independence, but have confined our-
selves to plain and correct narrative."[57] What seems
particularly remarkable is that after a full generation, "the
plot, dialogue and even character types of the 1790s bear
a striking resemblance to the drama of the pre-Revolutionary
era. . . .Other insistent mechanic demands thread through
the last three decades of the century: for democratic
participation, for social recognition, for protection for
American manufactures."[58] In a larger sense, the argument
in the 1790s was between radicals and conservatives and
concerned the proper locus of power in a free government.
And, as in the days before 1776, the question that divided
the two groups was still local versus foreign rule, only
now foreign meant Philadelphia, New York, and Washington
instead of London. Moreover, the Hamiltonian program to
expand the economy touched the sensitive nerve of the
radicals' self-interest. To the Jeffersonians such
machinations smacked of favors paid for with the taxes of
the "honest, hard-working part of the community," as
Representative Jabez Young Jackson of Georgia complained,
in order to "promote the ease and luxury of men of wealth."[59]
Though these social and economic forces were obvious
and potent, the ideas--the beliefs, assumptions, and
values of the people--were powerful too. This toughness

of men's ideas was demonstrated in the passionate exchanges between the embattled journeymen and their
masters; that these were more than rhetorical flourishes
is suggested by the intense reactions of the working class
to the new industrialism. Beginning about 1800 a process
was set going that was repugnant to an astonishingly large
section of American society; this dissatisfaction was clearly
evident among cabinetmakers and must have exerted subtle,
yet profound, pressures on taste and style within the craft
of cabinetmaking. Norman Ware has observed in his book
on the Industrial Worker: "The losses of the industrial
worker in the first half of the century were not comfort
losses solely, but losses, as he conceived it, of status
and independence. And no comfort gains could cancel
this debt."[60] A recent study of New York mechanics before
1801 indicates that "the mechanic was hardly a first-class
citizen. The very term 'mechanical' was employed in that
day with the connotation 'mean, base, pitiful.' The result
was a pervasive sense of social separateness, which
apparently grew stronger rather than weaker after the
Revolution."[61] In spite of a widening franchise to vote
and comparatively higher wages, the urban mechanic was
being pressured within, if not out of, cities where he had
to compete with cheap immigrant labor and foreign imports.
In New York the mechanics were becoming more proletarian
in character toward the end of the century. The population
of the city grew from just over 20,000 before and after the
War of Independence to 30,000 in 1790, 45,000 in 1795,
and finally 60,000 in 1800. "From about 1793 on there was
an influx of new immigrants of French, Irish, Scotch and
English background, most of whom joined the city's
working population in the lower ranks. . . .There were more
common laborers on the docks, more wage workers in
factories, more petty tradesmen, tea-water men, food
hawkers, chimney sweeps eking out a living."[62]
   The urban journeyman cabinetmaker, in spite of his
complaints, was well paid in comparison to his European
counterpart, and when the grievances expressed by mechanic
organizations began to be heard, they naturally invited the

importation of furniture from abroad.   As noted above, there
appeared in a New York newspaper in 1803 a serious proposal urging France to export "Cabinet Ware" from "Paris. . . .
where are such vast numbers of the most ingenious artists
in this branch." The article continued:

> At present, nearly the whole of their cabinetwork is
> manufactured by the Americans themselves. . .
> because they get the wood for it with more facility
> and at a cheaper rate than we do. . . .Some suppose
> that cabinet ware is too bulky to be sent so far over
> sea, and would be too expensive in its freight. But
> let it be remembered, as I said before, that American
> vessels in general return from the French ports only
> half loaded. . . .In pursuing this method, it is probable
> our goods of this sort will not only sell to advantage
> at first, but that in a short time it will in a great
> measure take place of the same manufacture in the
> United States, on account of the vast difference in
> the price of journeymen's labor in the two countries.[63]

This foreign competition was to be only a momentary
threat, for a long series of Continental wars were to disrupt
communications with the Old World and all but halt the flow
of goods and immigrants until after the signing of the Treaty
of Ghent in 1815. But this anonymous newspaper statement
illuminates in a graphic manner the critical phase through
which cabinetmaking was passing as the nineteenth century
dawned. The loosened connections with Europe and the
heightened interest in manufacturing during the Embargo
and the War of 1812 ushered the craft into a new phase
during which it was to flourish and find a new expression
as factory techniques and marketing skills developed. But
in the end it was this expansion of markets that threatened
the welfare of small groups of artisans and was primarily
responsible for extinguishing the style of artisan mannerism.
Independent craftsmen were unsympathetic to the spread
of the factory and improved transportation system,
because increased trade brought in competing goods that

took the bread out of their mouths. Working with their
hands, they were not in a position to expand their output.
The perennial shortage of cash frequently left them in
debt. The rural artisan was to become an increasingly
restless element in the population. Moving with the
spread of settlement into the newly opened regions and
setting up his workshop, he was protected in his local
market by the distance that raised the cost of competing
goods brought in from the East. There he had a large
measure of control over the price he obtained. It was
the transportation revolution that destroyed the comfortable
security of the individual workingman after 1820.

The Economics of Taste

This brings me to the fourth, and final, decade of
crisis, 1835 to 1845, when the sharp decline in the craft-
men's wages and status evoked a rising volume of complaints against the monopolies and spread of corporations
in transportation and in banking. As the westward movement
resumed after a pause during the panic of 1837, the artisan
found an outlet in the newly opened land of the country,
usually settling in new towns and cities where the transportation lag offered some security until the railroad came.
During this same period his counterpart, the industrial
worker in the factory, was rapidly losing ground. "The
problem of primary importance for the industrial worker
of the forties and fifties is to be found in the changes in
his status and standards of living," Norman Ware observed.

The depressions of 1837-39 left one third of the
working population of New York City unemployed. . . .
The New England mills were either closed down or
running only part-time and undermanned. Between
1839 and 1843 wages generally fell from thirty to
fifty per cent. . . .In 1844 the same amount of labor
that had once produced for the mechanic and his
family a comfortable subsistence was inadequate to
maintain his standards, and his only alternative was

increased effort or the reduction of his wants.[64]

This degradation of the worker in American society at
the opening of the Industrial Revolution, thought for so
long to be a nineteenth-century phenomenon, now appears,
from some recent studies, to have started early in the
eighteenth century. James A. Henretta's statistical work
has clearly traced the emergence of the seaport poor in
eighteenth-century Boston as a result of economic subordination of workers in a growing market of overseas
commerce. He discovered from the Boston tax rolls that:
"In 1687, 14 per cent of the total number of adult males
were without taxable property; by the eve of the Revolution,
the propertyless accounted for 29 per cent." That is, these
were wage earners in the full meaning of the term--the
laboring force of nondependent, propertyless workers. He
continued:

> The social consequences of this increase were
> manifold. For every wage earner who competed
> in the economy as an autonomous entity at the
> end of the seventeenth century, there were four
> in 1771; for every man who slept in the back of
> a shop, in a tavern, or in a rented room in 1687,
> there were four in the later period. The population
> of Boston had doubled, but the number of property-
> less men had increased fourfold.[65]

Another historian concluded from these astonishing
figures that "increasingly, colonial Boston was less a
place of equality and opportunity, more a place of social
stratification."[66] Earlier I mentioned the high degree of
geographical mobility of craftsmen in the eighteenth
century; the newspaper advertisements announced the move
or arrival of a cabinetmaker as often as they did the avail-
ability of a craftsman's wares. But did this translate into
vertical mobility? Was mobility out the same as mobility
up? In The Social Structure of Revolutionary America,
Jackson Turner Main uncovered a "proletariat" comprising

"nearly 40 percent" of the population. He offered figures
indicating that in pre-Revolutionary years 80 percent of
the indentured servants "died, became landless workers,
or returned to England." He concluded that "the long-
term tendency seems to have been toward greater in-
equality" and a "growing number of poor."[67] This economic
subordination of the working class in early America was
clearly to have profound effects on the democratic credo.
One labor historian concluded that the "Jeffersonian
Republicans of New York City. . .could claim that they
were heirs to the 'spirit of '76' and that the 'revolution of
1800' was indeed the consummation of the Revolution of
1776."[68] But another claimed that "throughout America
property qualifications excluded more and more people
from voting until a 'Jacksonian Revolution' was necessary
to overthrow what had become a very limited middle-class
'democracy' indeed."[69]

These economic maladjustments and their social by-
products in the lives of artisans, dating from early in the
eighteenth century, erupted in the labor protests of the
1840's, when workers as a class were rapidly losing ground.
With the introduction of "the machine into the garden," a
revolutionary process was set going, not only in the methods
of production, but also in the transition to the factory
system. The first was more obvious and dramatic--the
application of water- and steam-driven machinery to production that we now call the Industrial Revolution. The
other was the social revolution in which the sovereignty
of economic affairs passed into the keeping of a special
class, a group of owners of capital who had acquired
their wealth, not primarily as producers, but as distributors
in foreign and domestic trade.

What upset cabinetmakers in the 1840s was that just at
the moment when the term "wage" displaced the old term "price"
for his remuneration, regarded by him as a symbol of a
deeper change, that wage was continually shrinking.
The average journeyman could make from $12 to $15 a week
in 1836, whether he was paid wages or by the piece. By
1840 wages had fallen to $8, and by 1845 it was said the

majority of journeymen could earn no more than $5. The
very best cabinetmakers could command $8. By any
standard, this was an extraordinary drop in wages for
cabinetmakers. "The reason given for this falling-off
was the growth of wholesale work for the auction shops.
This work was done chiefly by Germans who were said to
'work rapidly, badly and for almost nothing.' The manu-
facturers were said to go on the immigrant ships as they
arrived in New York and engage these men for a year at
$20 or $30 and their board."[70] In 1843 a Philadelphia
journeyman cabinetmaker complained that "already by
the gradual reduction of the price of labor, the journeymen
are reduced to the necessity of laboring twelve and fourteen hours a day to gain a mere subsistence."[71] The condition of the workingman became oppressive by the 1840s,
and his first impulse was to escape: some to the frontier
and others into reform labor movements.

Conclusion

   I have tried to suggest that the cabinetmaker in the
preindustrial epoch, or between 1750 and 1850, merits
more careful historical study. The steady decline in his
income and his social position, the persistent deterioration
of his status and independence, the impact of the spreading
factory system on his behavior and attitudes, to say nothing
of its impact on his living conditions, and the occurrence of
all these trends in the face of a preindustrial society that
was suffering from a dropping per capita income and becoming increasingly rural (though not agrarian) in composition:
these problems assume considerable significance as deter-
minants of what, how, and why furniture was made. As you
have gathered, I do not believe that the consumer's taste
was very relevant; at least, it appears to have become less
relevant after 1800. I would even doubt that the price books,
with their infinite variations on form and design, were widely
known among the buying public. Rather they document the
bitter controversy surrounding the transition from payment
by the piece to wages (declining wages) for work done by

journeymen. But it is very hard to generalize about this
critical period after 1800 when we have so few compilations
of newspaper advertisements in published form to analyze.

This population drift to a rural setting would suggest that
in preindustrial America most cabinetwork--even some of
the high style, sophisticated furniture--was manufactured
outside the large urban centers. This raises, it seems to
me, fundamental questions about our definition of country
furniture, or what I prefer to call artisan mannerism. Was
it not more a matter of materials, skills, economics, and
demography, rather than a matter of city and country?

Notes

1. The Tastemakers (New York, 1954), p. 4.
2. Times Literary Supplement, Nov. 30, 1967, p. 1124.
3. Wharton, French Ways and Their Meanings.
4. Stevenson, Virginibus Puerisque (1881), quoted in
Lynes, pp. 180, 8.
5. I am indebted to Professor M. G. Kammen of Cornell
University for these thoughts on biformity; they have been
taken from a talk given at the Columbia University Seminar
in Early American History and Culture, March 11, 1969, and
will appear in his forthcoming book, People of Paradox.
6. Morning Chronicle, Feb. 24, 1803, quoted in Rita
Susswein Gottesman, The Arts and Crafts in New York,
1800-1804 (New York, 1965), p. 160.
7. The words "neat" and "neatness" in advertisements for
furniture appear as early as the 1730s and extend through the
eighteenth century. I believe that they gave "neat" the following meaning: "Characterized by elegance of form or arrangement, with freedom from all unnecessary additions or embell-
ishments; of agreeable but simple appearance; nicely made
or proportioned. In early use the handsomeness of the thing
appears to be the more prominent idea" (Oxford English
Dictionary).
8. South Carolina Gazette, March 22, 1740, quoted in
Alfred Cox Prime, The Arts & Crafts in Philadelphia, Maryland and South Carolina, 1721-1785, Gleanings from Newspapers (Topsfield, Mass., 1929), p. 163.
9. June 28, 1762, quoted in George Francis Dow, The
Arts & Crafts in New England, 1704-1775, Gleanings from
Boston Newspapers (Topsfield, Mass., 1927), p. 120.
10. The Americans in Their Moral, Social, and Political
Relations (1837), quoted in Carl Bode, The Anatomy of
American Popular Culture, 1840-1861 (Berkeley and Los
Angeles, 1959), p. 39.
11. Russell Hawes Kettell, The Pine Furniture of Early
New England (Garden City, N.Y., 1929), p. ix.
12. Ibid., p. xxvii.
13. William MacPherson Hornor, Jr., Blue Book:

Philadelphia Furniture, William Penn to George Washington
(Philadelphia, 1935), p. x.

14. See Jesse Lemisch, "The American Revolution Seen
from the Bottom Up," in Barton J. Bernstein, ed., Towards
a New Past: Dissenting Essays in American History (New
York, 1968), pp. 3-45.

15. Lynd, "The Mechanics in New York Politics, 1774-
1788," V (Fall 1964), 225-46; Young, "The Mechanics and
the Jeffersonians: New York, 1789-1801," ibid., pp. 247-76;
Champagne, "Liberty Boys and Mechanics of New York City,
1764-1774," VIII (Spring 1967), 115-35; Montgomery, "The
Working Classes of the Pre-Industrial American City, 1780-
1830," IX (Winter 1968), 3-22; Maurice F. Neufeld, "Realms
of Thought and Organized Labor in the Age of Jackson," X
(Winter 1969), 5-43.

16. Thompson, The Making of the English Working Class
(New York, 1964), pp. 12-13.

17. Lyman H. Butterfield et al., eds., Diary and Autobiography of John Adams (Cambridge, 1961), I, xiii.

18. Arthur Wherry Richards, Progress of Life and Thought
(Des Moines, 1892); Henry Wendler, Reminiscenses (written
by J. Orin Oliphant) (Cheney, Wash., 1926); Elizabeth A.
Ingerman, "Personal Experiences of an Old New York Cabinetmaker [Ernest Hagen]," Antiques, LXXXIV (Nov. 1963),
576-580; and Jocelyne Baty Goodman, ed., Victorian
Cabinet Maker [James Hopkinson] (London, 1968).

19. Lemisch, p. 6.

20. Thompson, pp. 12-13.

21. Third ser.,XXV (July 1968), 371-407.

22. P. 33.

23. Boston News-Letter, May 10-17, 1714, quoted in Dow,
p. 106.

24. South Carolina Gazette, August 5, 12, 1732, quoted
in Prime, Arts & Crafts, 1721-1785, pp. 161, 172.

25. South Carolina Gazette, March 22, 1740, quoted in
ibid., p. 163.

26. New-York Gazette or the Weekly Post-Boy, Dec. 31,
1753, quoted in Rita Susswein Gottesman, The Arts and
Crafts in New York, 1726-1776 (New York, 1938), pp. 122-23.

27. Pp. 38-39.

28. Boston Gazette, August 16, 1756, quoted in Dow, p. 115.

29. Boston News-Letter, April 20, 1758, quoted in Dow, p. 117.

30. New-York Mercury, Jan. 3, 1763, quoted in Gottesman, Arts and Crafts, 1726-1776, p. 124.

31. South Carolina Gazette, July 9, 1772, quoted in Prime, Arts & Crafts, 1721-1785, p. 176.

32. Maryland Gazette, June 22, 1762, quoted in ibid., pp. 166-67.

33. Pennsylvania Journal, May 17, 1775, quoted in ibid., pp. 205-6.

34. Delaware Gazette, June 23, 1798, quoted in Alfred Cox Prime, The Arts & Crafts in Philadelphia, Maryland and South Carolina, 1786-1800 (Topsfield, Mass., 1932), p. 192.

35. The Colonial Craftsman (New York, 1950), p. 66.

36. Ibid., p. 1.

37. P. 4.

38. Ibid., pp. 3-4.

39. Quoted in ibid.

40. New-York Gazette and the Weekly Mercury, Jan. 11, 1773, quoted in Gottesman, Arts and Crafts, 1726-1776, p. 111.

41. South Carolina Gazette, August 12, 1732, quoted in Prime, Arts & Crafts, 1721-1785, p. 161.

42. August 24, 1815, Lester J. Cappon, ed., The Adams-Jefferson Letters (Chapel Hill, 1959), p. 455.

43. (Cambridge, 1967), p. 22.

44. Hornor, p. 80.

45. Ibid., p. 81.

46. Letters from America, Historical and Descriptive; Comprising Occurrences from 1769, to 1777, Inclusive (London, 1792), pp. 112-13.

47. Pennsylvania Chronicle, Oct. 8, 1770, quoted in Prime, Arts & Crafts, 1721-1785, p. 206.

48. South Carolina Gazette, June 29, 1767, quoted in ibid., p. 187.

49. Hornor, pp. 74-77.

50. Ibid., p. 76.

51. Facing p. 321.

52. Hornor, p. 235.

53. Prime, Arts & Crafts, 1786-1800, pp. 204-8; Gottesman, Arts and Crafts, 1800-1804, pp. 145-47.

54. American Furniture: The Federal Period 1788-1825 (New York, 1966), pp. 19-26, 488.

55. Staughton Lynd and Alfred Young, "After Carl Becker: The Mechanics and New York City Politics, 1774-1801," Labor History, V (Fall 1964), 219.

56. Aurora, April 7, 1796, quoted in Prime, Arts & Crafts, 1786-1800, pp. 206-7.

57. American Citizen, Dec. 31, 1802, quoted in Gottesman, Arts and Crafts, 1800-1804, p. 147.

58. Young, "Mechanics and the Jeffersonians," p. 276.

59. Quoted in Carl N. Degler, Out of Our Past: The Forces That Shaped Modern America (New York, 1959), p. 92.

60. The Industrial Worker, 1840-1860: The Reaction of American Industrial Society to the Advance of the Industrial Revolution (Boston, 1924), p. x-xi.

61. Lynd and Young, "After Carl Becker," p. 220.

62. Ibid., p. 219.

63. Morning Chronicle, Feb. 24, 1803, quoted in Gottesman, Arts and Crafts, 1800-1804, pp. 159-60.

64. Pp. 26-27.

65. "Economic Development and Social Structure in Colonial Boston," William and Mary Quarterly, 3d ser., XXII (Jan. 1965), 85.

66. Lemisch, p. 8.

67. (Princeton, 1965), pp. 37, 49, 66, 156, 288, 291.

68. Young, "Mechanics and the Jeffersonians," p. 276.

69. Lemisch, p. 8.

70. Ware, pp. 66-67.

71. Ibid.

No. 7 on the Check List of Furniture exhibited during
the conference. Leather "elbo" chair, or "Boston"
chair, maker unknown, probably Boston area, 1710-
1725, red oak rails, soft maple legs and stiles,
H. 35 1/8"; W. 24"; D. 27½". Winterthur Museum
(58.553)

AN ART HISTORIAN'S VIEW
A COMMENTARY ON STYLE IN COUNTRY ART

R. Peter Mooz

AMONG the viewpoints from which we may examine American country furniture of the late seventeenth and eighteenth centuries is that of the art historian, using his techniques of formal analysis and iconography--the study of the meaning of images. For instance, studies of early fourteenth-century Madonnas in the style of Duccio di Buoninsegna by Enzo Carli, Cesari Brandi, John Martin, and James Stubblebine reveal a number of significant elements useful to the study of country art. These studies compare several Madonnas made in and near Siena, and reveal the differences between paintings done in outlying areas and those painted in the style center. Two paintings can illustrate the point: Pietro Lorenzetti's Madonna, now in the Philadelphia Museum of Art, and Lippo Memmi's Madonna, now in Washington. Both ultimately relate to Simone Martini's Maesta in the Palazzo Pubblico of Siena, painted in 1315-22. Pietro worked in Siena; Lippo in San Gimignano. Both painters reveal a tender, humanist approach to the Mother and Child, as well as new Gothic motifs. In both pictures the details of the donor in the corner and the position of Christ's feet are very similar. Pietro's Madonna is quite close to Simone's, but Lippo's Madonna looks less worldly than Simone's and carries on the older Ducesque tradition of the mushroom-dome head, Byzantine star on the shoulder, curved hands, and child's pose touching the head cloth.

These studies suggest that pictures might be graphed according to lines of influence and geographical relationships. Taking Siena as the center of Duccio's influence in the early fourteenth century, one could look at the Madonna and Child at Badia a Isola and understand the

changes that occurred as a function of the geographical and
cultural relationship to Siena.   Then if the Madonnas at
San Gimignano or Città di Castello were similarly compared
to their Sienese models, a pattern of influence could be
determined.

The idea that such a scheme could be developed for
American art in the eighteenth century follows logically,
because at that time America, like Italy in the fourteenth
century, had a number of separate style centers.   Each of
these centers developed a sphere of influence around it, and
each center was only loosely related to the others.   An
instance of contact between the separate style centers in
eighteenth-century America can be seen in the introduction
of the Philadelphia Hepplewhite style into Salem, Massachusetts, through an order in 1796 by Elias Haskett Derby,
the Salem China trade entrepreneur.   This contact is comparable to the painting of Madonna and Child by Duccio of
Siena being done for the Rucellai family in Florence.   Thus
the "molecular" style model, developed in studies of Italian
art, may operate equally well in studies of American art.
Although this model is not explored in the text of his book,
several charts in Allan Ludwig's Graven Images reveal the
operation of style patterns similar to those just suggested.[1]

According to Ludwig, the earliest known ornamental style
gravestone in America was one for John White, dated 1668,
in Haverhill, Massachusetts.   It established the convention
of coil volutes on the border panels, web rosettes, and a
winged effigy.   These designs were repeated by the so-
called Haverhill Carvers I, II, III, whose style spread
to Rowley and Ipswich as early as 1674.   The style was
popular in Rowley and remained in favor until the 1740s,
spreading to other towns in Essex County and to Harvard,
Massachusetts, in particular.   From Harvard, it passed to
the Worcester area and Lexington.   Ipswich styles were
also influenced by Haverhill although another stylistic
vocabulary was already well established, which included a
variant on the style that introduced birds.   The Thomas
Hart stone of 1674 is the best example of the Ipswich style.
A map in the appendix to Graven Images shows the spread

of the ornamental style to Connecticut.   This occurred via
Joshua Hempstead, who first carved gravestones on June 11,
1722.   The source for Hempstead's gravestones was
probably a stone from the North Shore of Massachusetts
Bay imported directly to New London.   His style was
quickly taken up in the areas north of New London, Norwich,
and Lebanon, the major style centers of Connecticut, from
where it spread throughout eastern Connecticut.[2]

Because the geographic origin of gravestones can usually
be precisely determined, their forms and iconography can be
compared.   The results are very similar to those found by
researchers in Italian trecento art.

The gravestone data are important, but ideas concerning
diffusion patterns originated in research now in progress on
Philadelphia country houses.   As with gravestones, the
original location of a house is known, and reasonably
accurate dates can usually be determined for it.   Finally,
lines of influence dictated by geographical factors can
easily be identified by plotting them on a topographical map.

The style center for country houses is obvious: Fairmount,
and the "Liberty" areas of Philadelphia.   The key monuments
of new form and iconography are a little less obvious.   It is
always possible that a house no longer standing was the
actual key monument.   In the interest of brevity, the roles
of three Pennsylvania houses; the Slate Roof house,
Pennsbury, and Stenton will not be discussed.   The role of
Mt. Pleasant in Fairmount Park, Philadelphia, is, however,
crucial to our study (fig. 1).

The most stylish house prior to Mt. Pleasant was Belmont,
built also in Fairmount in 1755.[3]   Woodford, still another
Philadelphia house, may have been built about this date,
but because internal structural evidence suggests a
possibility that the house was originally a single story,
following a long-established, two-room rural dwelling plan,
it was certainly not the most advanced.[4]   Today Woodford
boasts a Palladian motif over the doorway, but it would
appear that, rather than setting the style, it was following
a precedent established by Mt. Pleasant.

The owner of Belmont was William Peters, born in

Fig. 1. Mount Pleasant, Fairmount Park, Philadelphia,
ca. 1761-1762. (Photograph, Wayne Andrews)

Liverpool in 1702. He immigrated to Philadelphia about
1735 and married Mary Brientinall, a relative of the
Shoemaker family, in 1741. Registrar of the Admiralty,
judge of the Court of Common Pleas, and member of the
legislature from 1752 to 1756, he was an officer of the
crown and a member of the governor's circle at the time he
built Belmont.[5] The house has a central pediment and an
ell. The design relies strongly on the motifs of projecting
central area and side quoins. This arrangement may have
been inspired by Swan's The British Architect.[6] But the
prominence of the three-bay central facade makes unavoid-
able the conclusion that this country house was adapted
from the long-standing town house traditions. Thus the
facade can be read as a transplanted town house with two
short extensions on the right and on the left, uneasily
decorated with quoins.

Mt. Pleasant is a complete change. Conceived as a
country house, it owes almost nothing to earlier houses in
Philadelphia. The first owner, Captain John MacPherson,
who began it in 1761, was a Scottish sea captain who was
forced to settle on land after a serious accident.[7] He
brought with him a knowledge of Scottish country houses
and, as we shall see, a gentleman's taste derived from
architectural design books. He owned no town house;
Mt. Pleasant was his principal seat. Incidentally, he had
two daughters of marriageable age, and some think the
house was expected to establish them immediately in the
proper social circles. Thus, the house is the result of
certain new conditions which demanded a special solution
not previously available.

Of course, some of the elements of Mt. Pleasant cannot
be divorced from previous practice. The quoins, the
dressed stone cornices, the narrow central pavilion, and
the balustrade are not new. But the door is very new; the
Palladian window is new (it had been used only in public
buildings before); the dormers and the pediment top to the
pavilion are new. These are precisely the items that
establish a new iconography for the country house.

The term "iconography" needs further definition.

Iconography is generally used in conjunction with a study
of pictorial representations. But the root of iconography
is the study of images (icons). When a certain saint is
portrayed in a picture, items connected with the image of
the saint are included. For example, if a person is
shown with a shaggy tunic and book, he is St. John. It
should also be noted that even though St. John is characterized by both of these attributes, the hairy tunic alone is
enough to identify him. On the other hand, the book alone
is not enough because it is associated with other images.
Iconography, then, is concerned with the study of the
changes and spread of these images over time.

Iconography can also apply to architecture. For
example, the word "church" might bring to mind the image
of an enclosed rectangular space and a steeple. Of
course, that is not the only image that the word "church"
might convey. In the Renaissance the word may have
aroused an image of a circular building with a dome.
These variations are the concerns of iconographical
studies of architecture. Let us apply this system to the
present problem. What do the words "country house"
evoke? In 1920 maybe a Tudor or Norman house with a
round turret entrance and half timbering; today a colonial
farmhouse painted white with a red barn and a coach lamp.
In Philadelphia about 1750 the term probably evoked a low
one-story building or a large stone farmhouse. By 1762
it meant a large brick house with Palladian motif, central
pediment, hipped roof, balcony, dormers, and a round
arched doorway. Thus, if a Philadelphian wanted a
country house in 1765, unless he was very conservative or
completely unaware of MacPherson's home, he would build
a house with as many of Mt. Pleasant's features as
necessary to indicate to the viewer that it was a country
house. In most cases dormers and a Palladian window
were enough, although the more of the whole iconography
used, the better the image.

That Mt. Pleasant set a new precedent can be seen in
the very simple comparison of molding profiles in Mt.
Pleasant and Belmont drawn by Martin Wiel in his important
study of the Philadelphia country house.[8] The Belmont

molding is awkward; the profiles seem dictated by arithmetical means.   That of Mt. Pleasant is refined by more subtle modular relationships in the dimensions.   It is almost like comparing a sixth-century kouros with a fifth-century one.

This comparison of moldings is not the essence of the difference; it is only one of the symptoms of the real differences.   The modular proportions seen in the moldings are taken from a design book.   Design books may have been used in Philadelphia before 1762, but I am aware of no case in which the actual plates from a book were copies.   Because no precedent for this type of house existed, one is tempted to say that the designer of Mt. Pleasant went directly to the design book.   The ultimate reasons for the use of design books are probably more complicated than that.   For example, why did MacPherson go to James Gibbs, rather than to Batty Langley, Abraham Swan, or Robert Morris for the facades?[9]   The answer to this question may be important. However, if a simplification may be allowed, perhaps we may say MacPherson brought with him to Philadelphia a new idea of a country house, a new way of planning it, and a new large pocketbook to pay for it.

The first hint that the house came from a design book is given by the side elevations, which are left blank.   This lack of architectural articulation could be explained by the fact that side elevations were not given in the books. Definitive proof of the use of design books is found in the doors, windows, and woodwork.   The front door is taken directly from <u>A Book of Architecture</u> by James Gibbs published in London in 1728 (fig. 2).   Curiously, though the whole composition is shown in plate 34, the actual details were probably not taken from that plate but from plate 100 of the same book.   Notice that the door is a combination of the surround of example 1 and the rustication of example 3 shown on plate 100.   The probability that plate 100 rather than plate 34 was the real source is further supported by the design of the garden front doorway.   This doorway is composed of the rustication of example 1 and the surround of example 3 shown on plate 100.   In other words, two examples were used for two doors, but the designs of rustication and surrounds were interchanged.   The window motif

Fig. 2. Plate 100 from James Gibbs, A Book of
Architecture, London, 1728.

also comes from Gibbs's plate 68. The window is treated
like an ornament, not locked into the architecture by
structural scheme. It is placed on the surface and held up
by delicate consoles at the base of the uprights. This is
exactly the style seen in Gibbs's plate 68. The interior is
also one of the few precisely taken from a design book--in
this case from Abraham Swan's.

Let us see now what Mt. Pleasant reveals about a pattern
of style diffusion. Probably only three years after the
erection of Mt. Pleasant, Edward Stiles began Port Royal
(fig. 3). It was located on Frankford Creek north of Philadelphia, near the present North Philadelphia Station of the
Pennsylvania Central Railroad.[10] In its final years, little
of its original grandeur remained, but Port Royal still pro-
claimed a debt to Mt. Pleasant. Its iconography included
Palladian window, dormers, and round-arched-door motif
along with the balustrade and hip roof that were also seen at
Mt. Pleasant. But there is a difference. These features
neither copy Mt. Pleasant nor draw on an elaborate folio-
sized design book. Looking carefully at the Palladian motif,
for example, one sees that the window is set on a broad
projecting panel of brick surrounding the door. The method
of handling the Palladian motif comes not from a design book
but, like the basic iconography, from a building that could
have been observed in Philadelphia. Stiles's town house
was on Walnut between Third and Fourth Streets, facing
north.[11] Any native Philadelphian would know that, out of
his front window, Stiles would have seen Independence
Hall--specifically the first tower, completed to the cornice
by 1750 to 1753.[12] On this building a Palladian window was
set on top of a projecting brick panel, just like that at Port
Royal. The important thing there is not the sources but the
meaning of the change in sources. Port Royal is imitative.
It is not original; it depends on forms and iconography found
in other buildings in the style center. It follows the latest
iconography but adjusts and simplifies it. The basic impact
is almost the same as Mt. Pleasant, but when the two are
compared closely, we conclude that Port Royal is derivative
and simplified.

We can trace this trend down to its sad conclusion in

Fig. 3. Port Royal. Originally Frankford, Pennsyl-
vania, 1762. Destroyed 1928, partially restored at
Winterthur Museum. (Photograph, Archives, Winterthur
Museum)

graceless facades, simplified to the point of disinterest in some of the country houses. In all of these, however, the form is not drastically changed, and the rudimentary iconography remains. The workmanship and refinement are lost owing to economy.

In contrast to this vertical transmission near the style center, we can trace the horizontal spread to areas removed from the style center. Our first step might be Cliveden, the Chew mansion in "distant" Germantown, built between 1761 and 1768 (fig. 4).[13] At first glance the building seems another Mt. Pleasant. In fact, some have attributed it to the same workers. Yet Mt. Pleasant is only evoked. The iconography is followed, but the house is substantially different. Most importantly, the roof is a gable, there are double doors, and the urns, which came direct from England made from designs like Gibbs's, are overdone and almost giddy. How much closer in form is Cliveden to the Pastorius house of 1748, a mile or so down the road. Cliveden thus represents a combination of the iconography and forms of Mt. Pleasant with the stronger traditions of the locale. Cliveden's style, therefore, is completely a product of the historical circumstances at its place of origin.

More time would permit an analysis of style diffusion to other areas as represented in the George Read house of New Castle, Delaware, and Rock Hall of Lancaster, Pennsylvania. It suffices here to point out that, although these houses do follow the iconography of Mt. Pleasant, changes occur that are due to local historical circumstances. Both show also that distance, either physical or temporal, between the style center and the place of origin of an object will effect changes. By studying the forces which intervene between the style center and the object under consideration, the changes in the style can be identified and interpreted. Thus, as with the Madonnas and the gravestones, a model could be drawn showing lines of stylistic influence which could serve as an index of change caused by removal from the style center.

For the problem of style in country furniture, this model seems perfect. However, studying the influence of

Fig. 4. Cliveden. Germantown, Pennsylvania, ca. 1764-1765. (Photograph, Wayne Andrews)

historical circumstances at the place of origin and generat-
ing theories of regional characteristics are always
treacherous. Rudolph Wittkower observed that when an
art historian moves from describing a sequence of art events
to making conclusions, he becomes an art theorist and is
vulnerable to attack on the basis of the terminology he
chooses and the theoretical apparatus he adopts.[14]   In
furniture, this is doubly treacherous, since we must avoid
the Scylla of having few dates and known places of origin
to begin with and the Charybdis of the discovery of a dated
piece of known origin which completely contradicts the
theory.

In this study of furniture my starting point was a piece
owned by the Gratz family of Philadelphia, variously called
a dressing table, low chest, lowboy, or lobby table (fig. 5).[15]
The Gratz family is associated in a letter of 1806 with the
Van Pelt and the Turner familes, all of whom owned pieces
recognized as of the highest style.[16]   This dressing table
therefore is one of the style leaders, if not the principal
statement of the high style.   The dressing table is 28 3/4
inches high, 37 inches wide, and 18 3/4 inches deep.[17]
It is noticeably wider and lower than most, but its proportions are carefully related and based on a module of four
inches.   In fact, the whole dressing table is an infinitely
refined network of related proportions.   It is easy to
measure a piece and come up with some inadvertent
relationships in the dimensions.   But here the sizes were
so consciously made that relationships are not coincidental.
The width of the drawer is the same as the height of the
quarter round decoration on the corners and the height of
the legs up to the carving.   The height of the drawer is
repeated in the width of the carving of the knees and the
width of the ruffled shell.   On a larger scale, the proportion of the drawers, at 4 1/2 to 8 inches and the main case,
14 to 36 inches, follows golden section rules.

The ornament is rococo and displays the fullest interpenetration of spatial planes associated with the style.   No
specific design source has been located for it, but the
designs are similar in feeling to those found for metal objects.

Fig. 5. Dressing table, made for Michael Gratz,
maker unknown. Philadelphia, 1769. H. 28 3/4";
W. 37"; D. 18 3/4". Winterthur Museum (57.505)

The skirting is close to several designs for brass handles in Chippendale's Director of 1762, [18] and the streamers surrounding the shell, though they derive ultimately from the school of Grinling Gibbons (1648-1721) and the cartouche patterns of James Gibbs, relate to designs on iron stoves listed as "Venetian" stoves in Chippendale's Director and "Philadelphia" stoves in Ince and Mayhew's Universal Household System of 1762. [19]

If one takes this dressing table to represent the iconography in the same sense that we discussed iconography in building, the image of the dressing table is a rocaille skirt, cabriole legs, carved central drawer, and flanking lower drawers somewhat narrower than the central one.

The Philadelphia dressing table illustrated in figure 6 has such an iconography. [20] It is less wide and taller than the piece just discussed. But several other factors are more important. The top is not the single board with a chamfered edge. It has a molded edge similar to those found on high chests. Moreover, its dimensions do not follow any modular proportion scheme. Its carving lacks great interpenetration. Finally, the whole is reduced and simplified from our prototype. We must note, too, that the streamers are partially broken off, and some carving is missing in this example. Thus the piece reads "dressing table" in its iconography, but several refinements are missing, and the whole is simplified.

In the city this simplification can go to the extent of the dressing table made for the Paschall family of Cedar Grove, in 1774, and attributed to David Evans (fig. 7). [21] The Evans piece reveals that some pieces made in the city were of a very simplified nature. The principal factor is a reduction of embellishment. The proportions are not seriously altered, and the iconography of a wide central drawer, cabriole legs, and quarter round pillar is followed. No new or extraneous ornament is substituted or added to the piece.

Comparison of the Gratz and Paschall pieces raises the question of stylistic diffusion to nonurban areas outside centers. A dressing table from the Winterthur collection

Fig. 6. Dressing table, maker unknown. Philadelphia, 1765-1775. Mahogany. H. 31"; W. 33 3/4";
D. 21 1/2". Winterthur Museum (58.224)

Fig. 7. Dressing table, attributed to David Evans.
American Chippendale, Philadelphia, late eighteenth
century. Philadelphia Museum of Art

asks a similar question (fig. 8).[22]   Stylistic analysis of the
piece could produce three different evaluations: (1) The
shells on the knees, the lack of Chippendale rocaille
ornament, and the even spacing of the drawers combined
with claw-and-ball feet and the quarter round columnar
motif might suggest that the table is a transitional piece
dating from 1740 to 1755. (This is the interpretation of
Joseph Downs.) (2) It might be a simplified city piece, made
when claw-and-ball feet and fluted columns were well in
vogue but carrying over conservative ornament. (3) Still
another possibility is that the piece represents a synthesis
developed in an area removed from a style center but under
urban influence, for example, Annapolis, Maryland.   Each
of the three alternatives has points to recommend it, and
there is absolutely no documentation for the piece to
provide a clue to the right choice.   Nevertheless, careful
stylistic analysis of the form of the piece may point the
way to the proper conclusion.

Between 1740 and 1780 changes occurred in the basic
forms of the high chest and dressing chest.   Claw-and-ball
feet gradually replaced the pad and trifid foot, and rocaille
ornament replaced shell motifs.   But the most crucial
change occurred in pieces traditionally dated about 1765
and later.   In these pieces the top drawer which projected
up into the head area of the bonnet top in earlier pieces is
eliminated, and the newly created void in the head is
filled with rocaille ornament.   Second, the skirt receives
strong rocaille ornamentation in an attempt to retain visual
coherence between top and bottom, preserving the unity of
the piece.   Third, the pediment becomes purely a facade,
and the width of the opening in the bonnet top becomes
greater.   This causes the ornament drawer, whose width had
usually been determined by the width of the bonnet top
opening, to become wider.   Fourth, quarter columns are
extended down the entire piece to the lower portion.

The effect of these changes on the dressing table or
lowboy is fairly important.   First, the ornament drawer is
widened, making the flanking dresser drawers smaller,
and abandoning the former equality in drawer width.

Fig. 8. Dressing table, maker unknown. Philadelphia or Maryland, 1755-1765. H. 29 1/2"; W. 35";
D. 22 3/4". Winterthur Museum (59.634)

Second, the scalloping in the skirt projects below the
drawer line rather than up above it.   Also, quarter columns
are used to match the lower part of the high chest.   Returning to our problem dressing table, we can now better
analyze it.   Despite the old-fashioned shell, the ornament
drawer motif and the carved rocaillelike outline of the skirt
projecting below the drawers are contemporaneous with the
claw-and-ball feet and the quarter column previously
recognized as rather late elements.   Thus a date of 1755 to
1765 would be more appropriate than those suggested in the
first evaluation.

The last conclusion tends to make the interpretation of
this piece as a simplified conservative city piece (or a
Maryland one) more probable.   Direct proof of the origin of
the chest is not available, but one interesting lead is found
in the construction of the low chest.   In back of the
inverted shell, on the inner side of the skirt, are two
support brackets.   They extend down each side of the
ornament drawer and are cut off at an angle and shaped to
fit in back of the wooden curls in the skirt which resemble
an inverted handlebar mustache.   This structural element
has also been found on a low chest in the Baltimore
Museum.[23]   The size, shaping, and cut of the brackets
are nearly identical in every detail.   Incidentally, the
pattern of the skirt, the shape of the inverted shell, and the
form of the shell on the ornament drawer, a round one
inscribed in a dished circle, are the same on both pieces.
The Baltimore Museum example has streamers around the
shell which the Winterthur one does not have.   (This makes
a later date even more certain for the Baltimore piece despite
the Queen Anne overtones.)

Though not based on documents, the Baltimore Museum
chest was shown as a Maryland piece in a Queen Anne-
Chippendale exhibition held at the Baltimore Museum in
1968.   The reasons for this regional identification are
sound, and one is tempted to agree with them.   This would
suggest that the Winterthur example should be given the
third interpretation as a piece done outside a style center.
Its form and design are a product of slightly disparate

ornamental vocabularies characteristic of outlying districts.
It also has a pronounced insistence on playfulness as well
as the reduction of sophistication in ornamentation usually
associated with non-style-center pieces.   Finally, some
connoisseurs have observed that the double cutout on the
side skirt of these pieces is characteristic of Maryland
furniture.   Whether or not this particular piece was made
in Maryland cannot be positively determined.

Another low chest in the Winterthur collection is
certainly from Maryland.[24]   This is a marvelous piece,
complete with trifid feet, canted corners, pierced skirt,
and shell-carved knees (fig. 9).   That this piece is a
Maryland one is clear from the ornamentation of the chest.
The unusual canted corners have been associated with
Maryland craftsmanship.   But more detailed comparison to
pieces of known Maryland provenance make the origin even
clearer.   If we compare the ornament of the legs on this
piece with that on a high chest belonging to Mr. and Mrs.
Lennox Birckhead (and having continuous ownership in the
Baltimore Birckhead family) amazing similarities are seen.[25]
The unusual shell with attached bellflower and the unique
curled volute decoration of the corner blocks are very
similar.   The heart motif in the pierced skirt also has a
Maryland prototype.   The heart appears prominently in the
back of a Chippendale chair which has a very strong
tradition of manufacture in Annapolis based on its long ownership by the Pinkney family of that city.[26]   Incidentally,
the way in which the piercing of the chair revolves in
languid curves and varies in thickness of wood membering
seems to suggest the origin of the heretofore unexplained
unique skirt piercing of the table.

Finally, a dressing table shown in Baltimore in 1947,
at the first exhibition of Annapolis and Baltimore furniture,
is strikingly similar to the piece in figure 9 and has a long
history of ownership in Cecil County, Maryland.[27]   The
ornamented drawer is absolutely identical.   The streamers
are transformed into fernlike leaves.   They meander
expansively over the whole drawer front.   The shell, the
size of the drawers, and the shape of the legs are similar.
Finally, the 1947 exhibition catalog, Baltimore Furniture

Fig. 9. Dressing table, maker unknown. Probably
Maryland, 1760-1770. H. 31"; W. 33 1/2"; D. 20".
Winterthur Museum (59.34.10)

(page 182), notes that the skirt under the drawers is a
replacement.   How easy it is for a pierced skirt to be
broken off.   The skirt in the Museum's piece is still
sturdy, but a surface crack extends entirely across it.
This example of a dressing table with a strong Maryland
history supports the previous suggestion of a Maryland
origin for the almost identical Winterthur piece.   Because
of the shells, pierced skirt, and trifid feet, the Maryland
piece has been dated 1745 to 1760.   The other related
pieces we have seen are dated ca. 1765 to 1775.   Certainly
this piece is close to this date too.   The central drawer is
wider than the flanking drawers, and the skirt drops down
in a manner similar to the rocaille-ornamented pieces that
we have suggested belong to the late phase of low chest
production.   A possible companion high chest now united
with the piece in the Museum has a central drawer in the
bonnet area.   If this information is considered, the date
for the low chest should be 1760 to 1770.

But with this new date and with the realization that the
ornament used comes from two style periods, several
questions arise.   What conditions would produce such an
object?   Where would these conditions occur?   The answer
to the first question might be found through the following
observations:

1. The combination of ornament from different points
in time denotes either deliberate conservatism or lack
of full awareness of the correct usage of ornaments.

2. While not so conclusive, the use of walnut indicates
a nonurban outlook where the use of local wood for a
piece in a style based on another wood is often characteristic.

3. The introduction of completely nonacademic
motifs and their substitution for high-style ones is a
trait found outside style centers.   And, in this case,
the hearts and almost birdlike cutouts suggest a German
ornamental tradition.

4. Finally, in complete contradiction to the
observation above, the fineness of the dovetail joints,
the expertise of the cabinetmaking, the refinements of the

juncture of leg and case, the sureness of the carving,
even though not especially lively, and the crispness of
the moldings demand recognition of a very high quality
of craftsmanship.

Now, where could these conditions have occurred?
First, they must be outside the major style center.   Yet
they are not untrained.   More specifically it is unlikely
that they could be from a place like Annapolis where there
was a distinct awareness of correct coherent ornament and
the proper high style.   Western Maryland, near Frederick
County, is a possible location, but the craftsmanship seems
to be too refined for the really rural circumstances there.
The logical place of origin is Baltimore.   The culture of
Baltimore in the 1760s was subject to a peculiar combination
of influences.   It was a developing area removed from the
mainstream of styles, and it had little previous import in
cultural affairs.   But people of wealth and a desire for
sophisticated living were beginning to settle in Baltimore
at mid-century.

In 1754 Governor Sharpe wrote to Lord Baltimore:

I have taken an opportunity since my arrival of
visiting Baltimore which indeed has the appearance
of the most increasing Town in the Province,
though it scarcely answered the opinion I had
conceived of it: hardly as yet rivaling Annapolis
in number of buildings or inhabitants; its situation
as to pleasantness, air and prospect is inferior to
that of Annapolis, but if one considers it with
respect to trade, the extensive country beyond it
leaves no room for comparison; were a few gentlemen
of fortune to settle there and encourage the trade
it might soon become a florishing place but while
few besides the Germans (who are in general masters
of small fortunes) build and inhabit there I apprehend
that it cannot make any considerable figure.[28]

In the next decade a group of fine craftsmen from Philadelphia and the Pennsylvania German district came to

Baltimore to meet the demands. We are instantly reminded
of the April 9, 1767, advertisement in the Maryland Gazette:

> Girard Hopkins, son of Samuel, Cabinet and Chair-
> Maker from Philadelphia, at the Sign of the Tea
> Table and Chair in Gay Street Baltimore-Town Makes
> and sells the following goods in the best manner,
> and the newest Fashions in Mahogany, Walnut,
> Cherry-tree, and Maple Viz. Chests of drawers of
> various sorts, Desks, Bookcases, Scrutoires,
> Cloth-Presses, Tables of Various sorts, such as
> Bureaus, Card, Chamber, Parlor and Tea Tables.
> Chairs of various sorts such as easy, arm Parlor,
> Chamber or Corner Chairs, Settees, Clock-cases,
> Couches, Candle stands, Decanter stands, Tea
> Kettle stands, Dumb-Waiters, Tea-Boards, Bottle
> Boards, Bedsteads, etc., etc. N.B. Any of the
> above Articles to be done with or without carved
> work.

It must be admitted that no empirical proof of the origin
of the piece can be generated. But at this point let us
return to the ideas concerning architecture stated in the
first part of this paper. We noted how the style of domestic
structures could be understood by their geographical relation
to the style center. We noted that a building seemed to be
a direct product of its stylistic circumstances relative to the
center.

If we apply this idea to the present problem, let us look
at a Baltimore house of 1764. This is the Mt. Clare home
of the Carroll family (fig. 10). The house was formerly
thought to date from the 1740s, but intensive research on the
land records shows that 1764 should be the date.[29]

An analysis of the house sets forth some important points.
First, the house combines ornamental practices of an earlier
time with architectural features of a later one. The windows,
for example, are the segmental arched ones ultimately
derived from the French styles of the Regency hotels of the
1720s and the central Palladian motif is found in English
sources of the 1750s, like Morris, Swan, and Langley.

Fig. 10. Mount Clare. Baltimore, ca. 1764.
(Photograph from Richard Hubbard Howland,
The Architecture of Baltimore, Baltimore:
The Johns Hopkins Press, 1953)

Second, the central section unites a very high-style
architectural innovation with traditional local practices.
The Palladian window, as we have seen, became the image
of architectural sophistication in 1761 with the building
of Mt. Pleasant.   The porch, though updated with sophisticated Doric ornamentation, is an element incorporated into
Maryland house facades for many years, according to
H. C. Forman.[30]

Thus, we have (1) continuance of old ornament,
(2) introduction of high-style iconography, and (3) use of
traditional local, even rural, motifs.   How easy to compare
the shells with the segmental arch windows, the wide
ornament drawer with the Palladian window, and the hearts
and bird piercing with the porch.

Comparisons of this nature might seem to be art-historical
solipsism.   But they often serve to point the proper
direction for research.   For our purposes, they may not
settle questions empirically, but they do reveal where to
look to find the answer.   Professor Erwin Panofsky did look
further and felt such comparisons were nearly empirical.
He argued that by formal and iconographical analysis the
art historian could arrive at the intrinsic meaning of the
object.   After carefully studying the history of culture, he
suggested one could find the particular conditions that
produced objects with the intrinsic meaning previously
identified and discover when and where an object was made.[31]

Summarizing what we have seen in the furniture, we might
conclude that furniture follows the molecular pattern of style
seen in architecture.

1. Certain pieces set styles in style centers.

2. Within the style center certain pieces are produced
which are derivative of the style.   They reduce the total
amount of ornament and simplify the iconography, though
the forms are not greatly altered and there is not a great
disparity between the styles of ornaments used.

3. Pieces made outside the style center are edited and
changed in both form and ornament according to the historical
circumstances of the place of origin.

In conclusion, I wish my brief study to show, not that

this or that piece should be termed "country," but that a
piece of furniture, like a painting or a building, is a
product of its historical context.

No. 30 on the Check List of Furniture exhibited dur-
ing the conference. Dressing table, maker unknown,
Connecticut, 1750-1780, cherry. H. 32"; W. 39";
D. 24¼". Winterthur Museum (58.589)

Notes

1.   Allan Ludwig, Graven Images (Middletown, Conn.,
1966), map 4, p. 465.
2.   Ibid., pp. 358, 362, 369, 373.
3.   Robert C. Smith, "The Houses in Fairmount Park,"
Antiques, Nov. 1962, p. 535.
4.   Martin P. Snyder, "Woodford," Antiques,
Nov. 1962, pp. 515-18.
5.   Edgar P. Richardson, "Some Owners of Park Houses
and Their Portraits," Antiques, Nov. 1962, p. 508.
6.   Abraham Swan, The British Architect (London,
1745).
7.   Frank Cousins and Phil M. Riley, The Colonial
Architecture of Philadelphia (Boston, 1920), pp. 74-75.
8.   Martin E. Weil, "Interior Architectural Details
in Eighteenth Century Architectural Books and Philadelphia
Country Houses" (Master's thesis, Winterthur, 1967),
fig. 39.
9.   James Gibbs, A Book of Architecture (London,
1728); Batty Langley, The City and Country Builder's and
Workman's Treasury of Designs (London, 1740); Abraham
Swan, The British Architect (London, 1745); Robert Morris,
Select Architecture: Being Regular Designs or Plans and
Elevations Well Suited to Both Town and Country (London,
1755).
10.   Cousins and Riley, p. 36.
11.   Ibid.
12.   Hugh Morrison, Early American Architecture
(New York, 1952), p. 533.
13.   Cousins and Riley, p. 88.
14.   Rudolph Wittkower, "Art History as a Discipline,"
Winterthur Seminar on Museum Operation and Connoisseurship, 1959.
15.   William Macpherson Hornor, Jr., Philadelphia
Furniture: William Penn to George Washington with Special
Reference to the Philadelphia-Chippendale School
(Philadelphia, 1935), p. 112.
16.   Object file, Registrar's Office, Winterthur Museum.
17.   Joseph Downs, American Furniture: Queen Anne

and Chippendale Period, 1725-1788 (New York, 1952), p. 333.

18.   Thomas Chippendale, The Gentleman and
Cabinetmaker's Director (London, 1754).

19.   William Ince and Edgar deNoailles Mayhew,
The Universal System of Household Furniture (London,
1762), p. 11.

20.   Downs, p. 333.

21.   Hornor, p. 114.

22.   Downs, p. 329.

23.   William Elder, Maryland Queen Anne and
Chippendale Furniture of the Eighteenth Century (New York,
1968), p. 74.

24.   Downs, p. 324.

25.   Elder, p. 79.

26.   Ibid., p. 20.

27.   Baltimore Furniture, an exhibition catalog at the
Baltimore Museum of Art (Baltimore, 1947), p. 182.

28.   Dieter Cunz, The Maryland Germans (Princeton,
N.J., 1948), p. 97.

29.   Richard H. Howland and Eleanor P. Spencer,
The Architecture of Baltimore (Baltimore, 1953), p. 8.

30.   H. Chandlee Forman, Maryland Architecture
(Cambridge, Md., 1968), p. 11.

31.   Erwin Panofsky, Studies in Iconology: Humanistic
Themes in the Art of the Renaissance (New York, 1939),
p. 16.

A FOLKLORIST LOOKS AT THE TRADITIONAL CRAFTSMAN

Bruce R. Buckley

THE folklorist has found himself in a very interesting position
since the end of World War II.   It was at this time that he
began to change the concept of his field from the study of
oral tradition, which is part of his long history of scholarship, to the study of the total folk culture.   He found that
many people already were studying aspects of folk culture,
and were using terms which the folklorist is supposed to
define, but never had embraced as his.   Although there are
many books on folk art, I know of none written by a folklorist
except those by Louis C. Jones.[1]   As for folk architecture
or vernacular architecture, it is only recently that folklorists
have looked at it.

So in discussing folk art, I am working against pre-
conceptions held by scholars who are not folklorists.   I
therefore wish to share with you some of the operational
definitions and models that folklorists are using today that
may help you in looking at the questions concerning country
furniture.   I will include the historical background and meaning of folklore, and some of the folklorists' methodology; and
point out the ways that the cultural and art historians can use
this approach.

"Folklore" became an international word in 1846, when it
was invented by the English antiquarian, William Thoms.
In an anonymous article he stated that antiquarians were not
properly studying the kinds of things that were products of
the past.   The concept of objects as relics of the past,
instead of expressions of a living tradition, was not compat-
ible with his point of view.   He suggested that the word
"folklore" be used for living traditions in the country, such
as the songs, ballads, and beliefs that were current "among
the common people," rather than for traditions of the Middle

Ages, as the antiquarians, at that time, were looking at them.
The word "folklore" has become a part of the vocabulary of
almost every country of the world,with different shades of
meaning. It is primarily defined as the orally transmitted
aspect of culture. This is the primary meaning of "folklore"
in the English-speaking nations.

Another term of which I hope we will hear more and more,
is the term "folklife ," a new concept in the United States
since 1940.[2]   The folklorist interested in folklife is looking
at more than the oral tradition of his culture. His view
includes the material culture and the social interactions that
take place in traditional culture. This concept already
existed in Europe in the eighteenth century, primarily in
Germany, and the German word comparable to folklife, still
in use today, is Volkskunde. The American folklife person
is related somewhat to the Volkskunde movement of Central
Europe.

Another term, "regional ethnology," describes methodology
more than it does the essence or meaning of folklife. It is
the frame of reference for the study. This also is European,
a twentieth-century term, used by the Scandinavian folklorist
Sigurd Erixon.[3]   He defined it as "a comparable cultural
research on a regional basis with a sociological and historical orientation with certain psychological implications."
This definition therefore places regional ethnology in the
interdisciplinary field. It is one branch of general ethnology,
an anthropological discipline, applied to civilized people.
It differs somewhat from the anthropological approach, and
from general ethnology,in that it avoids large generalizations
of cultural patterns. It is historically oriented, checking
its field data with documents of history. Regional ethnology
was accepted in 1955 as an adequate name for the whole of
international European folk culture research by the international Arnhem congress.[4]

The word "folk" itself needs clear definition. Too often,
definitions have confined themselves to the lore and life of
people who were called "folk." But the definition never
indicated just who these people were. This is especially
true in the United States.

A typical oral traditional folklorist would say, "Well, there is lore, including ballads and songs, and we will collect the lore, and the people we collect it from are, therefore, folk, and the folk are the ones who create the ballads and songs." So the definition is still not clear, nor is it clear whether folk and country can be equated. All these terms with their various connotations have been part of the changing definition of folklore.

Europeans have always said, "This is a peasant culture." In our democracy, we do not use the word "peasant," even though we do have citizens comparable to this European class. So, although the word "peasant" has not been very useful to us in the past, you may hear it in the future. Anthropologists have rediscovered "peasant." Since Robert Redfield's works have been followed up with field research, we now have studies in international peasant societies that should generate some interesting theories for the future.[5]

Another connotation for "folk," and part of the common definition, is "old-fashioned" or "conservative"--words normally applicable in a rural-urban dichotomy. This use of "folk" is also European in its background, and it has been applied in the United States during the last three decades. However, it is being discarded by the folklorist as a basis for defining folk groups, because there is as much urban folk culture as rural folk culture in the United States today. It is difficult to say whether or not urban folk culture is a product of the twentieth century, or whether it projects further back in time.

Another useful term for us is "partial society," that is, not a total society but a group dependent upon a mainstream culture which satisfies certain of its cultural needs and allows it to continue in its traditional way. Again, this is an instance of anthropological and sociological usage in the United States. The works of Oscar Lewis imply partial culture in the twentieth century.[6]

The definition that I will follow is this: "Folk are a social group connected by a common tradition and a peculiar feeling of communication, based on a common historical background." Lyman H. Butterfield, although not talking

about folk, states it well in his introduction to the Adams
papers when he refers to people "who lived their lives below
the level of historical scrutiny."[7] These people are our
study as well.

The aspect of communication needs to be considered in
more detail. So, I shall try to develop a meaning for this
aspect, and then apply it.

Two primary premises accepted by most communications
theorists are that meanings are in people, and that perception
is functionally selective. Both of these premises are significant, I think, in defining the term "folk." No longer can we
speak of meaning in terms of qualities of objects or situations,
because a word does not "mean" nor does an object "mean."
The meaning is in the people who use the word or symbol plus
the acceptance by groups of commonly agreed upon definitions for these symbols. But, despite a commonly agreed
upon definition, no one can share the complete meaning of
the symbol; one can only approximate from his own experience
and observation of the use of the symbol what meaning another
person has for that symbol.

We laugh at the children depicted in jokes about perception or misperception in school situations, such as: "I pledge
allegiance to the flag of the United States of America and to
the republican for which it stands." But I think this is a
common indication of the learning-perception situation of the
student in grammar school who is looking for meaning. It
may not even be a mistake as far as he is concerned, because
he does not perceive it as a mistake.

We may also have several levels of meaning for the same
symbol. The term "apple," for example, may have private
meaning, such as the apple that made me sick as a boy, or
sweet apples, or sour apples, or wormy apples. We each
have our own meaning for "apple." It may be a shared meaning in a family situation, such as the apple pies that grand-
mother used to make, or the applejack that Uncle John made
during prohibition. It may be on the dictionary denotative
level, "the fleshy, rounded red or yellow pomme fruit of the
tree of the rose family." Or it may refer to the culture of the
Pennsylvania Germans in which art, artifacts, song, food, and

drink may be related to the symbol of Eve's forbidden fruit.[8]

Perception of events and realities are based on our meanings for the event or reality, and we functionally select our perceptions to fit our previous meanings and organize our perceptions to fit our attitudes, our wants, our cognitions. One needs only to think of the many ways people perceive and describe the Civil War, racial integration, academic freedom, the escalation of the war, or communism. These perceptions may cluster together into groups or patterns or interpretation, but each group will hold to its own truth, its own reality, and its own definition of the event.

Throughout time many levels of interpretation of events, including recognition of what an event is, have been formed, clustered, and patterned. It may be that the folk may be characterized as a group perceiving and interpreting reality on a traditional level. How then, can we describe this traditional level of interpretation, perception, meaning, attitude, and communication? Many areas of human production are already described in terms which imply levels of interpretation. Societies, for example, are described in terms of preliterate, folk societies and urban-technical or civilized societies.

Music is described as folk music, popular music, or classical music. Dance is folk, primitive, popular, classical. The arts, in general, are folk, popular, fine, or academic. Unfortunately, each of these contain the word that we are trying to look at, so we are right back to "a folk is a folk is a folk" unless we go a little deeper.

As a basis for further examination, the three levels of cultural communication (informal, formal, technical) used by the cultural anthropologist Edward Hall may be useful if considered and translated into: folk, popular, and classical or academic. The criteria for separating these levels according to Hall are (1) learning process, (2) awareness, (3) effect and emotion, (4) attitude towards change.[9]

Let us first consider Hall's formal or popular level of culture. This cultural communication level is defined as that level of culture learned by precept and admonition. Motivation for learning is imposed on the learner by an older

member of the culture in terms of: "Don't do that!   No, you
are wrong!   No, no, no!"   The learner learns by his mistakes.   The formal level of culture is constantly brought to
the awareness of the person who is involved in it, and deep
emotional ties are established for the support of the formal
structure.   This is usually expressed in terms of institution-
alization.   Change in the formal level is slow and restricted;
the status quo is institutionally supported and reinforced.
A significant exception in attitudes toward change in a formal
level of culture is that the culture itself has to define what
is important to it.   It may be that the fabric of the culture is
slow in changing, but the embroidery on the fabric normally
called fashion changes constantly.

The technical, academic, or classical level of culture,
whichever you wish to call it, is defined in terms of one-way
learning.   That is, the teacher, the specialist, the scientist,
is supreme.   It is the teacher's objective to analyze and
present the material to the learner, who may accept or reject
it.   But, it is a one-way flow.   We are in that kind of
situation now.   The technical level is characterized by
fully conscious behavior, with personal emotions suppressed
under the rule of objectivity.   This objectivity is lost only
when you break the rules of the academic level.   That is,
as long as you follow the rules of a discipline, no one is
going to get emotional about it.   But, if you break the rules
of a discipline, then someone will get emotional about it.
The technical level is change-oriented.   In the twentieth
century, at least, the technical level is dedicated to change.

The informal or folk level of culture is defined in terms of
imitative learning.   It is characterized by such statements
as, "Well, when you grow older you will understand a little
more."   Or, "Don't ask me.   Use your eyes.   See what
people are doing."   The person is almost unaware of this
aspect of his life, which tends to a high degree of patterning.
When you try to make someone aware of imitative learning in
interview situations, he often justifies his reluctance by
saying, "Well, I've always done it that way."   Or, "That's
the way my grandfather did it."   Emotional response to
aspects of culture communicated on this level is sensed, but

not necessarily brought to the surface. It is expressed in terms of uneasiness in a situation. Something is just not quite right. There is no verbalization level to allow this to come forth.

On the informal level, there is no resistance to change because there is no consciousness of change. This does not mean to imply that change does not take place on this level of communication; by imitative learning there is a slow change through time. It is also probable that the tradition bearer in this level of culture, that is, the singer of songs, the teller of tales, the craftsman, may have some con- sciousness of and some attitude towards change slightly different from those of other members of his community and yet be in agreement with the members of his group.

The interaction of these various levels of culture has been of interest to the folklorist of the past. An older German theory of "sunken culture" presupposes the one-way flow of cultural ideas from the higher to the lower level of culture. This one-way flow of culture is no longer acceptable in contemporary theory. In the contemporary view of culture there is a constant interaction between levels, and one level influences another. The folk level influences the popular, and the popular influences the folk; the academic is influ- enced by the folk, and vice versa; so it is not a one-way flow of ideas.

Before applying these theories to influences in country cabinetware and simple city furniture, the methodology of the folklorist in using these levels of cultural analysis should be considered. Folklorist methodology is primarily field-oriented, which means that it is based on contemporary culture and its roots in history. Like the student of other social sciences, the folklorist is interested in historical studies, but for differing reasons. One group of folklorists aims to establish levels historically, determining the peculiar characteristics of folk cultures for certain periods through field work and research into the documents of the time. Another group of folklorists studies historic documents to understand the present. They ask why we are where we are through the artifacts, the traditions, and the belief

systems that we currently possess.   The byword of the folk-
culture specialist is based on an old Chinese proverb: "From
a different line of work, my colleagues, I bring you an idea.
You smirk.   It is in the line of duty.   Wipe off that smile,
and as our grandfathers used to say: 'Ask the fellow who cut
the hay.'"

One aspect of the folklorist's methodology is similar to
that of the art historian or the cultural geographer, the so-
called historic-geographic approach.   Here, the folklorist
is looking for patterns and forms and the groupings of these
patterns and forms, their space diffusion, their time-
orientation, and the change through the diffusion in space
and time.   Among the various theories growing out of this
study of transmission is the wave-diffusion theory of cultural terms, similar to that used by the art historian.

Applying the folklorist's framework, with an awareness of
the interchange of ideas between city and country, let us
now turn to contrasting the Dominy family of craftsmen of
East Hampton, Long Island, with the Dunlaps of New
Hampshire.   It should be noted that this analysis is based
upon my reactions to the oral presentations given at this
conference rather than upon a detailed analysis of the craftsmen involved.

The folklorist might look upon the Dominys as a classic
example of the folk level of communication.   They lived in
an isolated community setting.   They had face-to-face
contact, and all of the members of the community knew each
other.   There was constant interacting.   They looked to
themselves rather than to New York City.   Although they
seem to have been both physically and culturally isolated
from the mainstream of popular culture of the time in many
aspects, only research into their history would determine
this with certainty.   The craftsmen themselves were not so
much following an apprentice system but learning by
imitating and working within the family situation.   The one
or two who became more skilled became the tradition bearers
for the next generation.   They were not necessarily apprenticed to a trained craftsman, and therefore belonged more
to the folk rather than the popular tradition.

It is interesting to note that other levels of cultural communication were available to this group of craftsmen. They knew New York City, they went to New York City, they knew what was being produced there, but this knowledge does not seem to have changed the communication they had within their own community. Our current appraisal would consider them to have been behind the times in styles and fashion. Perhaps we could say they had enough "common sense" to hang on to the traditions of the past rather than to follow the ever-changing fashions of the times. Consistency is important in the example of the Dominys, because clocks made thirteen or fourteen years apart, by two different craftsmen, were almost identical. The whole concept of clock, including the case, was passed on, even though no clocks were reported made within the fifteen-year period. Still, that meaning was consistent.

Another Dominy characteristic is partial craftsmanship, which is a part of the definition of a traditional craftsman. As a farmer, each craftsman did many things, and craft happened to be one of the services that his community, at that time, particularly needed. But he could not survive in this kind of community on craft only, for the need was not that great. If he were operating in a popular level of culture, he would look at his economy and say, "I have to produce more things and get a better trade system so that I can make money and do only my craft."

Although the Dominy articles are signed, they are almost anonymous in character. Unless they were signed and dated, it would be difficult to know which was made earlier, and whether they were made by different persons, or by the same person.

It is interesting to note that even a man in the economic upper class of the community chose the local craftsman. This person probably had enough money and contact to have made any choice as far as furniture was concerned, and yet, for that aspect of his culture, he picked the local tradesman, the local craftsman. He may not have chosen the local craftsman in other items. Why did the well-to-do man come to the local craftsman, and did he do everything traditionally

in every part of his life, or was he involved in trade in a
large urban center? What other aspects of life were
traditional for that person? These are the questions the
folklorist would ask in trying to evaluate the place of the
local craftsman.

Another question relates to the ship's captain within the
community who had available to him all the outside world,
who had perceived differences, and who still selected the
local craftsman. Why did he do this even when transportation held no problem for him?

Why then did these two types of people, who should be
functioning by prediction of economics or by prediction of
being open to other cultures and who should not be on a
communication level of tradition and folk culture, still go to
the traditional craftsman in the community?

In contrast, the description of the Dunlaps of New
Hampshire seems to place them on a popular level of culture.
The community seems to have been similar in physical
isolation to that of the Dominys, but the Dunlaps seem not
to have lived in the same self-cultural isolation. Apparently
they identified with both Boston attitudes and products. The
craftsmen themselves were not really imitative of tradition.
In the discussion of them, I think the word "unique" was
used. "Unique" does not have meaning in a traditional
folk level of culture. It does, however, have a great deal of
meaning in a popular level of culture, especially in fashion
and style. The uniqueness and individual stamp of the "style
setters" implies a nontraditional approach, which is more
of a formal popular approach. The Dunlaps seem to have
based their style on the fads of Boston, but to have translated them with the eye of country cousins of New Hampshire.

Let us contrast the simple city furniture of Boston and
Philadelphia. There seems to have been some dichotomy
between Boston and its outlying communities, stemming from
a certain dynamic tension there; whereas, in Philadelphia,
according to Mrs. Nancy Goyne Evans, there was one big
happy family, or a closer-knit interchange between city and
the country. Or it may be that it was even deeper than that.
Here the theory of development of cities based on the folk

level of communication may be of significance. If a city
grows out of its traditional background and serves the
people around it on the basis of this tradition, it is more
of a folk city than one which is established as a trade-
oriented, other-side-of-the-ocean-oriented, commerce-
oriented city, only incidentally serving the poor country
cousins. It was these two orders of city development,
very likely, that constituted the differences between the
Boston and Philadelphia areas. Those in and around Philadelphia could communicate with each other from the basis
of a common traditional background. For example, there
really was not as much dichotomy in the Philadelphia area
as has been implied between the Salem and Boston areas.

Therefore, when the folklorist is asked to look at what
the decorative art historian calls "country" or "simple city"
furniture, his first reaction may be that you are confusing
the folk and popular levels of cultural communications. If
this analysis is valid, it is important to the study of the
artifact because different theoretical premises and different
methodological approaches are necessary in studying folk
and popular levels. Popular culture is time-oriented, and
it follows that time and economic history, or the time-
oriented historical approach, is primary in understanding the
popular level of culture. As popular styles and traditional
styles are diffused from their centers, opposite results
appear. On a traditional level, the original style persists
even as the style is diffused. However, as the popular
style is diffused, there is a constant interaction and change.
The people who note these changes attribute them to the
element of time, and this is true about changes in furniture.
One says, "That is a furniture style of such and such a
period in such and such a place; it originated in London,
which was the style center fifty years ago." Therefore, on
reexamining artifacts in relation to the culture that produced
them, one may find that they can be classed as "country folk"
and "country popular" and "city folk" and "city popular"
styles. Differentiating between folk and popular rather than
between country and city may give us new and clearer insights into man and his creations.

Notes

1. Agnes Halsey and Louis C. Jones, New Found Folk
Art of the Young Republic (Cooperstown, N.Y., 1960); Louis
C. Jones and Marshall B. Davidson, American Folk Art in
Fenimore House, Cooperstown (New York, 1953).
2. For a brief review of the history of the term "folklife,"
see Don Yoder, "The Folklife Studies Movement,"
Pennsylvania Folklife (Lancaster), XIII, no. 3, 43-56.
3. Sigurd Erixon, "An Introduction to Folklife Research
or Nordic Ethnology," Folk-Liv (Stockholm, 1950-51), vols.
XIV-XV.
4. For a comprehensive discussion of the history and
meanings of terms used in the folk field, see Ake Hultkrantz,
General Ethnological Concepts, International Dictionary of
Regional European Ethnology and Folklore, vol. I (Copenhagen,
1960).
5. Robert Redfield, Peasant Society and Culture: An
Anthropological Approach to Civilization (Chicago, 1956), is
one among a dozen volumes by this author dealing with
primitive societies.
6. See Pedro Martinez: A Mexican Peasant and His
Family (New York, 1964) and La Vida: A Puerto Rican Family
in the Culture of Poverty (New York, 1965), among others.
7. Lyman H. Butterfield, Leonard C. Faber, and Wendell
D. Garrett, eds., Diary and Autobiography of John Adams,
The Adams Papers, 1st ser. (Cambridge, Mass., 1961), p. xiii.
8. Don Yoder, "Schnitz in Pennsylvania Folk Culture,"
Pennsylvania Folklife, XII, no. 2, 44-53.
9. Edward T. Hall, "The Major Triad," The Silent
Language (Greenwich, Conn., 1966), chap. 4.

CONCLUSIONS

CONCLUSIONS

High Style versus Country

Montgomery: Part of the difference between the work of high-style Boston cabinetmakers and the more simple styles made by the Dunlaps may stem from the dichotomy that Bruce Buckley has discussed. Apparently there were people in New Hampshire who were both traditional-minded on the one hand and popular-minded, or fashion-conscious, on the other. The Dunlaps catered to the fashion-conscious people, in terms of the flowered ogee moldings and other ornamentations. And yet Charles Parsons showed us several things that were traditional, but old-fashioned in approach. I think that the Dunlaps met the needs of two groups of people.

Evans: I do not think that the Dunlaps were filling the needs of two different kinds of people. Rather I think they were filling the needs of people that had dual needs. They were rooted in tradition; yet they were close enough to Boston to be influenced by the popular. They wanted a little of both. They did not want to leave the traditional because it was comfortable, but they recognized and were aware of the influence coming from Boston.

Parsons: They were not necessarily limited to Boston because there were also cabinetmakers in nearby Portsmouth and Exeter. The situation becomes complex when you try to compare furniture of different areas. That is why I avoided this question of how to compare Dunlap furniture with what was made in Boston.

Of course, one of the biggest considerations was distance. For the larger pieces transportation was so difficult that New Hampshire people would perhaps accept what was made locally if it was sufficiently attractive.

One example is the interior of Colonel Robert Meade's house. He was the wealthiest man in Amherst, New Hampshire, and he had the Dunlap fireplace and room-end put in there. Had he been in Boston, he might have chosen

something else, but in Amherst he had a Dunlap. Colonel
Meade started in Amherst, gained his wealth as a merchant
in Boston, and returned to Amherst. He had seen other
things, but he accepted locally made joinery.

Communication

Mooz: Mr. Parsons pointed out that the village in which
some of the Dunlap furniture was made exerted an almost
identifiable influence, and from that basis one could first
group styles in terms of villages and then look at topographical, geographical, and cultural relationships, including
linguistics. Art historians often talk about the articulation
of ornament, and architects and painters have special vocabularies. The type of communication in popular and traditional
cultures is also important. In popular culture communication
is often written fairly prescribed, whereas in folk cultures
it is unwritten and oral with more possibilities for change
in the execution of ideas. I think another factor that we
should consider is communication between areas and how
the interchange of ideas took place.

Buckley: I agree that communication is an important factor,
especially with the survival of only 10 percent of a man's
total production. Oral tradition, however, is governed by
the community and reshaped when the tradition bearer gets
out of line. It is possible that a piece of furniture was not
really acceptable to the community, but we do not know
this today. For example, I am sure that some of the folk
potters would be aghast at the kinds of things called folk
pottery today.

Hummel: Presumably, then, Mr. Buckley infers that one
person, even in a traditional society or culture, could be
functioning at different historic time levels depending on the
situation. For example, a woman in Islip, Long Island,
wrote to Felix Dominy and said, "Mr. Dominy, would you
please to make me a neat and fine clock and tell me how
much it will cost?" That is all the letter said. He answered

her and said, "Such a clock will cost $80." There was complete understanding between them about what she wanted and what she would get for that $80.

On the other hand, Felix or Nathaniel wrote an incredibly elaborate letter to David Gardiner telling him how to set up a clock. It was a well-written letter with a few spelling mistakes, which everybody made in the eighteenth century, and is still understandable today. In terms of that letter or communication, the writer was using a more popular level of communication. So I still believe that we need some more regional or specific studies before drawing generalizations.

Local Customs

Hummel: For further insight into local customs, I refer again to the very astute Timothy Dwight. He was president of Yale University from 1795 to 1817, and presumably knew what was going on not only in Connecticut but in the rest of the country. When he visited East Hampton, he talked about customs and social character as being regulated by the long-continued customs of this single spot rather than by the mutable, changeable, beautiful fashions of a great city. He spoke of the powerful influence of an extensive country, intimately connected in its parts and controlling by general opinion and practice the personal conduct of every inhabitant.

If you really want to answer that question about the Dunlaps, you would probably have to find out how economically dependent the people in that area were upon Boston, what they thought about Boston, and what Bostonians thought about them.

Survival

Another thing that should concern us in these analyses is the factor of survival, which Mr. Buckley has mentioned, and the percentages with which we are dealing. I have located about 10 percent of the Dominys' total output, so my judgment is based on 10 percent. I do not know what

a statistician would say about the reliability of a generali-
zation based on a 10 percent sampling. I suspect that you
could also calculate a percentage figure for the Dunlaps,
but we should keep in mind that we are dealing with
samplings and not the whole range. The whole range is not
available to us.

Garrett: It is surprising how few chairs remain from the
number that must have been turned out in the many chair
factories that existed in pre-1860 New England. I do not
think they were moved up into the attic and thrown out as
soon as we may have thought. For example, a large
collection of late nineteenth-century Boston interior
photographs taken in the Victorian period are now at the
Boston Athenaeum. They show slat-backed chairs in the
studies, libraries, and parlors of Boston homes. Even
pre-1900, cultivated, Beacon Street Bostonians would
absorb and juxtapose overstuffed furniture with slat-backed
chairs. It may be that more survive and are just waiting
to be recognized, codified, and studied. Mr. Parsons
says that no one has made a search in Portsmouth, and
this is probably true of many small towns and cities.

Artisan Mannerism or Country Style

Montgomery: Mr. Garrett has used the term "artisan
mannerism" which seems to me a better description of the
droopy pendants at the corners of the legs, the attenuation
of the legs, and the curious pediments on the Dunlap
furniture than the term "country furniture."

Garrett: The manneristic touch or artisan individuality
of the Dunlap furniture does seem a better explanation of
the exaggerated style characteristics than the simple
mathematics of distance from cultural centers.

Shepherd: In labeling furniture as country or city
furniture, we might consider the work of William Savery,
who made both very plain and very sophisticated styles.

It was the taste of the clientele, then, that decided his style rather than the locality of its manufacture.

Evans: This is true of the Philadelphia area. You have two types of furniture being made in the same area to satisfy various needs.

Montgomery: I believe the distinguishing ingredient is artisan mannerism. I do not believe you would get these exaggerations in furniture produced in a city. Mr. Buckley, do you think there would be a strong enough traditional culture in the city to promote artisan mannerism?

Buckley: In the twentieth century, yes; but whether you can project this back historically, I do not know. From our field work in the city today, we find as much tradition based in the city as there is in rural areas.

Montgomery: But is there the introduction of artisan mannerism in cities, if we accept that term, or "exaggeration," if you will?

Buckley: You are looking at it from a technical-cultural level, and saying this is an exaggeration. My question would be whether they looked upon this as exaggeration.

Hummel: I would hesitate to say you would never find artisan mannerism in the city. It is quite possible you might, but again you are dealing with survival. I wonder if survival in the city is the same as in a rural area like the one in which the Dominys worked. Is it an accident that the four best clocks they made have survived? In between there is a whole range of clocks which are gone. I do not know where they are. Then you reach a certain price level, and these survive, seemingly in abundance. But is only the best-made furniture surviving?

La Fond: I think one problem we may never solve is whose taste produced the rural or simple furniture. For instance, did the cabinetmaker produce only what pleased himself or did he work to please his neighbors and customers who were paying the bills?

But is it likely that the style of each individual area was conditioned by individual circumstances? For example, if the Dunlaps, with their skills--and they definitely were extremely skilled craftsmen--had turned up in Chester County, what would have been the result? I think that certain areas were more likely to produce certain things. Possibly, through analysis of folk culture, we may be able to discover likelihoods for furniture whose individualisms have baffled us.

Popular or Folk

Buckley: Perhaps the terms "popular" and "folk" can be clarified in terms of an object. In his new book, Patterns of Folk Culture in the Eastern United States, Henry Vase cites the banjo. The banjo probably originating in Africa, developed into the so-called five-string banjo with certain stylistic or form characteristics: it is a very small drum covered with the skin of a local animal and it has no frets. In contrast, the four-string banjo, a product of popular culture used during the blackface minstrel days, is a fretted instrument with a large head, a tightly stretched drum, four strings instead of five, and completely different musical characteristics. The second banjo is an object of popular culture; the first banjo is a product of folk culture. Both have the same origin.

Folk Idea and Classical Proportions

Buckley: I think that in the same way that pattern books, based on the academic, classical background, form the basis of the popular order, the oral tradition is the basis for folk art.

Forman: From my point of view, the origin of classical architectural proportions in furniture rises from the dual

nature of the joiner in the seventeenth century as both
furniture maker and interior woodworker: his architectural
training is reflected in the furniture. This is borne out in
Batty Langley's City and Country Builder's Treasury (1740),
in which he states that not one cabinetmaker in fifty is able
to make a bookcase indispensably true, according to any
of the five orders, without having a joiner to set out
the work for him.

Buckley: Through time the classical may have become part
of the traditional, but the people looked at it as "the way
it had always been done," rather than as part of the
classical tradition.

Hummel: I am in complete agreement with Mr. Buckley.
I find without question that the Dominys are traditional
craftsmen. Apparently one of the children in each generation
was chosen to pass on traditional ideas. John Lyon
Gardiner did patronize local craftsmen. Apparently he did
not buy his silver in New York City; he went to Elias
Pelletreau in Southampton, which was in the same regional
area and had the same tradition. But John Lyon Gardiner
was also conscious of, and had, outside contacts. He had
bookplates, for example, done by Paul Revere. He was
aware of what was going on elsewhere.

Future Studies

Gilborn: What generalizations can be drawn to establish
a model for future studies of what we have labeled country
cabinetwork and simple city furniture?
     Mr. Buckley gave us the concept of popular and folk
culture as an influence in style. Mr. Garrett prefers the
term "artisan mannerism" to denote an indigenous American
style, and he feels that the furniture styles were more a
result of "materials, skills, economics, and demography"
than of origin in city and country. Is there a specific
single model that would summarize our collected
findings?

<u>Mooz:</u>   I agree with historian Michael Kraus that today's researchers should be able to project themselves back into the society of their interest; should be able to walk into a coffeehouse or other public institution and talk to people without being considered an outsider. If a generalization is to be drawn, it would be to use every one of the techniques and methods discussed without looking for one model alone to explain traditional, popular, or folk furniture as opposed to the presence of artisan mannerism in furniture.

I do not think that we will ever find a broad general approach that will make uniform what has happened all over the country in terms of furniture production. I think we have to study it in individual units.

<u>Fleming:</u>   Both Mr. Garrett and Mr. Mooz have urged the same approach; Garrett, in terms of his periodization, advocates taking small periods of fifteen and twenty-five years and zeroing in on them; Mooz, in terms of the historical circumstances of the place or origin, believes you should get right down to local and specific cases.

Following up Craig Gilborn's point on generalizations or models, I would like to ask for conclusions on the use of the rural-urban division with which we began. To what extent is it useful to retain the rural-urban terms, either in supplement to or in place of the popular or the folk, or of anything else?

<u>Forman:</u>   There is another aspect that may be more basic, and that is the concentric-circle idea or concept. Starting with London as the style setter, and with Philadelphia as a regional style center, there is radiation on out into rural areas, with consequent changes. Do the many points of view which have been presented here leave this concept intact?

<u>Buckley:</u>   If you are talking about the folk level of culture, then one type of wave-diffusion pattern takes place. If you are talking about popular culture, I think style

diffuses in the concentric-circle manner.

Montgomery: I agree that it would require careful and
exact analysis of individual cases to know whether you
were dealing with a popular level, a folk level, or a
traditional level. It would take a lot more of the kind of
study that Charles Hummel has done, or of the documentation
done by Charles Parsons, to separate them.

Fleming: Perhaps our country furniture should be divided
into two groups: one group well proportioned and well
constructed as to dovetails and other details and the other
less well constructed and conceived. The first group could
be called plain or ornamented; the second group, country,
if we must keep this term.
       I am reminded of Peter Manigault's remark to his London
agent on ordering furniture about 1770, "The plainer the
better so that they are fashionable."

Forman: I do not think there is necessarily any correlation
between the degree of finish or quality of craftsmanship
and the imagination shown in decoration. The Van Pelt
highboy, for example, is not necessarily a better work of
art than one of the Dunlap pieces.

Montgomery: I agree. Without question, we can continue
and will continue to discuss the subject of country furniture
for a long time to come. During the past two days, we
have heard detailed reports by Benno Forman, Charles
Hummel, Nancy Evans, and Charles Parsons on representative makers of country furniture, and we have been shown
in slides and in the exhibition in the Rotunda the character
of the product of country furniture makers. We have heard
explanations of culture transfer and of transmission of
ideas of form both from generation to generation and from
London to Boston to New Hampshire, or from London to
Philadelphia to Chester County.
       From these studies it is apparent that many, many
variables are involved. The ideas invoked by the term

"country" are not precise. The kinds of people who lived in the country varied. "Country" has not one but numerous meanings. Country people may have bought the bulk of their furniture custom-made from local craftsmen, but they also bought furniture from several other sources--on direct order from city craftsmen or city merchants or from country merchants who bought their stocks from both country and city artisans. Sometimes articles from the latter were assembled or decorated after arriving in the country.

Even furniture produced by country craftsmen was subject to wide variation because the training and backgrounds of country artisans varied greatly. Some, after training by cabinetmakers in the city, set up shop in the country. Others, after serving apprenticeships under cabinetmakers in the country, continued to work there. Others, trained by carpenters, made furniture as well as built houses in the country. Still others were self-taught without formal training. For these reasons, furniture used in the country is not one kind of furniture but many kinds of furniture. Country furniture is a confusing term. If we are to continue to use it, I think we must agree on its definition. I propose that we restrict the use of the term to furniture actually made in small towns and rural areas. That is, in fact, what most of us picture in our minds when we hear the term.

Peter Mooz has suggested that it may be, and probably is, impossible to find a broad approach that will provide generalizations for the furniture used in rural areas all over the country, that is to say, the North American continent, from the time of first settlement up to 1850. He advocates case studies of country furniture on a piece-by-piece and maker-by-maker basis to gather evidence of "individual units" from which explanations of a more specific nature may be deduced.

Mr. Buckley's suggestion of differentiating and exploring furniture according to the approaches of the folk culturist is an exciting one with great promise. But as he made clear it will not be a simple plan to carry out. He foresees the necessity of a great deal of systematic exploration before

one can isolate and explain the two strains, the popular
and the folk in furniture, or just how much these particular
strains in furniture are indebted to the high-style furniture
sometimes referred to as "academic furniture."

Much of the furniture we have been exploring may vary
in the quality of its craftsmanship and the degree of its
individuality, but often it seems to reflect an elusive
something that I believe is aptly described by Mr. Garrett's
term "artisan mannerism." That term appeals to me. It
sounds like art. And, as we close this conference, I
think we can agree that more than a little of this country
furniture is art.

No. 1 on the Check List of Furniture exhibited during the conference. Cabinet, possibly made by James Symonds for Thomas and Sarah Buffington ? , Salem, Massachusetts, 1676. Red oak, red cedar, soft maple. H. 17¼"; W. 17"; D. 9 7/8". Winterthur Museum (58.526)

COUNTRY FURNITURE--AS ADVERTISED

The following quotations from advertisements in nineteenth-
century newspapers are a by-product of research done in the
office of Charles F. Montgomery by a student-assistant,
Elaine Lees. We publish them because we think they enlighten
several aspects of this subject. Ed.

Few people in the "Towns and Parishes adjacent" to
Middletown, Connecticut,[1] regarded country furniture "made
and ornamented in the newest fashion and best manner"[2] "at
the old Stand in the Main-street on the corner"[3] as only
"middling and common."[4] Some of them, however, resisted
the claim that it was "of the same quality as can be purchased
in the city of New York, or elsewhere."[5] Nevertheless,
country cabinetmakers promised that "All orders"[6] would be
"executed with promptness and in a workmanlike manner"[7] and
that "all kinds of Cabinet work from the Cradle to the Coffin"[8]
would be manufactured "to order on short notice"[9] and that
"furniture needing repair will receive immediate attention."[10]
One cabinetmaker offered to "receive salt and whiskey, in
exchange for his work,"[11] and everyone could be "most advan-
tageously accommodated for cash or short credit"[12] or for
"Lumber and most kinds of Produce."[13] Samuel M. Dockum of
Portsmouth, New Hampshire, who "purchased 900 unpainted
Chairs (from Boston?)"[14] did "not hesitate to say they are the
best article ever offered for sale in this market."[15]
In 1825, Rand and Abbott of Bedford, New Hampshire, announced "A GOOD CHANCE FOR A MECHANIC"[16] and offered
the public "a complete set of Cabinetmaker's Tools, with two
good Turning Lathes, Circular Saw, ¢c. &c."[17] and "a large
and convenient shop"[18] located on "a good stream of never
failing water...about one and half miles below Piscataquog
Village in Bedford, N.H. near Merrimack river"[19] from which
"furniture may be easily and very cheaply transported to
Boston by water."[20]
Westward, William E. Willis of Erie, Pennsylvania, sold
"Chairs, or any other work in his line done to order, on short
notice"[21] and stated flatly that "if people think they cannot

get work done here like which comes from the east, where
they boast of getting it cheap, let them fetch a sample and
pay me the cash, and if I do not make my work as good and
as cheap, I will not charge a cent for it."[22] He added "N.B.
I will always have the latest fashions."[23]

A few years later, Ashley and Williston of Syracuse, New
York, offered "Cane, Flag and Woodseat Chairs, of our own
manufacutre, warranted good; also Boston Rocking and Sewing
chairs, ditto, besides a small lot of Eeastern (sic) manufacture,
which will be sold VERY CHEAP to get rid of them."[24]

1. Elizur Barns, _Middlesex Gazette,_ Middletown,
Connecticut, June 23, 1808.

2. James B. Chapman, John B. Merrit, _Connecticut Herald,_
New Haven, Connecticut, April 18, 1809.

3. See No. 1.

4. Albert J. Steele, _New Haven Palladium,_ New Haven,
Connecticut, October 9, 1841.

5. Blair and Bowditch, _New Haven Palladium,_ March 30,
1830.

6,7. Jones and Durfee, _Calhoon County Patriot,_ Marshall,
Michigan, January 20, 1838.

8. See No. 2.

9. Leonard Whitney, William P. Derby, _Niles Gazette,_
Niles, Michigan, July 19, 1837.

10. See No. 6.

11. Elijah Mock, _Western Monitor & Boonslick Correspon-
dent,_ Fayette, Missouri, March 15, 1828.

12. F. W. Bushnell, _Norwich Courier,_ Norwich, Connecticut, January 28, 1824.

13. Thomas Thompson, _Trumansburg Advertiser,_ Trumans-
burg, New York, February 1, 1837.

14, 15. Samuel M. Dockum, _Portsmouth Journal,_ Portsmouth,
New Hampshire, January 1, 1835.

16, 17, 18, 19, 20. Rand & Abbott, _New Hampshire Patriot,_
Bedford, New Hampshire, October 15, 1825.

21, 22, 23. William E. Willis, _Erie Observer,_ Erie, Pennsylvania, April 20, 1833.

24. Ashley & Williston, _Syracuse Weekly Journal,_
Syracuse, New York, May 14, 1851.

No. 6 on the Check List of Furniture exhibited during
the conference. Chest on frame, maker unknown. Cabinet section, Ipswich, Mass., 1690 (?)-1708, walnut.
H. 44½"; W. 22¼"; D. 13 3/4". Frame section, Boston
or Roxbury, 1727-1728, walnut, white pine. Winterthur
Museum (57.1111)

CONSERVATION OF FURNITURE

INTRODUCTION

THEORIES about furniture care are as varied as the numerous waxes, varnishes, oils, and miracle polishes currently on the market. Insofar as a systematic study is concerned, this is a neglected area that needs a great deal of basic research. Considerable knowledge on fixing furniture and making it look good exists among craftsmen. But this is shop knowledge, passed on from one craftsman to another through seeing and doing. Few craftsmen, however, have the opportunity to assess their work and materials against long periods of aging and wear. Consequently, expedient treatment, dependent on shop knowledge, is generally the fate of most furniture.

Considering furniture as works of art, museum personnel make every effort to diagnose and treat wooden objects with special regard to the following conservation guidelines:

1. Treatment should take into account all the various materials of the object and should increase the lifetime and stability of all its components.

2. Materials used in conservation should be reversible. Whatever is "done" should permit "undoing" at some future date--without damage to the original parts of the object.

3. Thorough written and pictorial records of conservation and restoration work should be kept.

4. While restoration of losses is sometimes made to confuse the eye and persuade the casual viewer that losses or damage are minimal, the intent of restoration is basically to unify a damaged object rather than to deceive the viewer.

Many more conservation guidelines could be cited, but these few should suffice for a beginning. Practitioners are only now more fully realizing the complexity of reactions between various materials used in making furniture--the shrinkage of wood and relationships between glues, fillers, stains, gesso, size, and so forth. Since we could not hope to cover all furniture conservation problems in a day, we somewhat arbitrarily decided to restrict our discussion to films, varnishes, paints, and other surfacing agents that are easily altered or destroyed.

The panel membership was selected on the strength of experience and interest in the problems of furniture conservation. But since we are still trying to solve basic problems in furniture care, whatever was said cannot be considered definitive. Our session was extemporaneous. More thorough information on the subjects covered may be found in various writings about conservation, for while our intentions were good, we could not possibly be as exact or as informative as we would have liked to be in the short time allowed for discussion. Everyone involved with the care of art objects should be thoroughly familiar with that excellent publication <u>Studies in Conservation</u>, which is the journal of the International Institute of Conservation, and Dr. Harold J. Plenderleith's book <u>Conservation of Antiquities and Works of Art</u>. To direct the beginner in conservation, a list of selected works in the Winterthur Library are appended.

The first problem is really a moral one. How far should we go in trying to restore an object to what we believe was its original appearance, fully aware that in so doing we may unconsciously be imposing our twentieth-century values and taste?

Jonathan L. Fairbanks

PRESERVATION OR RESTORATION

The Moral Question

Forman: To what extent is the preservation or restoration of antique furniture a moral question? The museum curator or historian is interested in seeing the piece in its original finish and as it was originally made. He wishes to preserve evidence of previous finishes, and therefore to use no treatment that is irreversible. His aim is to discover the truth, in as minute detail as possible, about how the cabinetmakers of the time worked, what were the materials and the methods they used, and then to conserve each piece according to documented proof. It is a question of adhering to historic fact rather than of imposing twentieth-century values and taste. Although a museum cannot tell a private collector or a dealer what he has to do, it can set the standards and act as a source of information. The collector or dealer is free to restore a piece the way he wants it to look.

Penn: The historian's impulse is to put his knowledge into practical application, but this is not always the solution we use today. First of all, the materials available to the cabinet-maker of days gone by have, in some instances, been replaced by superior materials. Nothing is used today that can be guaranteed to be the same as what was being used in the seventeenth- and eighteenth-century finishes, which were particularly suited to the furniture made at that time. Let us assume that there was exact color balancing of the parts of a chair. Some parts would require bleaching and others darkening. In addition to stain, a dyed varnish may have been necessary to achieve the desired color combination. The part was made spotless by staining and filling the pores with stain. Many coats of finish were applied until the surface resembled a sparkling sheet of glass. The patination sought today may be completely different from what cabinetmakers were trying to achieve in the eighteenth century.

<u>Fairbanks</u>: In cleaning old varnish from a piece of furniture, we must be aware that we are probably involved with more than a single simple layer when we take off the alligatored surface. But a surface that destroys the original beauty of the furniture should be removed. There is nothing sacred about an old layer of dammar or shellac or varnish which is completely disintegrated and is no longer visually pleasing. If the piece is of museum quality, it is suggested that, for analysis or identification purposes, one could bottle and save the material removed and keep a record of what was done. So-called reflow cleaning is not a wise practice. It only invites trouble to reapply the dissolved material because the same discoloring, checking, and alligatoring will probably happen again.

<u>Forman</u>: It is my impression that much of the alligatoring which we see today on eighteenth-century furniture represents a subsequent refinishing job done in the nineteenth or twentieth century without first removing the waxes, oils, and other materials used in treating furniture in the home through the years. The later varnish could not bind to these substances and must have begun to alligator almost immediately.

Identification of Finish

<u>Melody</u>: Identifying the finish can be done by a rule-of-thumb method. If it checks in rectangles, it is probably lacquer; if it puddles and has a reddish brown behind it, shellac is indicated. Varnishes tend to crack in squares. Linseed oil is apt to grow hard and horny because the small molecules form larger molecules. Wax may whiten after a number of years especially in the lines of a carved piece where it could not easily be polished, but wax is readily removable.

<u>Barr</u>: Although it is almost impossible to identify original formulas in finishes, it is possible to classify modern finishes in terms of major function groups and to date the finish or to make a reasonable prediction about the authenticity of the finish. The inorganic constituents in finishes are more readily identifiable than the organic. Any finish is made up of a

number of ingredients, and each ingredient was chosen to provide some necessary function not covered by the other ingredients. For example, a plasticizer is necessary in some finishes,
but it may cause yellowing. Yellowing, among other unde-
sirable results of some finish formulas, is to be avoided in any
case.

Why A Removable Finish?

Barr: A removable finish, one that does not penetrate or cause
changes in the wood, is preferable to a nonremovable one because the original finish can be more easily determined and
preserved in the manner in which it was created. Such a finish also facilitates future refinishing.

Forman: Since furniture in a museum is not subject to wear and
abrasion, as it is when in everyday use, there is no reason
why a contemporary finish cannot combine (1) removability,
(2) protection of the surface, and (3) the desired optical qualities. The answer to protection, however, seems to reside less
in finish and more in temperature and humidity controls within
a museum. The desired optical qualities are quite a different
problem. Should the object look as it did the day it left the
shop or should it look old and patinated? In short, is the museum a repository of recreated historical fact or is it a place
to which an audience comes for an aesthetic experience?

Solvents

Jayne: The type of solvent to be used in removing a finish
is determined by the finish you wish to remove. A solvent's
strength is in direct relation to the material it is to dissolve.
For example, turpentine removes beeswax, but acetone, which
is usually called a stronger solvent, does not. It is best then
to say that a given solvent is a strong solvent of a particular
material. Our way of testing is simple. We start with water
on a small Q tip.
     Xylene can be tried next. It is better than turpentine in
that it has no resins, which might possibly tend to discolor.
However, it may not remove anything except wax.

Toluene and diacetone probably will not remove wax. They
have proved effective on shellac or dammar but not on copal.

Acetone is volatile and cleans quickly without dissolving
the surface beneath. Yet it does not dissolve beeswax.

Morpholine or dimethylformamide are called eaters or
destroyers because they break down a surface. Sometimes
they are required when weaker substances have failed.

As is apparent, finishes are still removed by rule of thumb
or by trial and error rather than by absolute scientific proce-
dures for each individual case.

TRADITIONAL FINISHES

Linseed Oil

Candee: Would linseed oil be objectionable because it is
basically an acid and tends to darken the wood? Is that intended to heighten the patina?

Jayne: Although no finish has surpassed linseed oil in
pleasing visual quality, it cures or polymerizes, and will not
redissolve in any known solvent.

Application

Fairbanks: An important consideration in choosing any material is the method of application. Reservations about linseed
oil can be somewhat modified if the oil is wiped off thoroughly
so that only a thin film remains. It should never be applied in
quantity and left on in thick layers. Linseed oil will turn paint
and goldleaf ornament dark. It is difficult to remove without
removing whatever is below. For this reason painted and gold-
leafed furniture should not be oiled, nor should a gessoed
piece.

Jayne: I like to think of a finish as a protective window that
leaves the pattern of the wood clearly visible. The best
finish is one that can be removed with a very light solvent that
attacks that finish and no other. As a painting restorer, I can
say that the surface of a painting protected by linseed oil cannot be easily cleaned without damage to the work itself. While
linseed oil does have a tendency to yellow with age, it remains
consistent with the lights and darks in the colors of the painting.

Lemon Oil

Barr: The modern lemon oil is reconstituted and probably will
not darken with age as easily as natural lemon oil because
impurities which tend to darken with age are removed.

Castor Oil

Barr: Castor oil is mainly a saturated oil, has no double bond, and therefore has very little reactivity. It is a long-lasting, nondrying oil which does not form a polymer. It is soluble in a wide variety of solvents and therefore removable. Knowledge of the chemistry of these finishes enables one to predict what is likely to be removable; it will save a lot of time in testing.

Shellac

Melody: We have not yet come up with a finish that is perfect for every case. I rely on shellac for most of my touch-up jobs. It is easily removed. The general tendency is to use white shellac, but the choice depends on the object and on whether you are trying to maintain a certain color. Orange shellac can darken a white wood, for instance, more than white shellac does.

Lacquer

Jayne: A lacquered surface by its very nature is hard to re-pair. Even visually, it is shiny like glass. There are very few things that will cause glass to adhere to glass. When there is peeling, it is difficult to create a tooth underneath that will make the lacquer stick. You can put a liquid adhesive under-neath and press the lacquer down and keep it there for two months and when you take the weight off, it may pop up again. If all of the lacquer is removed and the piece is sanded down to the original coat, and if the back side of the lacquer is sanded and readhered to this newly created support, then the traditional materials inside are lost, but the surface is preserved.

The memory of lacquer is like a steel spring. Once it has begun to curl it wants to stay that way. The molecules have taken a new form in the curling, and that is the way they want to stay. A damp cloth cannot be used to clean a lacquer sur-face because the lacquer may be adhering to a paper or a fragile ground, and any loss of size on that paper would cause peeling. Lacquer is impervious to most solvents.

Fairbanks: Ordinary household Renusit is sometimes useful in cleaning and restoring a shiny luster to lacquer.

Melody: For readhering lacquer to its backing board, some
persons have suggested building a box to contain the entire
item and putting a monomer material in by pressure. When
the pressure is sufficient, it should be treated by radiation,
which would cause the monomer to harden suddenly and then
everything would adhere.

Montgomery: In trying to restore a lacquered piece for my own
use, I tried putting epoxy glue underneath and heating the re-
applied lacquer with an iron. The heat had to be sufficiently
controlled not to burn the surface, but the lacquer did adhere
even though I was dealing with a very difficult crazed surface.
Heat is effective, but too high a temperature causes the
lacquer to crumble.

Japanning

Fairbanks: The finish on the Pim highboy at Winterthur is an
example of a japanned surface. Made in Boston about 1750, its
finish is an imitation of lacquer with paint, gesso, gold leaf,
and simulated tortoise shell. It has been badly touched up
with paint in several areas and is a major conservation problem because of the many different materials involved. A
good preventive measure for japanned surfaces that have gesso
dropping off is control of the humidity. There is no easy practical solution for this at Winterthur right now, because the
50 percent relative humidity that we try to maintain for other
objects is too low for the Pim highboy.

Varnish

Fairbanks: There are two basic groups of varnishes: spirit
and oil. A spirit varnish is dry to the touch when the solvent
evaporates, while an oil varnish cures slowly and hardens as
linseed oil does.

Penn: Some varnishes set up a partial vapor or gas barrier,
making it more difficult for air, which has a continuous oxidizing effect on wood or metal, and water to get through the finish
into the wood. A varnished chair may show a network of veins
or traction tracks where the finish layer is split. Air gets
through more readily at this spot, oxidizing the wood beneath
it.

Wax

Melody: Butcher's wax, which contains carnauba, is easily
removable, and gives a pleasing optical effect. I have waxed
many different objects with Butcher's wax. Simoniz is sometimes used, but this contains silicone, which can be abrasive
in a polishing agent and which hardens in time. Products whose
contents are unknown should not be used.

We are leaning more and more toward waxes, although we
have not given up the use of linseed oil entirely. We are
running tests on it. I am a firm believer in linseed oil. I was
trained to use it and, to me, it is an impossible finish to beat.

Fairbanks: As has been pointed out, linseed oil should not be
used on painted furniture if you want to save the natural appearance of the paint. It darkens the wood at the same time that it
heightens the patina. It must not be used on gold leaf or on
gessoed pieces.

One material useful in cleansing and surfacing painted
furniture is a wax called Renaissance, produced by Picreator
Enterprises, Ltd., 44 Park View Gardens, Hendon, London
NW 4, England. We are not as yet recommending it, but we
are running tests with it and have found it satisfactory for many
jobs.

Linseed Oil, Vinegar, Turpentine Emulsion

Fairbanks: In answering a question from the audience regarding the oil-vinegar-turpentine (in equal parts) formula, I repeat
that much of the value of this formula depends upon its application; how you use it and how much you wipe off. This formula

is no longer in general use at Winterthur, and while we have
not yet developed an ideal finish with a broad range of uses,
a likely candidate is a wax formulation dissolved in spirits.

Melody: Timothy Jayne has said, in connection with linseed
oil, that you put on three parts and you wipe off six parts. I
think that covers the situation beautifully. Not everyone un-
derstands this when they are applying linseed oil. I never like
the use of vinegar in an oil treatment. I omit the vinegar and
make use of raw linseed oil cut in half with turpentine. I
then use boiled oil over this for a second treatment.

Binders, Adhesives, Media

Jayne: As a painting restorer talking about painted furniture,
I think of binders or adhesives as sticky, wet materials, to
which some colored powder is added, to be applied as a protective film. Probably every sticky material has been used to
color something at some time, and the ones that are still in use
are those easily cleaned and artistically worthy of use or
aesthetically pleasing. Thousands, including lacquer, shellac,
gum arabic, linseed oil, sugar, molasses, and honey, have been
used.

Egg

Jayne: The egg was a favorite binder among early Flemish and
Italian painters. They found that water could be added to the
egg and still leave the media intact, but after a time the painting done with egg media was not really soluble in water. Time
has proved egg a medium of great endurance and of clarity which
makes us marvel when we stand in front of an early Flemish
painting or manuscript.

Gum

Jayne: Another natural binder is the gum from trees. Alone,
it remains somewhat soluble, but it soon becomes brittle, dis-
colors, and shines. Another defect is poor longevity. However,

gum dissolved in a mild spirit and then applied to a picture
surface becomes a protective barrier easily removable with
solvents, and it presents no danger to the painted surface.
Dammar, mastic, and copal gum are used by the artist in painting and by the furniture maker. Gum arabic is another medium
important to the painter, although it remains soluble in water and
and is easily damaged. Someone believing it to be washable
like egg may wash it away; it may also be severely injured by
moisture in the air.

AW2

Montgomery: With what can you treat a painted and decorated
surface to bring out the luster, to preserve it? Specifically, I
am thinking of a painted Baltimore tier table with glit decoration. It has pigment coming to the surface, and it is chalking
so that it has lost its original luster and glow. None of the
natural grain is showing.

Jayne: If the piece of furniture is not going to be used, you
could use AW2 varnish to give a very glittery and shiny surface. AW2 is easily removed and gives a nice color. It will,
however, darken. Shellac, preferably white, could be used,
but it also would age in time. As long as the painted decoration is insoluble to acetone alcohol, you could then remove
superficial layers of shellac, dammar, or AW2 with acetone
alcohol.

Comparative Aging

Barr: I have conducted some experiments in accelerated
weathering for the purpose of establishing a standard for the
prediction of the aging of different finishes. Wood panels
were painted both with the old, familiar dammar, mastic, copal,
and linseed finishes and with some modern, synthetic ones.
Sections of each panel were exposed to intense ultraviolet light
for 300 hours, other sections for 800 hours. The latter is
roughly equivalent to 100 years for a piece of furniture under
normal conditions of museum lighting. Linseed showed

considerable darkening at 800 hours, while the modern urethane
darkened but slightly. Carnauba, or Butcher's wax, did not
darken although the uncoated wood bleached or lightened. The
nitrocellulose finish, in use since 1920, did not darken. Beeswax darkened slightly, and copal to a greater degree. Modern
nitrocellulose finishes are generally free of the impurities which
tended to cause darkening when such finishes were applied
twenty years or more ago.

Penn: With a relatively pure wax we would not expect to see
much checking or cracking, even after a hundred years. Such
a wax would be a finish superior to the initial polymer, which
would crack easily. It is almost impossible to achieve an
impermeable film or to stop the wood from breathing. Moisture does get through even plastic and polymers. It is impossible to stop it.

Original Finish

Forman: Much of the discussion at this seminar has
centered around the phrase "original finish," but there are
several reasons why the phrase is misleading. I dare say
that there are not a dozen early chairs or high chests in
American museums which have their original finish on them
unless they are painted examples whose finish has been
preserved under subsequent layers of paint. Research into
the articles that were in colonial cabinetmakers' shops and
investigation of shop practices, indicates that several
kinds of finishes were available to customers. These
finishes ranged from a quick lick and a promise of shellac or
varnish to a hand-rubbed finish with oil pressed from the meat
of walnuts. It is obvious, however, that the latter treatment
would cost several times as much as the former because of
the amount of time involved in applying it. The hand treatment
would be enhanced over the years by successive applications
of beeswax. The shellac or varnish finish could stand up
to more than a half century's worth of wear and abrasion.
Very likely pieces done with shellac or varnish have been
refinished several times since the eighteenth century.

TODAY'S POLYMERS

<u>Barr:</u>   It would seem unwise to continue to use unsatisfactory traditional finishes when, through testing, a suitable new finish that is quite stable chemically over hundreds of years may be found. The new ones we have been experimenting with are synthetic polymers. A polymer can be a naturally occurring or a synthetic chemical compound formed by the joining of small molecules or much larger ones or the union of two monomers. The complexity of modern polymer or resin chemistry and the thousands of types of synthetic resins already known have produced commercial finishes for nearly every conceivable use. In general, the three basic classes of resins applicable to restoration uses are the natural ones: dammar, copal, and mastic; the natural resins modified by chemical process to produce new resins with new properties for new uses; and the synthetic polymers or mixtures of synthetic polymers which also have new and individual properties. The process of modifying natural resins is so simple that it could have been done centuries ago.

Nitrocellulose

<u>Barr:</u>   Nitrocellulose, which did not show age in my accelerated exposure experiments, is made from cotton or wood into a highly purified nitrate, and it is because of its purity that it does not darken on exposure to ultraviolet. It does not harden or react and probably would not polymerize further; hence it should be removable even after several hundred years. Therefore, a modern, commercial nitrocellulose-based finish of good quality should offer good protection, ease of application, stability against discoloration, and removability with relatively mild solvents.

<u>Fairbanks:</u>   We are experimenting with these things, but not yet recommending them. Back in 1926, a little book called <u>Furniture Yesterday and Tomorrow</u> stated that the nitrocellulose-base material for finishing furniture represented a radical change not only in materials used but in durability obtained.

Conservators, generally speaking, have shied away from considering nitrocellulose for furniture care, but we are testing
it.

Barr: I would like to have at least the minimum kind of protection you get with something like nitrocellulose, and there
are finishes which are far superior to this in hardness and in
protective quality. All of these have good optical properties
and can be removed if you make a mistake in applying them.
Most modern finishes, however, are "cross-linked" and therefore not suitable for museum use.

Cross-linked Polymers

Barr: Cross-linking, a process wherein polymer chains are
tied together to form an insoluble material such as the poly-
urethane class of finishes, provides a good "marine" finish.
Urethan-based finishes are the extremely hard, impermeable
finishes needed on boats. Because they must be broken off
mechanically, they are not suitable for museum use.

Linear Polymers

Barr: Linear polymers are those with a long chain of molecules
in the same pattern. Polyethylene glycol is an example of a
linear polymer, and its advantage is that, like nitrocellulose,
it can be removed easily with a variety of solvents. In general
such linear polymers are suitable for museum use. As for specific new finishes that should be avoided, the only way to
avoid danger is to read the label. Most lacquers and varnishes
have labels that explain the nature of the chemicals used, and
you are usually safe with the products of reputable manufac-
turers. One may, however, consult a chemist, a curator, or a
conservator with specific questions on specific objects.

SUMMARY

Barr: In summary, what, after all, is the purpose of a finish?
It should give the wood a sheen or a gloss that is optically
pleasing or reproduce the aesthetics of the original finish. But
it should also preserve without being impossible to remove.
Polymer finishes can be considered as binders, filling up pores,
strengthening both the surface and the wood in depth. Nitrocellulose finishes applied commercially are made to stay on
the surface and to give a high sheen. It is an easy finish to
apply at the factory by spraying and is inexpensive. Little is
lost as little soaks in; therefore, it is not effective protection
from abrasion. Urethane, for example, is a finish that soaks
in, cures chemically, gives a harder finish than nitrocellulose,
and can be applied by spray or brush; but it cannot be removed
easily.
    Finishes have different degrees of impermeability. Some
natural finishes crack easily and become checkered; hence they
are not much of a barrier to moisture. But if a relatively pure
wax is used as a finish, little checking or cracking would be
expected, even after a hundred years. Wax can be made to stay
on the surface if it is properly formulated and applied. Therefore, a special wax formulation may be a superior finish for
conservation in museums because abrasion resistance is not a
primary requirement for museum use. The film left by the finish will probably affect the aesthetic aspect of an object. A
finish can, however, be formulated to match the appearance of
weathered surfaces and prevent further deterioration.
    I believe that from a linear polymer resin or a wax or both
can be formulated a finish for museum use which will give only
limited abrasion protection but will provide impermeability to
harmful vapor. In addition, such a finish should not show age,
such as color changes, cracking, and the like, and it should
be capable of giving the curator just the degree of gloss he
wants to match an existing finish or a period. Still other characteristics which I won't name are desirable in an ideal museum
finish. Such a finish has not yet been produced, but continued
scientific experimentation at Winterthur will, we hope, produce
an ideal finish for protective use.

GLOSSARY

Acetone: "a solvent which dissolves synthetic resins, natural soft resins, and certain waxes; and shellac to more than 80 percent."--Gettens and Stout, Painting Materials

AW2: Polycyclohexanone resin, a synthetic varnish similar to dammar and now used by many restorers to replace this natural resin.

Alligator: "to develop intersecting cracks and ridges."--Webster

Beeswax: "a wax obtained as a yellow to brown solid by melting honeycomb with boiling water, straining and cooling, and used especially in polishes."--Webster

Covalent bond: "a chemical bond formed by the sharing of one or more electrons, expecially pairs of electrons, between atoms."--American Heritage Dictionary

Crazed: "a pattern of fine cracks."--American Heritage Dictionary

Double bond: "a chemical bond consisting of two covalent bonds between two atoms in a molecule."--Webster

Japan: "a black enamel or lacquer of a type originating in the orient, used to produce a durable glossy finish."--American Heritage Dictionary

Lacquer: "any glossy, often resinous material used as a surface coating, such as the exudation of the lacquer tree."--American Heritage Dictionary

Lac: "a resinous secretion of the lac insect, used in making shellac."--American Heritage Dictionary

Linseed oil: "the most important of the vegetable drying oils, is obtained from the seeds of the flax, the same plant that furnishes linen fiber."--Gettens and Stout, Painting Materials

Monomer: "the simple unpolymerized form of a chemical compound having relatively low molecular weight."--Webster

Morpholine: "a strong solvent for dyes, waxes, shellac, and for casein."--Gettens and Stout, Painting Materials

Nitrocellulose: "a pulpy or cottonlike polymer derived from cellulose treated with sulfuric and nitric acids."--American Heritage Dictionary

Plasticizer: " a chemical substance added to natural and synthetic rubbers and resins to impart flexibility, workability, or distensibility."--Webster

Polymer: "a natural or synthetic chemical compound or mixture of compounds formed by polymerization, and consisting essentially of repeating structural units."--Webster

Reconstitute: "to build up again by putting back together the original parts or elements."--Webster

Shellac: "a purified lac formed into thin yellow or orange flakes, often bleached white and widely used in varnishes, paints, stains, inks, and sealing wax, as a binder."-- American Heritage Dictionary

Varnish: "an oil-based paint containing a solvent and an oxidizing or an evaporating binder, used to coat a surface with a hard, glossy, thin film."--American Heritage Dictionary

Definitions quoted by permission of G. & C. Merriam Co., Publishers of the Merriam-Webster Dictionaries (Wester's Third New International Dictionary, 1966), and the American Heritage Publishing Co., Inc. (The American Heritage Dictionary, 1969).

SUGGESTED WORKS ON CONSERVATION OF ART OBJECTS

Brommelle, N. S., and Moncrieff, A. J., "Deterioration and Treatment of Wood." London, 1969.

Feller, Robert L., Stolow, Nathan, and Jones, Elizabeth H., On Picture Varnishes and Their Solvents. Oberlin, Ohio, 1959.

Gettens, Rutherford J., and Stout, George L., Painting Materials: A Short Encyclopedia. New York, 1947. Reprinted by Dover Publications, 1966.

Keck, Sheldon, "Mechanical Alteration of the Paint Film," Studies in Conservation, XIV (February 1969), 9-30.

Plenderleith, Harold J., Conservation of Antiquities and Works of Art. London and New York, 1956.